EPHESIANS

LIFE AND LOVE IN CHRIST

BY R.S. BEAL JR. & EARL D. RADMACHER

*To Don and Phyllis,
Faithful servants and wonderful
friends,
Dick Beal*

August 2012

Copyright: © 2012 by R.S. Beal, Jr.

All rights reserved. No part of this book may be reproduced in any manner without permission of the author, except in the case of quotes used in critical articles and reviews.

R. S. Beal Jr.
821 Briarwood Drive
East Wenatchee, WA 98802
E-mail: rsbeal@nwi.net

Earl D. Radmacher
8333 SE Astor
Milwaukie, OR 97267
E-mail: drr10@comcast.net

Biblical text from The Holy Bible, English Standard Bible. Copyright 2000, 2001 by Crossway Bibles, a ministry of Good News Publishers. Used by permission. All rights reserved.

Book design: a.zuccarello@gmail.com

ISBN: (13 digit) 978-0-9838455-1-5

This book was printed in the USA by:
ONE WORLD PRESS
890 Staley Lane
Chino Valley, AZ 86323
800-250-8171
printmybook@oneworldpress.com
www.oneworldpress.com

In memory of Zane Clark Hodges

Teacher, Friend, and Outstanding Student of the Word

TABLE OF CONTENTS

Abbreviations Used i

Authors' Preface. iii

Introductory Considerations. viii

The Salutation 1

Division A_1 Identified With Christ. 4

Division B_1 Be Subordinate In Awe Of Christ. 46

Division C_1 Made Alive In Christ 69

Division D_1 United In Christ 91

Focus: The Fervent Central Prayer 131

Division D_2 Live In Unity 144

Division C_2 Arise From The Dead. 175

Division B_2 Be Subordinate To One
    Another In Awe Of Christ 215

Division A_2 Find Strength In Christ. 247

Conclusion. 266

Special Observations 270

Index Of Authors 291

Index Of Subjects. 294

ABBREVIATIONS USED

ASV *American Standard Version*

AV *Authorized Version of the Bible* (Oxford: University Press, n. d.)

BAG   Walter Bauer, William F. Arndt, and F. Wilbur Gingrich, *A Greek-English Lexicon of the New Testament* (Chicago: Univ. of Chicago, 1957)

BAGD   Walter Bauer, *A Greek-English Lexicon of the New Testament and Other Early Christian Literature.* Revised and edited by Frederick William Danker. 3d ed. (Chicago: University of Chicago Press, 2000).

ESV *Holy Bible, English Standard Version* (Wheaton, IL: Good News Publishers, 2001)

HCSB *Holman Christian Standard Bible* (Nashville: Holman Bible Publishers, 1999)

NAB *New American Bible* with *The Revised Book of Psalms* and *The Revised New Testament* (Totowa, NJ: World Catholic Press, 1987)

NASB *New American Standard Bible* (Nashville: Thomas Nelson, 1977).

NEB *New English Bible New Testament* (Oxford: University Press, 1966)

NET *New English Translation* (Internet address: Biblical

i

Studies Press, L.L.C., 1998)

NIV *New International Version* (Grand Rapids: Zondervan, 1978)

NKJV *New King James Version* (Nashville: Thomas Nelson, 1991)

NRSV *New Revised Standard Version* (New York: Oxford University Press, 1989)

RSV *Holy Bible, Revised Standard Version* (Grand Rapids: Zondervan, 1952)

AUTHORS' PREFACE

For individuals who prayerfully and studiously think through every sentence, possibly no book yields richer and more gratifying rewards than the Epistle to the Ephesians. The authors have been immeasurably enriched by searching out the meaning of each word. Anyone who seriously inquires into what God has revealed in this epistle will surely be constrained to voice the same testimony.

Why write a commentary on the Epistle to the Ephesians when both popular and scholarly commentaries abound? Briefly, our purpose of is to provide a substantive commentary of use to pastors and adult Bible class teachers with special concern for those who lack a reading knowledge of Greek or whose Greek is mostly forgotten. This book will also be of value for those who want a more detailed explanation of the text than is available in most popular commentaries. The commentary seeks to lay bare the astonishingly radical nature of Christian faith and life as developed in Ephesians. The believer's irrevocable union with Christ is glossed over in most commentaries. Many commentaries find some rationale for keeping the believer under the "moral" law, even though it is contrary to the Apostle Paul's clear teaching. Few commentaries develop the significance of love as the standard for all Christian behavior, even though it is of overriding importance in Ephesians.

In writing this study, we have complete confidence in the text itself. The various English translations, when compared, usually provide a good understanding of what the apostle wrote. Yet we have needed recourse to the Greek text, for this was the writer's own language.[1]

Nevertheless, we have not done full justice to the majestic themes of the epistle. No one really can. It is the epistle itself that needs to be absorbed by the Christian. Perhaps the most a commentary can do, and what we have sought to do, is to remove impediments to an understanding of Paul's letter. Some impediments are inescapably there because few of us read the language that Paul used and none have experienced firsthand the culture in which he lived. Other impediments stem from different traditions and philosophical views which lack biblical justification. Yet some of these views are so deeply embedded in the thinking of modern Christendom that it is difficult for many expositors to appreciate what Paul really taught. So our goal has been to understand and to explain his words as we think he would explain them were he here today.

A student who has some background in Greek and who wants to go beyond what is written here will find considerable profit through consulting the exhaustive study by Harold W. Hoehner.[2] Knowing Greek is not essential for following arguments in the two-volume work by Markus Barth,[3] or

---

[1] The Greek text followed is that in the Nestle-Aland Greek Testament, 27th ed. (Peabody, MA: Hendrickson, 2006).
[2] Harold W. Hoehner, *Ephesians: an Exegetical Commentary* (Grand Rapids: Baker Academic, 2002).
[3] Markus Barth, *Ephesians: Introduction, Translation, and Commentary on Chapters 1-3*, ed. William Foxwell Albright and David Noel Freedman (Garden City, NY: Doubleday & Co., 1974), and idem., *Ephesians: Translation and Commentary on Chapters 4-6*, ed. William Foxwell Albright and David Noel Freedman (Garden City, NY: Doubleday & Co., 1974).

in the one-volume work by Peter T. O'Brien.[4] Each of these authors carefully explains for the English reader almost all the significant meanings of phrases, clauses, and sentences in the text, and then tells why he has chosen a particular understanding. Although a reader might disagree with some of their interpretations (as frequently we have), each has comments worth considering.

We have chosen to use the text of the *English Standard Version* (ESV). There is value in each of our common versions of the Bible, for each one has been produced through the careful and reflective thought of one or a number of translators. With almost no exceptions, the meaning of the Greek words is well understood. Differences between translations occur in large part because each to a greater or lesser degree represents the translator's interpretation of the thought of the original authors. A translator cannot avoid coming to the text as an interpreter, although some studiously try to be as neutral as possible. Furthermore translators come to the text with different backgrounds and inescapable biases. Unfortunately translations that seek to render the Greek of the New Testament into English as faithfully and exactly as possible, of which the precise American Revised Version of 1901 is a prime example, manage to produce a reading that is painfully wooden. Consequently all recent translations represent something of a compromise between accuracy and readability. Some modern English translations succeed admirably in being reader friendly and are wonderfully adapted to conveying thoughts for rapid reading. Nevertheless the more a translator seeks to produce the most readable English ver-

---

4   Peter T. O'Brien, *The Letter to the Ephesians*, Pillar New Testament Commentary, ed. D. A. Carson (Grand Rapids: Eerdmans, 1999).

sion expressing the general concept rather than the meaning of the words (so-called "dynamic" translations), the less likely the result will convey the rich meaning and nuances of the original and will often introduce thoughts foreign to the original. Given these problems, it seems to us the ESV is the best compromise. While being quite readable, it includes the fewest passages needing explanatory comments or clarification. Although in a small number of places our interpretation differs with the interpretation of the editors of the ESV, each phrase represents a point of view held by careful scholars and deserves consideration alongside our observations.

We make no claim to originality in our exposition other than in our development of the structure of the Epistle. We have tried to evaluate and use the best thoughts of other authors. Beyond published studies, we especially appreciate those who have had a hand in our own growth in understanding God's grace and then of the Epistle to the Ephesians.

R. S. Beal Jr. notes the following. "From years long past I owe a major debt of gratitude to the late Dr. Lewis Sperry Chafer of Dallas Theological Seminary in whose classes I learned the rich meaning and amazing scope of God's grace. In recent years, as I sought to put my thinking to paper, several individuals contributed generously to my efforts. I express my deepest thanks to the following, who have read and helpfully commented on drafts of a single or several divisions or of the entire book, improving my writing style, pointing out obscure sentences, or criticizing my interpretations: <u>Norman P. Anderson,</u> David P. Beal, L. David Beckman, the late Keith Fredrickson and his wife Judith, the late S. Lewis Johnson Jr., Ted Inabnit, and William Fraatz. Each made worthwhile suggestions which usually

I was pleased to adopt. A few of our reviewers disagreed with some of our positions, and their observations were quite valuable, for they constrained us to reexamine our thinking. I thank Frank Ames for bringing to our attention an interesting piece of literature on the epistle. I am particularly grateful to Max H. James, my esteemed colleague at Northern Arizona University, where we both taught before retirement and where he served as chair of the Department of English. His investment of time in working on the text led to its substantial improvement. I am most grateful to Dr. Radmacher for his critical analysis and his sharp understanding of the Word. I thank Alan Krause, Hope Engle, and Marilyn Stelting for some invaluable computer help. Above all, I am especially grateful to my wife Evorine for her constant encouragement and patient endurance the many hours I was glued to my computer or pouring over books."

Earl D. Radmacher notes, "I want to thank Dr. Beal for inviting me to share in a rewriting of the commentary, for after reading his manuscript I was tremendously impressed with his accurate grasp of the Epistle and his vocabulary, so easy to read and unlike that found in most modern commentaries."

We both are particularly grateful to Dr. Roy B. Zuck for his helpful and painstaking work as our texteditor.

INTRODUCTORY CONSIDERATIONS

Comments are provided on each sentence in Ephesians to the extent they are likely to be of help to a Bible teacher but with an effort not to be overwhelming. A Bible teacher or pastor who wants to expound Ephesians in great detail, perhaps taking no more than one or two verses at a time, will need to go to other sources, perhaps to one of the commentaries listed in footnotes 2, 3, and 4.

We have not included a discussion of the authorship of the epistle. We are convinced the Apostle Paul was the sole author. This we believe in spite of a number of scholarly commentators who argue that the letter was written by someone else or that Paul authored only a core of the epistle to which someone else penned substantial additions. Those who are concerned about such matters will find Paul's authorship ably defended in the three commentaries listed in notes 2, 3, and 4. An adequate defense of Pauline authorship is also given in commentaries by F. F. Bruce[5] and William Hendriksen.[6]

A subject to which we have given considerable space is the literary structure of the epistle. Not only do we believe this is interesting in itself, but we are convinced it is the key to the major theme of the epistle. It shines a new light on Paul's reason for writing the epistle. In our judgment the divisions proposed here represent the outline Paul himself

---

5   F. F. Bruce, *The Epistles to the Colossians, to Philemon, and to the Ephesians*. The New International Commentary on the New Testament, ed. F. F. Bruce (Grand Rapids: Eerdmans, 1984), 240-46.
6   William Hendriksen, *Exposition of Ephesians*, New Testament Commentary, ed. D. A. Carson, (Grand Rapids: Baker, 1967), 32-56.

Introductory Considerations

would have used had he wanted to exhibit the topics of the letter. So the commentary is not divided into chapters but is broken into divisions that follow this structure.

At various places in the text are footnotes. These are added where we needed to attribute a quotation to an authority or a source of information beyond the limit of our personal investigations. A reader interested in the extensive literature on the epistle will do well to consult the commentary by Hoehner or for a more up-to-date list of references to consult the Bibliography of John Paul Heil.[7]

At the end of the book are six special observations that are too extensive to be included within the comments or footnotes. They are included to justify several positions we have taken in this work.

I. CHARACTER AND PURPOSE OF THE EPISTLE

In many respects Ephesians is unlike other letters bearing the name of the Apostle Paul. Ernest Best, who does not think that Paul himself was the author, sought to compare its moral teachings with that of the "genuine" Pauline letters. He asserted that the last half is "prosaic and lacks his sparkle."[8] However, if the tone is different from that of his other compositions, it is simply that the mood of this letter is one of praise, devotion, and prayer. Ephesians is not polemic

---

7   John Paul Heil, *Ephesians: Empowerment to Walk in Love for the Unity of All in Christ* (Atlanta: GA, Society of Biblical Literature, 2007), 318-36.

8   Ernest Best, *A Critical and Exegetical Commentary on Ephesians*, The International Critical Commentary, ed. J. A. Emerton, C. E. B. Cranfield, and G. N. Stanton (Edinburgh: T. & T. Clark, 1998).

or confrontational as are some of his other epistles, for he is not facing a crisis of doctrine or behavior in a church but is reflecting on some of the deepest realities of the Christian life.

What are these deep realities? The apostles' foundational teaching, addressed in the first three chapters, is that the believer in the Lord Jesus receives from God an astounding station, one in which he or she has been fully forgiven and is indissolubly united with Christ. God provides this bounty through His great love. His love is unveiled in Christ's death on the cross. It is expressed in His absolute grace, grace poured out in measure beyond comprehension. The truth of God's love leads Paul to teach what love amounts to in the relationship each believer should have toward others, which is the major burden of the last three chapters.[9] Practicing love toward fellow believers does not purchase salvation. Instead God's grace, when truly understood and accepted, leads compellingly to a life of love.

The doctrine of the Church occupies a large part of the letter, and well it should. The truth of the Church, Christ's body, follows from what God has done through uniting each believer with Christ. In turn this means that all believers are united to each other, so it is not surprising that members of the body should receive careful instruction in their relationships to each other. Given the Christian's calling (4:1), the believer is urged to live a corresponding life of love, especially with respect to those in the household of faith (Gal.

---

[9] Heil, *Ephesians: Empowerment to Walk in Love for the Unity of All in Christ*, seems to be the first modern commentator to recognize that the primary theme of Ephesians is the doctrine of love shown by God and expected in the life of each believer.

6:10).

Dealing with the unity of believers, Paul found it necessary to address the question of how believing Jews and believing Gentiles are related to one another before God. The Jews lived under the Mosaic law, and this automatically separated them from lawless Gentiles. How believing Jews and Gentiles can enter into a common union has only one resolution, and this is the annulment of the law through the cross. It is the entire body of the Law that was annulled, a theme Paul also expounded in Romans, 2 Corinthians, and Galatians, but a theme many expositors find difficult to accept.

II. INTERPRETING THE EPISTLE

Because it addresses genuine needs of Christians everywhere, Ephesians is loved and respected. In spite of its familiarity, when its doctrines are accurately exhibited, they are more astounding than most readers realize. For English readers a certain degree of interpretation is necessary.

As with any ordinary letter today, Ephesians is to be understood in its normal, grammatical sense. The normal sense is the straightforward meaning conveyed by its language. This means the letter should not be read as a series of spiritual maxims but as an interconnected whole. Each sentence is part of the flow of the apostle's teaching, so no sentence is to be taken by itself, isolated from what goes before and what comes after.

For a reader who wants a rich understanding of the apostle's words, a Bible dictionary and a commentary are useful adjuncts. This is because Paul, writing in Greek, used certain expressions in a sense not fully translatable in English without adding a number of additional words. Yet when such additions are supplied, they often imply ideas not there. Also some expressions in Ephesians are flavored by the culture in which Paul lived, a culture foreign to our way of thinking. The commentary that follows is written to clarify the issues to the best of the authors' ability. More importantly, it is written to show the practical importance of every passage for twenty-first-century Christians.

Some Christians are likely to object, "Why should I need human help in understanding the epistle? Jesus promised in John 16:13 that when the Spirit of truth comes, 'He will guide you into all the truth.' So all I need is to read the verses and accept the impression the Holy Spirit gives me." As much as we might wish, God does not work this way. The Holy Spirit inspired the precise wording of the epistle. He did this so that believers might be taught, reproved, corrected, and trained in righteousness (2 Tim. 3:16). There is no alternative to receiving the words just as they have been given. The Spirit's present ministry is not to lead the devout reader to some sense beyond what is already provided but to lead the Christian to apprehend the relevance of the epistle's truths to his or her life. Our task is to understand clearly what He has already presented.

III. TIME, PLACE, AND CIRCUMSTANCES OF WRITING

Among scholars who accept the authenticity of Ephesians, there is fairly general agreement that the epistle was written by Paul from Rome between A. D. 61 and 63. Another choice accepted by a few is that the epistle was written in Caesarea where Paul was imprisoned two or three years earlier. Still a few other writers suppose that Paul was imprisoned in Ephesus about the middle of the 50s and that he wrote the epistle from there. The silence of Acts regarding an imprisonment in Ephesus renders the latter supposition rather improbable, although Paul's account of trouble in Asia (2 Cor. 1:8-10) conceivably refers to an imprisonment. The totally different tone of Ephesians and the words expressed by Paul at his last visit with the elders in Ephesus (Acts 20) not long before his imprisonment in Caesarea is at least suggestive that a later and more reflective period saw the writing of Ephesians, but there is no proof.

Every scholarly commentator has observed the many similarities between Ephesians and Colossians. This has convinced theologically liberal commentators that Colossians was written before Ephesians, then sometime later, perhaps decades later, an unknown author copied many of Paul's ideas from Colossians, tried to imitate Paul's style, and sent out Ephesians under Paul's name. These scholars suggest that the author wanted to get some points across and knew they would not be accepted under his or her own name. Also these writers assume that the different style of Ephesians is the key to its pseudonymous authorship.

Many of the similarities as well as differences between Ephesians and Colossians can be accounted for by the following simple assumption. Paul planned and wrote the Ephesian letter over a period of time, giving a great deal of thought to its literary structure and artistic composition. In places he chose particular words and expressions that were not a part of his normal writing vocabulary. As is true of the writing of any accomplished author, it is easy to find substantial differences when examining an author's more hastily written documents and documents written with preparatory thought and care. Paul evidently wrote Ephesians with the thought that it would be a formal statement of certain doctrines. He intended it for circulation among several churches. At or near the completion of the epistle, word came concerning doctrinal errors among the Christians in Colossae. That prompted a hurried letter in which he repeated many of the thoughts found in the Ephesian letter, shortening the language, and omitting issues irrelevant to circumstances of the Colossian church but adding other items of pressing concern.

Is this assumption correct? No one in Rome left a record of Paul's daily activities, so we can never know for sure.

IV. THE SAINTS FOR WHOM THE LETTER WAS WRITTEN

Possibly (and even probably) Ephesians was intended to be circulated among a number of churches, possibly in Ephesus and its environs and even extending into the Lycus Valley. The great likelihood is that there were a number of house churches in the city, which then probably numbered a quarter of a million. O'Brien notes that it would be astonishing to find all Christians in Ephesus jammed into one megachurch.[10] In many of these house churches there would be believers who certainly knew of Paul but who had never seen him in person. That it was a circular letter is supported by the following four considerations.

(1) According to 1:15, Paul had "heard" of their faith and love. This is unlike his letters to the Corinthians, the Phi-

---

10 O'Brien, *Letter to the Ephesians,* 48.

Introductory Considerations

lippians, and the Thessalonians, where he wrote of their conduct not from hearsay but from firsthand knowledge. When he wrote to the Colossians, a church he seems not to have personally visited (Col. 2:1), he tells them, "we have heard" of your faith and love. If Ephesians was a letter intended for several churches in Asia Minor, only from the reports of others would he have known things about those he addressed.

(2) He had ministered more than a year in Ephesus and knew the people there quite well, but probably only those in an individual congregation or two. If the letter was intended for people where he originally ministered, it is surprising that he would not have mentioned people there by name or made some reference to them. This fact alone is enough to convince many scholars that Ephesians was not penned by Paul. The only other way to account for the omission is by supposing it was a circular letter intended largely for congregations with which he was unacquainted.

(3) He does not remind the recipients that he is their "father" in the faith, as he wrote to other churches where he had evangelized. There must have been many people in Ephesians whom he had personally led to the Lord. Such an expression would have been included if the letter was essentially intended for those to whom he originally ministered.

(4) An interesting comment is found in Col. 4:16, "and see that you also read the letter from Laodicea." Was there a Pauline letter to the Laodiceans which has been lost? Or is this a reference to the Ephesian letter? The second-century Gnostic heretic Marcion listed what he believed to be the books representing the true Word of God. In his compilation Ephesians was entitled "To the Laodiceans." In view of this, some have proposed that Ephesians was originally

xv

addressed only to the church at Laodicea. Most scholars, however, reject this notion in view of the lack of references in Ephesians to any of the people of Laodicea. On the other hand, if Paul himself directed that copies of the Ephesian letter be made with one sent to the church at Laodicea, it is at least possible that in Colossians 4:16 he did have reference to the Ephesian letter.

Presumably militating against Ephesians being a circular letter is Paul's closing comment in 6:21-22, "Tychicus the beloved brother and faithful minister in the Lord will tell you everything. I have sent him to you for this very purpose, that you may know how we are, and that he may encourage your hearts." Yet this is not proof that Tychicus could not have traveled from one church to another. If it was a circular letter, Tychicus himself could have been instructed to deliver copies to each congregation with personal encouragement and information about Paul.

Many uncertainties about such matters will continue unless a first century manuscript is discovered or some first century witness is found describing the epistle and its origin. Until then it seems reasonable to think of Ephesians as a circular letter written by Paul and intended for a number of churches.

V. OVERVIEW OF SOME GREEK VERB TENSES

Is it necessary to think about Greek grammar when all we really want is get into God's Word itself? Occasionally in the commentary it is necessary to delve a bit into Greek verbs. Therefore it will save space and time if we can cover some introductory concepts at the beginning. Then

Introductory Considerations

when reference is made to one or another of these verbs, the reader without a background in Greek will have a grasp of the ideas involved.

For English speakers to follow the fine nuances of first century Greek is difficult at best. At the heart of first-century Greek is the complex system of verbs, of which there are three fundamental kinds. One kind is found in what are called the *present* and the *imperfect* tenses. The Greek present tense is not at all like our English present. If a friend says in English, "I hunt in these woods," he is using the present tense. You understand that it is action at the present time, although you do not know whether it is continuing action over years or something he is uniquely doing now. In contrast, the Greek present tense does not necessarily mean "at the present." It carries the basic sense of something going on over and over. It represents action that happens repeatedly or continuously. Without some associated words, the reader would not know whether it is continuing action centuries ago, whether it is happening now, or whether it is anticipated in centuries to come. It is action without beginning or end in view.

The imperfect tense, just like the present, is used for continuing action, but it is action in the past. These two tenses can be compared to seeing a videotape or TV picture of a car traveling along a highway. It is in motion, but by itself you know nothing more. It might be noted, however, that the kind of action represented by the present tense can be altered by the meaning of the verb itself or by the context.

A second kind of tense is termed the *aorist*. The best way to think about the aorist is seeing a photograph. A photograph can be of a small object, perhaps a minute flower, or a larger object, possibly a family portrait, or a vast landscape. The aorist looks at a situation as if looking at a snapshot. In the verb itself there is no motion involved. This is the situation in John 18:22: "One of the officers standing by struck Jesus with his hand." "Struck" is in the aorist tense, because the blow took place at a point in time. The aorist does not tell us what time, only that Jesus was struck. The context tells us when. The same aorist form may be used for something that has continued for a time but has boundaries, much like a landscape picture. It can be thought of as a circle that views the action, of however long duration, as a single point. The verb does not describe what is in the circle. That is the duty of the context. In Acts 15:12 we find the aorist verb "fell silent." The aorist form of the verb embraces a period--a point--from beginning to end that the assembly listened while Barnabas and Paul spoke. It does not tell us how long they spoke; it only gives us a picture of people quietly listening as long as Barnabas and Paul were speaking.

The third kind of tense includes the *perfect* and the *pluperfect*. These tenses commonly describe something that occurred but with an effect that continues afterward. This can be thought of as a still picture in a television ad. Viewers watch it a second or two, then suddenly a person or a car in the picture begins to move. A delightful example of the use of the perfect tense is found in John 1:41, where Andrew finds his brother Simeon and says to him, "We have found the Messiah." The significance of the verb is not only that they found the Messiah at a particular point in time, but that the results of having found him continue. The tense describes a state or situation resulting from a past event.

The pluperfect, like the perfect, describes an event

Introductory Considerations

with results that continue, only the pluperfect looks only at the results continuing in the past. The results may or may not continue in the present, but only the continuing effect in the past is in view.

The aorist tense needs further consideration. Most commonly it refers to action that happened in the past with respect to the person who is doing the reporting. (For the benefit of language aficionados, this is only when the aorist is in the indicative mood.) That it commonly refers to past events should be obvious, for if someone is picturing an event, the person presumably has knowledge of an event that has already taken place. Nevertheless the verb can be modified immensely by the character of the verb itself and the way the verb is colored by the descriptive elements that surround it. Hence it is not always or necessarily a past event.

With these verbs in our minds, it will be simpler to picture some of the marvelous things the apostle teaches in his epistle.

VI. LITERARY STRUCTURE OF THE BOOK

Ephesians is divided into two major parts: a doctrinal section and a practical section. The first establishes certain essential facts of the Christian faith: *the Christian's status and privileges.* This sets forth the richness of God's love, which is so clearly seen through his grace with all its incredible benefits. The second points out what it is for a Christian to put his or her faith into practice: *the Christian's responsibilities.* The Christian's responsibilities are manifested in unfailing love toward others. The two major sections are divided by an exclamation of praise to God. The praise is in the form of a fervent prayer for the saints with a short doxology. As in all Pauline epistles the book begins with an epistolary salutation and concludes with a personal communication and benediction.

Many different outlines have been suggested for Ephesians, and probably most have some merit. The outline proposed here demonstrates how topics within each of the two sections correspond with each other in a systematic pattern. The following comparisons of the sections explain how this correspondence works out. (See Figure 1 and Observation I: The Literary Structure in Ephesians. p. 270) The first division of the letter corresponds to the last, the second to the next to last, and so forth. When the topics are arranged in order, they form a pattern that resembles half of the Greek letter *chi*, which is like our English letter X. Scholars term this a *chiastic* structure.

In addition to showing Paul's design as he composed the epistle, the following brief comparison of the corresponding sections is designed to help the reader see the strategy of the epistle. One critical commentator wrote, "No letter of Paul is so confused and confusing in its form and structure." One might think as much without observing the pattern of correspondences in the letter. The structure clearly points to one central theme, the surpassing love of Christ, which by the power of the Holy Spirit becomes available for the life of the believer.

Figure 1

THE LITERARY STRUCTURE OF EPHESIANS

Salutation (1:1-2)

THE CHRISTIAN'S PRIVILEGES AND STATUS

A_1 Identified with Christ (1:3-14)
    B_1 Subordinate to Christ (1:15-23)
        C_1 Made Alive in Christ (2:1-10)
            D_1 United in Christ (2:11-3:13)
                (1) Unity of the Body (2:11-22)
                (2) Paul the Minister of this Truth (3:1-13)

THE FERVENT PRAYER (3:14-21)

THE CHRISTIAN'S RESPONSIBILITIES

            D_2 Live in Unity (4:1-16)
                (1) Unity of the Body (4:1-16)
                (2) Christ the Minister of Gifts (4:7-16)
        C_2 Arise from the Dead (4:17-5:20)
    B_2 Be Subordinate to One Another (5:21-6:9)
A_2 Find Strength in Christ (6:16-20)

Conclusion (6:21-24)

The first division (A_1, 1:3-14) announces God's commitment to every believer. It belongs to him or her through being united to the Savior. The apostle cannot stress this union strongly enough. Over and over he affirms that what we possess we have *in him, in Christ, in the Beloved.* Every benefit is a consequence of God having identified us in a most remarkable way with the Lord Jesus.

A_1 is God's commitment to the believer and correspondingly A_2 is the believer's commitment to God. A_1 speaks of what God has done with finality, A_2 speaks of what the believer is to do with finality. Both are once-for-all: the first what God has done once-for-all, the second what the Christian is to do once-for-all.

Divisions B_1 (1:15-23) and B_2 (5:22-6:9) are both about subordination, the first, subordination to Christ, the second subordination to other believers. They obviously correspond in that each division speaks specifically of Christ and the Church.

Both Division C_1 (2:1-10) and Division C_2 (4:17-5:21) have to do with life in God. Both begin by reminding readers of the spiritual death in which everyone began and in which unbelievers still exist. C_1 describes God's grace bringing spiritual life. Division C_2 (4:17-5:21) urges the believer to enter a new kind of life in practice.

The primary thought of Divisions D_1 (2:11-3:13) and D_2 (4:1-16) is unity in the Church. Each consists of two corresponding parts, the second being (a) Paul the minister of the truth of this unity (3:7-13) and (b) the unity made practical through Christ conveying spiritual gifts to members of the body (4:7-16).

Introductory Considerations

As the central element in the structure of the book (3:14-21), this short passage defines the apostle's major purpose in writing. In a chiastic structure the reader's attention is focused on the central element.[11] This is important, for if the structure we have proposed is the Apostle's plan, then the primary thrust of the epistle is different than what has usually been assumed. This thrust is that the Christian might know the surpassing love of Christ, and through this, by the power of the Holy Spirit, be rooted and grounded in the practice of love. The whole sense of the epistle, as well as its literary structure, leads convincingly to this conclusion.

Details of the structure will be found in the discussion of each division in the following pages.

---

11   David A. Dorsey, *The Literary Structure of the Old Testament* (Grand Rapids,: Baker, 1999), 31. See also Ian H Thomson, *Chiasmus in the Pauline Letters* (Journal For the Study of the New Testament Supplement Series 111 (Sheffield: Sheffield Academic Press, 1995), 43.

Ephesians | *Life and Love in Christ*

THE SALUTATION
(1:1-2)

Only two verses are included in the salutation, which is true of the salutations in other epistles of the Apostle Paul. Yet this is deserving of spiritual reflection.

¹Paul, an apostle of Christ Jesus by the will of God,
Following the letter-writing custom of his time, the author placed his name first instead of at the end. The author was the same Paul who once had been a devout Pharisee and who had zealously persecuted Jewish followers of Christ. Following his conversion on the road to Damascus, he changed his name from Saul to Paul, a name which means "little." The name expressed his deep humility on recognizing that his acceptance by God was none of his doing but was wholly an act of God's grace.

"Apostle" primarily means "one sent out." Derived meanings are "delegate," "envoy," and "messenger." As Paul used it, "missionary" would be an appropriate synonym. In New Testament times the twelve who had been with Jesus were a specially recognized class, highly esteemed for their work. They were not the only ones devoted to evangelizing the nations and not the only ones termed apostles, but the original apostles had an intimate knowledge of Jesus, and had been commissioned by him. Paul himself had received a unique vision of the Lord and had received a commission to be a witness for him (Acts 22:6-21). It was God's specific will that he should be a missionary to the Gentiles.

To the saints who are in Ephesus, and are faithful in Christ Jesus:

The word "saints" can properly be translated "holy ones," but who are these? We know that God is called "the Holy One" (I John 2:20), and Jesus is designated the "Holy One" (Acts 3:14). Angels are termed "holy" (Mark 8:38). Astonishingly Paul is writing here of all those who have trusted the risen Christ. A derived meaning of "holy ones," and the meaning it has here, is "ones set apart for a holy purpose." Every Christian is set apart by God for a holy purpose, and this is true whether the Christian keeps this set-apart commission or not.

Commentators question whether the words "who are also faithful" should be translated this way or translated "who are believers." The latter is undoubtedly correct. The HCSB correctly translates, "To the saints and believers in Christ Jesus at Ephesus." Nothing suggests there were two classes among the Christians addressed in the letter, "those faithful" and "those not faithful." Indeed, the letter is addressed to saints who were less than wholly faithful. This is the burden of Paul beginning with 4:17.

One might ask, is Paul being redundant if the clause means "who are believers," since saints in the New Testament *are* believers? In secular Greek, the word for saint (*hagios*) simply meant "the quality possessed by things and persons that could approach a divinity."[12] Someone approved to approach a pagan god would be termed a "saint" by the Greeks. This is the way it would easily be understood, or perhaps misunderstood, by new Ephesian converts. Hence Paul made his meaning of "saints" unmistakable--he wrote of believers in Christ.[13]

---

12   BAGD, 10.
13   William J. Larkin, *Ephesians: A Handbook on the Greek Text*

The Salutation

If there is any question, the verses that follow plainly state that Paul was writing to all believers, not to some special class of believers understood as saints. In 1:13 he refers to "those who have believed in him." In 2:8 he mentions those who have been "saved through faith." How gratifying to know that however little we have *practiced* being saints, in his unending favor God has granted each of us who believes the *standing* of being a saint. Sainthood is not something reserved for the few canonized by an ecclesiastical organization, but for every single born-again person!

² *Grace to you and peace from God our Father and the Lord Jesus Christ.*

This initial address is characteristic of Greek letters in the time of Paul. It has no verb, but "be" is understood. Under what conditions grace and peace come is not stated here but this will be fully answered in the chapters that follow.

The blessings of grace and peace, as well as all the blessings that follow in verses 3-14, are from both the Father and the Lord Jesus Christ. This statement would have been impossible if the apostle had not held Christ to be of the same rank with God the Father or in a remarkably unique relation to Him. Whatever concept sophisticated modern humans may have of Jesus, to Paul he was far more than an ordinary human.

(Waco, TX: Baylor University Press, 2009), 2.

DIVISION A₁, IDENTIFIED WITH CHRIST
(1:3-14)

The masses of Christendom understand so little of the precious truths of these verses, truths of the Christian's permanent relationship to God through the Lord Jesus Christ. Central words of this division, *forgiven* and *redemption*, are of course, more or less familiar to Christians. They are heard in creeds and liturgical affirmations and even find their way into sermons. Seldom are they heard with the amazing scope and significance given them here. Other doctrines of this passage are ignored by many preachers and by authors of much of the devotional and religious literature of our day.

Most commentators consider this section to be a Jewish prayer of blessing (a *berachah*), since it blesses God and speaks of God's blessing on His people. Yet a careful study of the division shows it to be *instruction*. It is a declaration of what God in grace has done, not a prayer requesting grace. Verses 11-14 are clearly not a prayer of blessing, even though they are part of the single, long sentence in the Greek that begins with verse 3. There is no reason why Paul could not have assimilated the language of a Jewish prayer into his working vocabulary and used some of it without intending the division as a prayer.

.This first division (1:3-14) presents the magnificent grace of God, which in love provides the believer with every spiritual blessing.

³*Blessed be the God and Father of our Lord Jesus Christ, who has blessed us in Christ with every spiritual blessing in the heavenly places.*

This third verse epitomizes the rest of the passage. If it is true that Paul means certain ones have been blessed with every conceivable spiritual blessing, the statement is remarkable indeed. Some suggest that Paul does not mean every imaginable spiritual blessing but rather that he is exaggerating for effect. But no, as we consider the verses that follow, we must conclude this is what he expressly intends!

Clearly Paul includes himself among those who have this invaluable boon. He writes, "who has blessed *us* with every spiritual blessing." Someone earnestly seeking God's blessing cannot help asking who else besides Paul is included in that little but important pronoun *us*. The first verse states that the epistle is written to the saints, but if we limit our inquiry to the first eleven verses, we will not discover who the saints are or what qualifications are expected of one who would achieve sainthood. We only know that the saints are included in the pronoun *us*. As we continue our reading, we do not find an immediate answer. Seven times in the following verses the pronouns *we*, *us*, and *our* are used without any indication of who is intended.

In verse 12 the whole matter is clarified. It is *we who first hoped in Christ*. To remove all doubt, verse 15 explains that it is those who have *faith in the Lord Jesus*. In verse 19 it is *us who believe*. And 2:8 states that those who are included are those who *have been saved through faith*. Whatever the blessings are that Paul is delineating, they belong to every single person who has taken God at His word, believing in His holy Son whom He sent into the world.

This almost incomprehensible truth affords a troubled heart great relief. Some may fear they have missed out on God's blessings since they lack the emotional thrill that possessed them after first hearing and receiving the message of salvation. Some for the first time may see themselves for what they really are, and wonder how a fully righteous God could possibly bestow any good on them. Then with plainest reassurance they are told in this division that however their feelings in the matter may fluctuate, if they "first hoped in Christ," if they believed in the Father's blessed Son, they indeed have every spiritual blessing. On God's promise, every believer is included in that simple pronoun "*we*."

The expression *in Christ* is critical to verse 3, and for that matter to the whole Book of Ephesians and the rest of Paul's writings. Its importance is easily seen by noting how often the phrases *in Christ, in him, in whom* (when referring to Christ), and *in the beloved* are repeated in verses 3-14. *In Christ* means something other than "by means of Christ," although the words are usually read in this sense. If we understand that the things listed here are done "by means of Christ," we shall not be totally wrong, for it is surely true that our salvation comes by means of Christ. The expression *in Christ* does not arrest our attention as it would that of first-century Greek readers. Our English word "in" is used more loosely than was the Greek word *en*, which it translates. Normally *en* was used to refer to someone located within a city, within a house, or in a boat, but not ordinarily of someone's person being *within someone else's person*. Paul's Ephesian readers would accept the phrase as good Greek, but they would stop for a second look at the surprising concept.

When we follow Paul's use of the expression, we discover that to be *in Christ* means that in a real sense the Christian has been placed, located, *within* Christ. *In Christ* signifies that whatever Jesus Christ is before God the Father, *the believer shares his identity*, because he or she is *within* the Savior. It is the Father giving the believer the same exalted status that Christ in all His glory now holds. It is the Christian's *full identification with Jesus Christ* in the eyes of the Father.

This does not imply that everyone is identical with God and needs only to become conscious of the supposed fact (as some religious systems teach). The believer does not become God or Christ by *nature* (that is, in essence) but is one with Christ in a personal standing before God. Paul used a corresponding comparison in Romans 8:29, where the Christians status is that of a member of the family of Christ, Christ being the older brother.

A brief overview of some key passages establishes the way the apostle used the phrase. A beginning is found in Colossians 2:9, "For in him [that is, in Christ] the whole fullness of deity dwells bodily." Jesus was completely identified with God the Father. This verse (among many others) establishes the unity of the Father and the Son. His humanity is unquestioned by almost everyone today, but this verse affirms what is also true, His full identification with the Father, hence His absolute deity. Following this, Colossians 2:10 applies the same concept to the believer: "And you have been filled *in him*, who is the head of all rule and authority." Fullness is saying that the believer has received everything, every spiritual blessing, through being identified with Christ.

Second Corinthians 5:17 adds to an understanding of the phrase: "Therefore if anyone is in Christ, he is a new creation. The old has passed away, behold, the new has come." In what way is the person *in Christ* a new creation? Obviously the Christian has not lost a certain propensity to sin.

Temptations constantly confront the believer, and they represent possibilities that are terribly real. If this were not so, the Ephesian letter would not have made such an issue of the Christian's obligation to put off fleshly practices, to put away falsehood, to desist from stealing, and the like. Grievous as the fact is, the Christian can sin, does sin, and a few Christians, most deplorably, sin often. Nevertheless the Scriptures declare that the believer is a new creation. Two things make him or her so. One is the fact that the Christian truly has a new inner resource, a divinely given power to live a new kind of life. This is asserted in Ephesians 1:19. The second is the fact that he or she has a totally new standing before God. God no longer counts that person's trespasses against him or her (2 Cor. 5:19). Not that the Christian is without trespasses. Rather, God does not view the Christian for what he or she is in practice. He sees the Christian for what the Christian is as the result of the cross. This means that God not only removes the believer's guilt, but also that he adds total righteousness to his or her heavenly account. He considers that person as righteous--as good--as Jesus Christ (2 Cor. 5:21).[14]
.   In virtue of being "in Christ," the believer is stated to have every spiritual blessing. However, this verse does not promise every conceivable blessing. The blessings guaranteed to the believer are those limited to *the heavenly places* (in various versions translated "the heavens" and "the heavenlies.") To understand what these are, observe Paul's usage of the expression in this epistle, which provides four additional truths about the *heavenly places*.

      1:20, They are the places of Christ's abode.
      2:6, They are the places where the believer is now "sitting."

---

14   For details on this concept refer to Observation II: In Christ. (p. 272)

3:10, They are occupied by "rulers and authorities," the realm of spirit beings.

6:1 2, "Spiritual forces of evil" operate in this realm. What sort of place includes all of these? We can assume they all refer to the same place. It seems apparent from 6:12 that they cannot be heaven itself, for heaven is the place of God's holy presence where the Christian rests forever delivered from sin and the presence of evil.

Heavenly places is not an expression of contradictions. Think of them as those realms where both good and wicked spiritual forces are at work. The heavenly places are where both God's Spirit and Satan are struggling for the soul of the Christian. Precisely here unquenchable blessings belong to the Christian. Because the Christian is "blessed with every spiritual blessing," he or she cannot ultimately fall. Satan cannot get the final victory.

The statement in 2:6 is not an exception to this concept. Sitting in the *heavenly places* is associated with being raised up with Christ. Obviously a literal resurrection is an experience no believer has yet enjoyed, but it is one that belongs to the Christian's *standing* before God. Similarly being made to "sit with him in the heavenly places in Christ Jesus" is a reference to the believer's *standing*. The believer has been seated so that in the coming ages God "might show the immeasurable riches of his grace in kindness toward us in Christ Jesus" (2.7). Because of this relationship, even though threatened by the forces of evil, the believer will be victorious by God's grace. Satan cannot get the final victory.

If we are tempted to think God is hesitant to dole out his blessings, we need to consider every word through verse 14. The apostle lists the blessings that are actually in the possession of the believer. When verse 3 states that God "has blessed us," this means that the blessings are already granted. *The blessings Paul writes about are those received by the Christian the moment he or she enters a new relationship with God through believing in Jesus the Messiah for salvation.* (John 20:31). That person may know very little about the blessings other than the fact that God has extended forgiveness to him or her. The blessings are not the kind one immediately feels, senses, or experiences. Because they relate the Christian to the providential care of the Father, experiences definitely will follow. Nevertheless the blessings belong to every believer regardless of feelings or emotions. Even though they are not immediately experienced, they are no less real, true, and valuable.

Verse 3 begins with the words, "Blessed be the God and Father of our Lord Jesus Christ." Someone might ask, "Is it not arrogant for a mere human to presume to bless the Almighty God?" Not at all, not when we understand that two Greek words in the New Testament are both translated "blessed." One is *makarios*, which means "happy." This is the word translated "blessed" in the Beatitudes (Matt. 5:3-11). Surely it would be presumptuous for any human to pray for God's happiness. The word used in Ephesians 1:3 is *eulogetos*. It derives from *eu*, "good," and *legō*, "to speak." The English word "eulogize" comes from it. It means "spoken well of." God "speaks well" of us in His gracious actions toward us. In turn we "speak well" of God by acknowledging His truth, His greatness, and His right to receive our constant adoration. We cannot help but bless God in the sense of "speaking well" of Him when we grasp the tremendous scope of the six significant blessings unfolded in the verses that follow.

I. Holy and Blameless (1:4)
⁴even as he chose us in him before the foundation of the world, that we should be holy and blameless before him.
 This verse says believers were chosen. When did this take place? In whatever sense individuals were chosen "before the foundation of the world," the choosing extends beyond some initial point, for it constitutes the believer "holy and blameless" before God. The aorist "chose" is a circle with boundaries that embrace at least a certain period of time. What are the limits of the boundaries? That remains to be explained in verses to follow.

A. The Unnecessary Controversy over God's Choosing (His Election)
 Few intellectual subjects have generated more passionate arguments among Christians than the question of whether God chooses individuals to believe and be saved or whether it is the individual's personal choice to believe and be saved. This is an issue that historically separated many Christian denominations from each other. On one side John Calvin, famous French theologian of the sixteenth century, and his followers preached the inexorable sovereignty of God in which He elected only certain ones to salvation, and others, the non elect, are unavoidably bound for hell. Everyone's eternal destiny was settled before creation itself. In the centuries to follow, Presbyterian, Puritan (including their successors, the Congregationalists), and Reformed churches gave this doctrine their allegiance. On the other side the Dutch theologian Jacobus Arminius, born fifty-one years af-

ter Calvin, could not escape the "whosoever will" verses of the Bible. He insisted that not only did Christ die for all but that God in His love made it possible for anyone for whom Christ died to come to him by his or her own choice. Each one makes a personal decision to be saved or lost. If this is true and humans can make free choices, it would seem that for salvation humans must also have the responsibility of cooperating with God. Further, a Christian may choose to remove himself or herself from the fold of salvation by unbelief or by gross sin. Methodist, Churches of Christ, and many other denominations built upon this conviction. Among early Baptists, the Particular Baptists of England followed Calvin's view, and the General Baptists of England adhered to the view of Arminius.

Many writers seek to harmonize the election verses with the whosoever will verses of Scripture by thinking of them as opposite sides of an irreconcilable paradox (or at least one opaque to us). An oft-heard illustration is that predestination and free will are to be compared to the two sides of an arch over the gate of salvation. One about to enter sees the words written outside the arch, "Whosoever will may come." After entering, one looks back and on the other side of the arch sees the words, "You did not choose me, but I chose you." It may be comforting for Christians to think this way, but does not the thinking contradict itself?

Is harmony possible? True, God is inscrutable except insofar as He has chosen to reveal Himself. But when His revelation seems to be self-contradictory, do not believers have some obligation to seek a resolution? Would God give us a revelation with contradictions, even if the contradictions are soft-pedaled by calling them "in tension"?

Verse 4 clearly speaks of God choosing every believer. Does not the word "chose" favor Calvin's view, especially when the verse says that the choosing took place "before the foundation of the world"?

To get around the problem, some Wesleyan commentators and theologians hold that election is primarily a *corporate* term. This is not the same concept as the corporate election of the Church, a doctrine developed further along in this study. Taking a view acceptable to Wesleyan theologians, Marcus Barth wrote, "The phrase [in Christ] denotes the relationship formed by Jesus Christ between God and God's people, rather than a bond established by faith or sacraments between Christ and individuals only."[15] Supposedly nothing in Ephesians 1 is about individuals; rather, the text looks at the Church, people as a group who are "in Christ." This view is plainly an error, for forgiveness in verse 7 is clearly something God does for the individual, not for the Church corporately. "Believed in him," verse 13, is part of the same sentence as verse 4. There the choosing refers to individuals who believe, not a corporate body.

The issue, in this passage at least, has a suitable resolution. It is one that follows neither Calvinist nor contemporary Arminian/Wesleyan theologies. Interestingly the explanation, in a critical part, is right in front of our eyes, although many respected Bible scholars have missed it. To understand the apostle's thinking, we must first recall that our Lord Je-

---

15 M. Barth, *Ephesians, Introduction, Translation, and Commentary on Chapters 1-3*, 70. Since it a relationship between God and God's people collectively, a believer is free to abandon his salvation. See also Klyne Snodgrass, *Ephesians*, The NIV Application Commentary (Grand Rapids: Zondervan,1996), 49.

sus was chosen, foreordained, elected to be the Savior from all eternity. Peter declared in Acts 2:23 that "this Jesus" was "delivered up according to the definite plan and foreknowledge of God." In 1 Peter 1:20 he explains that Jesus "was destined before the foundation of the world." This affirmation by Peter was nothing surprising or unexpected by the Christian community, for the Lord, speaking to his Servant in Isaiah 49:7 had announced, "the Holy One of Israel, who has *chosen* you." The predicted Messiah was clearly understood to be chosen before His advent: Luke 9:35; 23:35. Paul unquestionably echoed this truth in 2 Timothy 1:9, where he wrote of our salvation given us "in Christ Jesus ages ago."

God destined Jesus before the foundation of the world, but did God ages ago also choose certain individuals to become believers? Did he then work in such a way that the chosen would irresistibly believe and others, not chosen, simply could not believe? Ephesians does not make such a specific statement, although many who take this position find their basic proof in Ephesians 1:4-5 and 1:11.

What does verse 4 say? Note again these simple but pointed words, "in him." Many expositors take them as meaning "by means of him," but we have seen (v.3) that they signify *complete identification with Christ*. This is the key. Without it everything in verses 3-14 is easily misunderstood. (See Observation II, p. 272.)

Understanding the key, every person trusting in Christ should be able to voice the following statements. Before I believed, I was *not* identified with Him. In no respect could I have been one of those chosen, for I was one of the "children of wrath" (Eph. 2:3). When I believed, at that point I was placed *in Christ*. I became in God's sight what Jesus is. At the time of my conscious act of faith, through becoming one with Christ, I was chosen *in Him*. I was not chosen to believe, but having believed I was chosen for *all that He is*. Is Christ without sin in the reckoning of the Father? So am I (Eph. 1:4, 7). Is Christ risen from the dead? In the reckoning of God, even now so am I (Eph. 2:6), although the event waits the Lord's reappearing (1 Cor. 15:51-52). Was Christ chosen before the foundation of the world? So am I, although my being chosen did not take place until the day that through faith I was placed "in him." As a believer I was chosen "before the foundation of the world," but only through being "in Him."[16]

B. The Meaning of Being "Holy and Blameless before Him"

The purpose of our having been chosen is that we might be "holy and blameless before him." But what does this mean? Those of us willing to examine our lives under the searching scrutiny of Scripture are constantly reminded how often we sin, if not in overt acts of commission, then in covert acts of selfishness that reveal how little we have entered into the full measure of the love of Christ. It may be possible to be "holy and blameless" as far as our friends and associates are concerned. But the Scriptures here are speaking about being holy and blameless *before God*. Can anyone

---

16 Karl Barth, *Church Dogmatics*, Vol. II "The Doctirne of God," ed. G. W. Bromiley and T. F. Torrance, trans. G. W. Bromiley, J. C. Campbell, Iain Wilson, J. Strathearn McNab, Harold Knight, R. A. Stewart (Edinburgh: T. & T. Clark, 1957), 94-145. The authors do not agree with much of Barth's theology, but he sought to understand the meaning of the Scriptures. Especially helpful is Barth's translation on pp. 108-110 of a passage from Athanasius (c. 293-373), one of the church fathers who expressed this concept.

qualify?

In our daily practice there is no question but that God wants us to be holy and blameless. The same two words are found together in 5:27, which states that Christ's great sacrifice was made with the express purpose that the Church, the assembly of His people, might be holy and blameless ("without blemish" in the ESV). In 1:4, however, all those who are "in him," all who believe, are *in fact* "holy and blameless." Is this reality?

The words "holy and blameless" do not refer to the Christian's character. They have to do with the Christian's standing (or position). They state how God regards the believer, seeing him or her as being united with Christ. At this point the apostle is not concerned with the Christian's behavior. To be acceptable to God, an acceptable standing is an absolute prerequisite. The question of character or of practices cannot enter, because no one has an acceptable character. Before a God of moral perfection, the least peccadillo disqualifies, condemns. But to the undeserving sinner who comes to Christ in faith, God grants a perfect standing.

Some commentators suppose that the phrase "before Him" refers not to what the believer is in this life but to the character the Christian will have when standing perfected before God in glory. Certainly every believer will be blameless when presented to the Father in heaven. What the apostle declares is that this perfect standing belongs to the believer *now*. It is "before Him!" Everyone stands constantly before the omnipresent God. Some stand before Him condemned; others stand before Him with perfect righteousness. There is no middle ground.

II. Placed as Sons (1:5-6)

In love ⁵he predestined us for adoption through Jesus Christ, according to the purpose of his will, ⁶to the praise of his glorious grace, with which he has blessed us in the Beloved.

The result of "predestined," an aorist participle, is that believers are constituted sons of God. The circle described by the aorist is large. As sons of God it extends until the time of the believer's resurrection. In verse 6 the aorist verb "blessed" (or "graced") tells us something was done at a point in time. Is it a point no larger than a pin prick, the point of conversion, or is it a circle embracing a great span? By itself the verb does not say. The implication is that it is a large circle, for it was something done for the purpose of bringing glory to God, and surely that glory was not for the brief moment of one's conversion.

In verse 5, the ESV and some other modern versions have the translation "adoption." Other versions use "adopted as sons." The RSV, NIV, NKJV, and a few others translate "placed as sons" or simply "sons." Which should we choose? The Greek word (*huiothesia*) is a compound of two words, "sons" + "placing." We can think of believers as being adopted, but to translate it this way implies a concept that may be foreign to Paul's thinking, since it overlooks a number of other passages about sonship where the idea of adoption is absent.[17] The verse should be translated, "he predes-

---

17 George C. Gianoulis, "Is Sonship in Romans 8:14-17 a Link with Romans 9?" *Bibliotheca Sacra* 166 (January-March 2009): 70-83, summarizes efforts by scholars to determine whether the concept of adoption had its origin in Greek law, Roman law, or the Old Testament. The question is, Was it a common enough practice among Greeks in Ephesus that it would have been used in any legal sense by the Apostle? It seems much simpler to see Paul using it as the new status into which all believ-

tined us for sonship."

We are not by nature the sons of God. The concept of the universal fatherhood of God and the universal brotherhood of man did not come from the Bible. Unquestionably it was not included in the belief system of the apostle, who wrote that before becoming Christians all of us were among the "sons of disobedience" (2:2). As such, we had no claim of any kind to a personal relationship with God.

What is described here in 1:6 is an act of God, who put us into His family in a way that is completely untrue of those who are not believers (John 1:12). As God constitutes us sons, we become, in His reckoning, on the same plane as the One who is His Son by nature, Jesus Christ Himself. What is so wonderful about sonship is that it is a standing to which we have no right. It would have been an act of infinite grace had God made us simply servants. Yet in an incomprehensible act of pure grace He has made us sons!

Believers are here called "sons," not "children." Believers are often referred to in Scripture as God's children, a term that denotes the affection with which God holds them. Sonship, on the other hand, conveys the idea of status and position of a family, which in turn reflects the glory of Christ, the Head of the family.

The status of sonship (and daughtership, insofar as these earthly distinctions are important) means that in every

---

ers have been placed by faith. See the summary in Douglas J. Moo, *The Epistle to the Romans* (Grand Rapids: Eerdmans, 1996) 501, n. 26. Moo questions whether Paul used the word to mean the act of adoption or the status of sonship. The reading "placed as sons" or "sonship" seems much less likely to lead to erroneous conclusions. Some recent translators have chosen "adoption" presumably to avoid sexist language suggested by the word "sons" or "sonship."

way believers are the objects of God's concern. He will not abandon us. He will continue to lead, plead, chasten, and work providentially to draw our hearts closer to himself. A brief survey of doctrine embraced under the term son is instructive. Sonship required the suffering of Jesus and the price he paid at Calvary (Gal. 4:4-5; Heb. 2:10). It is entered by faith (Gal. 3:7, 26). It makes the believer the object of God's constant care, which includes (a) the bestowal of good gifts (Matt. 7:9-11) and (b) the discipline of chastening (Heb. 12:5-8). It confers freedom on the believer in this life (Matt. 17:26) and heirship of the kingdom in the future (Gal. 4:7; Rev. 21:7). It has now the testimony of God's Spirit (Rom. 8:16-17; Gal. 4:6). It will be fully revealed at the resurrection (Luke 20:36; Rom. 8:18, 23, 29).

Not only are we sons. The Word says that he *predestined* us to be His sons. Can the believer, once granted sonship, later forfeit his or her sonship? Happily, the answer is no. The *context* of these verses conveys the thought of a once-for-all act. If sonship can be forfeited, either by a lapse of faith or a fall into sin, then the word "predestined" is meaningless. Had the Holy Spirit intended it to be contingent, another verbal tense or another word would have been chosen.

The Greek word for "predestined" simply means to be "marked out beforehand."[18] The word was precisely chosen to introduce four aspects of divine preparation for sonship. There were things that necessarily had to precede our sonship. What these are is plain from the four particulars

---

18 See the lexical study of "to predestinate" (*proorizein*) by C. Gordon Olson, *Getting the Gospel Right: A Balanced View of Salvation Truth* (Cedar Knolls, NJ: Global Gospel Publishers, 2005), 267-73.

with which Paul qualifies sonship.

(a) *We are marked out for sonship by God's passion.* Sonship originates with God's passionate love. For English readers this fact is clear from the punctuation and word order found in the ESV but not from the punctuation and word order in many other versions. The AV, for example, reads as if it is the love in our character that makes us holy and blameless. Fortunately the ESV put the word "love" where it belongs.[19] This division of the epistle is about what God has done for us. We are destined to be sons, not because of *our* love but because of *God's* love. NET appropriately translates, "For he lovingly chose us in Christ." The NASB and the NIV correctly have "in love He predestined us" (vv. 4b-5a), except that the NIV does not capitalize "He.".

This matter of love is of outstanding importance, if we wish to understand much of Paul's message in Ephesians, not only in this passage but throughout the epistle. The word used here for love is *agapē*, a familiar word among Christian audiences. Its full significance is often missed. It stands for a total concern for the welfare, good, and interests of another person *without any expectation of recompense or reward*. It is the love that God had for us when He gave His son to take our place in death. It is the love God now has for all mankind. (See Observation III, The Biblical Meaning of Love, for a further explanation and comparison with other Greek words for love, p. 276).

(b) *We are marked out for sonship through a person.* This is none other than Jesus Himself. Why is it that here Paul wrote, He destined us in love to be His sons "*through* Jesus Christ" instead of *in* Jesus Christ? Nowhere else in

---

19 Larkin, *Ephesians: A Handbook on the Greek Text*, 7.

the epistle is this phrase used. The answer is clear, when we recognize that "in love" belongs to verse 5 and not verse 4. "In love" modifies "predestined," not "that we should be." Before we could be *in Christ*, the love of God had to provide a means by which the demands of divine justice could be averted and we could be made acceptable to him. Guilty of sin, we could never be placed *in Christ*. So in his incredibly great love, God sent his Son to suffer the agony of Golgotha that *through* that awful judgment we might be made acceptable. Thus God's love, working "through Jesus Christ," did what was necessary for us to become sons.

Understanding that we are granted sonship through the person of Jesus Christ, the word *predestined* cannot hold that dread interpretation according to which, long in advance, God selected a few to salvation but by failing to select the rest, consigned the great balance of mankind to inevitable and everlasting torment. The odium of such an interpretation is not relieved by insisting, as some do, that God elects some and merely leaves others to their own inevitable choice. If God chooses not to provide most of mankind an "effective call," God surely chooses the rest for hell. What other rational conclusion is there? This verse, supposedly a prooftext for this view, does not make such a doctrine necessary.

God's plan making our sonship possible was done through the predestination of Jesus Christ. It was not provided uniquely for the few whom God presumably elected, but in God's love the provision was made for the whole world. Each of us became a recipient of the grace of sonship when by faith we were placed *in Christ*

At the end of the Civil War, General Robert E. Lee was seeking to escape Grant's overwhelmingly more numerous forces by a westward march from Petersburg. On Palm Sunday morning, he found his path on the west blocked by the infantry of Union generals Ord and Griffin. Almost to a man, Lee's remaining troops were loyal to him and were willing to continue fighting, even though it would mean certain death. Obviously, Lee had to make a choice. He could continue the struggle toward inevitable annihilation, or surrender and win life for his men. Out of concern for his troops, he chose to surrender. The decision was made before his troops knew what he was thinking. When he signed the surrender papers in McLean's house at Appomattox, he predetermined his soldiers to life. Yet each individual, after being informed of the act, had to ratify that destiny by accepting a parole. By turning in his weapons and accepting a parole, the individual soldier settled his own destiny.[20] No less for us, when by faith we accept God's work through Jesus Christ, who previously earned our destiny for us, we are granted salvation. At the moment of faith we enter life as sons. Henceforth we can look forward to the full and certain realization of that sonship in the resurrection.

(c) *We are marked out for sonship for a purpose.* It is "according to the purpose of his will." The word "purpose," used in the ESV is not wholly adequate, because it omits the idea of "good," which is in the original word, *eudokia*. The AV, the NKJV, and the NRSV translate the original word by "good pleasure," but this leaves out the idea of purpose. "Good purpose" or "kindly intent" would do better. God's

---

20   In the interest of historical accuracy, it might be noted that Lee's officers were given individual paroles, but to expedite the surrender, each officer in command of a body of troops listed the men under his command and to effect their paroles signed the list for them.

will, Paul is explaining, is not arbitrary or capricious, but is part of a design, and that design is eminently good.

In the midst of a culture guided mainly by a hedonistic quest for pleasure, there are young souls who desperately need a purpose in life. They cry out for meaning, but can find nothing more significant than preserving animal rights or campaigning for zero population growth. In becoming a son of God, an individual aligns himself or herself with the highest of all purposes, purposes directed by God who has all knowledge and from whose guidance the greatest possible good can and does emerge. Here alone can a person truly find oneself, find a genuine identity.

(d) *We are marked out for sonship to God's praise.* The question may have occurred to some, Why did God go to the trouble of making us sons? Was it primarily for the benefits that accrue to us? Or was it for the sake of the good works that we might do? Undoubtedly both are good reasons for His saving us. But here we are told that the primary reason is that God might be known and praised for His grace. The glory of God is at stake.

Curiously the ESV (and the RSV and the NIV) omits the phrase "for himself," a phrase that is in the Greek text. Verse 5 should read, "He destined us in love to be his sons through Jesus Christ *for himself.*" Perhaps the editors thought that including it was redundant and failed to add any new thought to the discourse. It is important, however, for it emphasizes the thought of verse 6, that God made us sons for His sake rather than primarily for ours. We are, of course, the benefactors, but He far more so.

"To the praise of his glorious grace." The idea of grace is not complicated. In English we commonly use the word to refer to an action or deed that is gracious or a form that is graceful or pleasing. For example, "What grace she has on her skates." The Greek word was used in the same way. But the Greek word was also used of kindness or good will exercised by one person toward another. This is precisely how it is used here. It is the free, unearned favor that God pours out on those who lack the worth to claim it. If God asked for the least human deed to gain His favor, He would no longer be a God of limitless grace. What this God of grace asks, and what He in his infinite power has a right to ask, is that He might receive the praise of the universe for being the God of such grace.

III. Redeemed (1:7-8)
[7] In him we have redemption through his blood, the forgiveness of our trespasses, according to the riches of his grace, [8] which he lavished upon us in all wisdom and insight

"Lavished" in verse 8 is an aorist-tense verb specifying what God did through the riches of His grace. As we have seen, the aorist may refer to a minute pencil-point in time or a large circle. How large is the circle here? God's grace must be more than momentary. Again the implication is a circle, not a brief point in the past.

Interestingly, in verses 7 the main verb is 'have." It is the only main verb in the present tense in the whole sentence. It has the sense of "continue having." This is a significant exception to the long string of aorist verbs. To continue having redemption means that the benefits of God's grace continue to apply, even if God's child should fall into sin--as at times any of us may do!

This third invaluable blessing belonging to the believer is that of redemption. The meaning of redemption is critical, for our eternal salvation depends on it. The Greek word used by Paul (*apolutrōsis*) had two meanings, one "release from torture" (Heb. 11:35) and "release from some constraint, usually by payment of a price." It is this latter sense which Paul uses in 1:7. What was purchased was the dismissal of the sinner's guilt. The passage is meaningless, unless God the Father is the one who, because the price was paid, is rendered capable of dismissing the sinner's guilt. God's judgment, which we deserve, was mercifully excluded when we came under the protection of the cross.

Here it is necessary to correct a particular error with regard to redemption. To Paul the price paid was the death of Jesus--nothing less, nothing more. This is obvious from the explicit statement that it was "through his blood." Also this is the sense in which the word is used in Romans 3:24-25 and Hebrews 9:15. Our English word is perfectly adequate to express the meaning of the word. Yet the emasculated sense attached to it in much current religious literature is entirely different. Authors write piously of the Church needing to "live redemptively." By this they mean that Christians should accept a concern for social action. The price is the personal inconvenience one may suffer. In the same breath they speak of Christ "living and dying redemptively," as though His death was that of a heroic martyr who suffered rather than surrender His concern for His fellow man, a category of heroism that in some measure we His followers are to emulate. Now to be sure, the Christian ought to be ready to suffer any extent of personal inconvenience, suffer actual pain if need be, even death, for the sake of another. May God help Christians who, lacking love, are deaf to the cries of those in need. But to use the word "redemption" to describe this responsibility is to take a word rich in meaning and reduce it to poverty. The subject here is our relationship to God, not society. The expositor S. D. F. Salmond, commenting on "through his blood" in this verse, stated it accurately: "Its primary idea, as is shown by usage and by O. T. analogy, is not that of receiving power or moral effect, but that of expiation, the removal of guilt, the restoration of broken relations with God."[21]

When the Apostle writes of the redemption rendered by our Lord, he unquestionably refers to His death and His death alone. The phrase "through his blood" was not intended to be an abbreviation for "through his blood, sweat, and tears." It does not mean His total life with all its trials and sorrows. It is not a redemptive life that is put before us, but a redemptive *death*. When Paul described the institution of the Lord's Supper, he wrote of the cup, which the Lord gave, as the New Covenant "in my blood." He immediately explained that it was the proclamation of the "Lord's death" (I Cor. 11:26). Not the proclamation of His life, as valuable and as significant as His life is for the believer, not the proclamation of His life plus his death, but specifically and pointedly, His death alone.

The words in verse 7, "through his blood," have sometimes been invested with a meaning the Scriptures never intended. Both in sacerdotal forms of Christianity and in popular modern pietism the substance blood, the very plasma and corpuscles that ran from the wounds of Christ,

---

21   S. D. F. Salmond, "The Epistle of Paul to the Ephesians" in *The Expositor's Greek Testament*, ed. W. Robertson Nicoll (London: Hodder and Staughton, 1903), 3: 253-54.

is considered to have saving virtue. His death is regarded as almost incidental to the shedding of His blood. That this confusion should arise is not surprising, since in the Old Testament blood was assigned such a central role. The blood of a sacrifice was sprinkled on the altar, blood of a bull and of a goat was sprinkled on and before the mercy seat, blood of a sacrifice was applied to a leper for his cleansing, and so forth. Nevertheless in the Old Testament the blood in every instance was representative of the *death* that was given. "For the life of the flesh is in the blood . . . for it is the blood that makes atonement" (Lev. 17:11). Significantly the verse goes on to explain, "by reason of the life." The loss of that life was symbolized in the sprinkling of the blood. The sacrifice of Christ's life, His death at Calvary, saves. The blood in a graphic metonomy speaks of that sacrifice. Yet "blood" stands for more than mere cessation of life. It pictures the violent and agonizing death the Savior endured at the hands of those bent on His destruction.

The apostle added the following two things about redemption. Each is important for understanding Ephesians in its setting.

(a) Redemption is a *forgiving* act. Forgiveness and redemption refer to the same gift of God, for "the forgiveness of our trespasses" stands in apposition to "redemption through his blood." Yet someone might ask, If they both refer to God's dismissal of sin, why did Paul use two terms? Reflection suggests the emotional impact each would have on new Gentile converts in Ephesus. "Redemption" is a judicial act. Although its consequences are tremendous, it lacks the warmth of "forgiveness," a word meaning the act of freeing someone from an obligation, guilt, or punishment. The one is legal, arising from the necessity of God's justice; the other is intimate, speaking of God's great love.

(b) Redemption is a *gracious* act. Did Paul forget that in the preceding verse he had already praised God for His grace? No. He simply cannot cease voicing his amazement that it is all a favor from God. In this list of benefits, not one comes by personal striving or virtue.

On this side of the Cross, it is easy enough for us to look back and understand the many Old Testament highways leading to the Cross. To the most devout Old Testament saint, however, it was all a mystery. Who was the redeemer of Job 19:25-26? Who was the suffering Servant of Isaiah 53? What could the promised Messiah, the great deliverer anticipated by Israel, have to do with the suffering Servant? These things were not explained. Not so much as a hint spoke of the purposes of God in manifesting His grace. Now this mystery is unfolded in all its magnificence. The death of Jesus has made the design of God marvelously clear.

Prior to the Wright brothers, men had observed the flight of birds, and imaginative dreamers guessed that someday man might build a machine to lift himself from the ground. Most people (including the grandfather of one of the authors) scoffed at the notion that man might ever fly. But when the Wright brothers showed by actually flying that it could be done, the whole picture changed. Similarly, when Jesus gave His life on the Cross, there was, in effect, a public announcement, first of God's deep concern for man, and second, of the fact that God did something to erase the guilt that held humans fast. Romans 3:25-26 amplifies this truth of the Cross being God's public justification and announcement of His righteousness.

His grace was "lavished upon us." The Greek verb translated "lavished" has as its primary meaning "more than enough." However wicked our past, the grace of God, made possible by the death of the Savior, is more than sufficient to erase every remembrance of sin. Significantly, the verb is an aorist. It happened at the point of our faith. .

Does "wisdom and insight" refer to God's wisdom and insight in lavishing His grace on us, or does it refer to the human wisdom and insight God in grace gives? Some expositors see wisdom and insight as benefits enabling a Christian to live wisely. However, the context is about God's grace in salvation. Included is God's wisdom and insight in providing us with His grace, not God's grace providing us with wisdom. Verse 9 which follows is about what God has made known to us, not about an ability he has provided for our knowledge. True, God wants the believer to experience wisdom and insight and to live accordingly. In Colossians 1:9 Paul prayed that the saints in that city might have "wisdom and understanding." But there Paul was concerned with human wisdom and insight, whereas in Ephesians 1:8 he is concerned with God's notable wisdom and insight.

IV. **Enlightened** (1:9-10)
⁹Making known to us the mystery of his will, according to his purpose which he set forth in Christ ¹⁰as a plan for the fullness of time, to unite all things in him, things in heaven and things on earth.

As we have examined the verbs beginning with verse 4, we have seen that they are aorists with the context indicating enduring time. According to verse 9, God "set forth" His purpose, another aorist verb. His purpose was to make known the mystery of His will, something inferring a very large circle.

Verse 9 states that God has made known to us what could never be discovered by intuition, logic, observation, or experimentation. Since it could not be discovered by human ingenuity, it is a *mystery*. The word "mystery" is used five additional times in Ephesians (3:3, 4, 9; 5:32; 6:19), obviously a significant word for the apostle. It means that what was previously either unknown or at best a silhouette vaguely seen is now clearly visible. God has now chosen to reveal His great purpose through Christ, a purpose that was not imagined by Old Testament saints.

What mystery of God's will is now revealed to us? It is His purpose "to unite all things in him." Sin created terrible disunity in the universe. In what sense are all things to be united? Are all beings, those in hell as well as those in heaven, ultimately to be restored in one common salvation? The passage does not say this, even though some have viewed it that way. The word translated "unite" (*anakephalaiōsasthai*) is an interesting word used only one other place in the New Testament, Romans 13:9. It is a word used for what a Roman or Greek orator did when he summarized his points at the end of a speech. The summary brought all his points together coherently *under one head.* This is Paul's announcement here. God is going to unify everything in the universe under one head. This will be for Himself, and this will be done in intimate connection with the Lord Jesus Christ. Everything will have purpose and meaning, even the necessity of eternal judgment itself, when all of God's purposes are seen "in Christ."

Reading verse 7, we should have no trouble recognizing that God's purpose can be accomplished only "through his blood." And only in the light of the Cross can it be discerned. This is a central concern of the apostle, not only here but in other epistles as well. Every apparent contradiction, every moral paradox, every spiritual question has a final and satisfying elucidation in the Cross. Is God unjust in granting total forgiveness to a wretched sinner who has done nothing worthwhile? Yes, He can do so because of the Cross. Is God unjust in condemning a man who is reckoned good by society and whose sins have been nowhere as gross as those of others, simply because that person failed to trust in Jesus? God can pronounce judgment and be completely just, since a free gate was opened at the Cross, but that gate was rejected.

In verse 10 the word "time" in the Greek is actually plural: "fullness of the times." God's plan for the fullness of the times looks to a point when the various epochs of history will be consummated. The times, that is the point when the realization that His purposes are completed, will be when the Messiah comes to rule on earth.[22] Is not this the end-point for which biblically-minded believers are longing?

Can we truly say that every believer, even the newest babe in Christ, is enlightened with an understanding of God's purposes? No, but every believer holds the key to such an understanding. Encountering the various circumstances of life, almost every believer wonders about God's purposes. Events are often perplexing, and one cannot see how a loving God could possibly be using them for good. There are many questions about the purposes of God a person would like to ask. The answers may not all be available in this life, but as the Christian grows in grace, the opaque becomes clearer

---

22 Hoehner, *Ephesians, An Exegetical Commentary*, 218-19.

through understanding the Savior's great sacrifice. Someday every believer will have the answers, and when we do, even the most tortuous questions will be answered in relation to the Father's wise design centered about the Cross.

V. **Made a Treasured Possession** (1:11-12)

[11]In him we have obtained an inheritance, having been predestined according to the purpose of him who works all things according to the counsel of his will, [12]so that we who were the first to hope in Christ might be to the praise of his glory.

The first clause of verse 11 more accurately translated reads, "In him we were made a heritage." This is preferable to the translations chosen by editors of the ESV, the AV, the NASB, the NRSV, and the NIV.[23] The verb, "we were made," is in the aorist tense. Does the aorist here imply a minute point in time or a large circle of time? How large a circle? By itself the aorist does not say. The context, that God has claimed us for His heritage, surely implies a very long period, presumably for endless aeons.

Two main thoughts come through in these verses. The primary statement is that God has claimed believers as His heritage. The second is the reason why God did so, namely, that we might be to the praise of his glory.

Most translations, including the ESV, construe the words to teach that God has given believers an inheritance. However, the promise of an inheritance reserved for believers in a life to come is found in verse 14. We indeed look forward to receiving the glorious wonders God has reserved

---

23   Ibid., 225-27. Larkin, *Ephesians: A Handbok on the Greek Text*, 13, explains why he disagrees. .

for us. But here is something entirely different. Paul uses a word found only here in the New Testament (*klēroō*). Paul asserted the unimaginable. In the sight of God, we ourselves are a fortune of such rare and precious value that He has fastened His claim on *us* as His special *heritage*.

Is any of us dejected because we are one of the nobodies of this world? Or because we will never leave our mark on society, not even on our own neighborhood? Have any of us been rejected and left to ourselves because we are unattractive or lacking in charm? How can people outside the faith know what God has made us? They can't. But from these words we know that God Himself has made us His own particular treasure!

The further sense of the passage is this: The believer's very existence as an individual with sins blotted out and a perfect standing in his sight is *in itself* a praise to God. The redeemed sinner is a wonder and a joy that glorifies God.

While considering these two verses, we should note they tell us truths about God making this praise possible. One is that He is a self-determining God. He carries out all things in accord with the "counsel of his will." He makes decisions for Himself. This statement might appear a tautology. If God is God, it ought to be obvious that He makes His own decisions. Nevertheless many people who talk and write about God believe in a God who is part of the universe and to a large extent is controlled *by* it rather than a God who is sovereign *over* the universe. The god they believe in is not the God of the Bible but a god who has come to them from the mind of philosophers.

A second striking truth is the fact of God's power. This passage says that he "works all things" according to the counsel of his will. The word "works" might more literally be translated "energizes." Some have taken this to mean that God is maintaining every activity of the universe, even including the physical energy of the atoms. Such may indeed be true, but what Paul is referring to here is not God's support of the physical universe but His activity on behalf of His people, activity that united us with Christ Himself. The word "works" is used a number of times in the New Testament of what God does (e.g., 1 Cor. 12:6; Gal. 3:5; Phil. 2:13), but always of God's personal power operating to produce all that He wants for those of us who believe. Surely this is a truth for which we can praise him. His power for our good is limitless.

A third truth is that God predestined us with a purpose. His purpose was that by our salvation we might be to the praise of his glory. When a sin-condemned individual places his or her trust in Christ, that person is predestined not only to all the astounding benefits of salvation but becomes God's heritage. Thereby God is glorified for his grace.

Whom did God claim as His heritage? The answer in the ESV is, "We who were the first to hope in Christ." This could be misleading. It would have been much better if the editors had written, "we who first hoped in Christ." The translation in the ESV is seemingly based on the notion that in verses 3-12 Paul was writing about Jewish Christians. Then in verses 13-14 he wrote of Gentile believers. This concept is found in a number of scholarly commentaries but is a mistake, as will be pointed out below. What the passage says is that God's heritage is limited to those who began with hope in Jesus. There are no exceptions.

VI. Sealed (1:13-14)

[13] In him you also, who have heard the word of truth, the gospel of your salvation, and have believed in him, were sealed with the promised Holy Spirit, [14] which is the guarantee of our inheritance until we acquire possession of it, to the praise of his glory.

"Were sealed" in verse 13 is the capstone of the series of aorist verbs in this division. It leaves us in no doubt at all. It is something that lasts at least from the time a person becomes a believer until that believer acquires possession of his or her inheritance. The circle described in the verse is one lasting from the new birth until the future resurrection. In this climactic statement, and implied or inferred throughout verses 3-14, everything listed with an aorist is something that God does *once for all*. The verbs taken alone do not say so, but they are most definitely colored this way by their contexts.

"In him you also" may seem an odd way of introducing this sixth major benefit granted those united to Christ. The previous verses all speak of what "we" have in Christ. Suddenly Paul writes of what "you" have. Not a few commentators suggest that Paul was writing in the preceding verses of what "we true Jews" have. Then in this verse Paul turns his attention to believing Gentiles to describe what they possess along with the Jews. Richard Weymouth went so far as to translate verse 11 "In Him we Jews have been made heirs," and to translate verse 13, "And in Him you Gentiles also."[24] Markus Barth wrote that the words are to show that there are two levels of authority in the Church. At the top

---

24 Richard Francis Weymouth, *New Testament in Modern Speech*, 3d ed., ed. and rev. Ernest Hampden-Cook (Boston: Pilgrim Press, 1909).

level of authority are those Jews who were first entrusted with the gospel. Then the Gentile believers are found at the next level.[25]

This is decidedly a wrong turn, even though the interpretation goes all the way back to Pelagius in the fifth century. Actually the Jew/Gentile theme does not become a part of Paul's discussion until 2:11, and when it does, it is to show that both Jews and Gentiles are part of one body, being brought into one true commonwealth. Furthermore there is not the least intimation of a Jew/Gentile level of authority anywhere in the book. In 4:11 we find implications of levels of authority, but these are based not on national origin but on spiritual gifts[26].

Why does Paul now abruptly write not of "us" but now of "you"? This is a common rhetorical device, well known among Greek writers. It directs the reader's thoughts to a matter needing particular attention. It is the same thing practiced by public speakers today. A preacher may be describing to his congregation what "we" have done in supporting missionary work in the former Soviet Union, how "we" have contributed to the support of a missionary in Russia plus one in the Ukraine and two in Byelorussia. The litany is almost monotonous when he unexpectedly says, "*You* need to think about taking on a responsibility for great, unmet, spiritual needs in Tadzhikistan." Did he mean that he and perhaps the assistant pastor and the choir director had been supporting the other missionaries and now the congre-

---

25 M. Barth, *Ephesians: Introduction, Translation and Commentary on Chapters 1-3*, 76, 92.
26 See Larkin, *Ephesians: A Handbook on the Greek Text*, 15, for a defense of this point of view.

gation has a responsibility for a new missionary endeavor? Of course not. First, he wanted to show what good things had already been done and next to exhibit emphatically an additional opportunity and responsibility. In the same way Paul is saying, "Look, we have all these things; now won't *you* (each of you in particular as well as all of you in general) think about this wonderful additional manifestation of God's grace."

This sixth principal benefit is a sealing that guarantees the final, resplendent outcome of our salvation. This benefit can be considered under five headings.

1. *The recipients of the sealing.* This is those who have heard "the word of truth, the gospel of your salvation," and who have believed it. Why does Paul say "the word of truth" instead of simply the gospel of your salvation? In Paul's day, just as in ours, there were many who were peddling other gospels. The only true gospel was the declaration of salvation by grace through faith alone in Christ alone! In order to believe, a person must hear clearly what to believe. Paul wrote in Romans 10:17, "So faith comes from what is heard, and what is heard comes by the preaching of Christ."

The benefit is plainly limited to those who "have believed in him." One may most sincerely believe in some other messiah, some other system, some other god, or one may believe deeply that God will honor every effort to be good. Yet nothing will suffice other than faith in Jesus Christ, the Redeemer. He is the only way. This is the unmistakable proclamation of these words.

Is God unjust in limiting salvation to those who have heard of and believed in Christ? What about those who have never heard? Do they not have a chance? This frequently asked question is not answered here. It is answered, at least in part, in Romans 1. It is beside the point to introduce the answer here. What the author is emphasizing is not who fails to get salvation, but the fact that it is extended to all who do believe. It is conditioned on nothing else, no other term, than simple faith. It has to be so. If it were not so, it would not be by grace.

What is meant by faith, or by believing? (It might be noted that both are translations of the Greek word, *pistis* or its verb *pisteuō*.) Both modern Arminian (including Wesleyan) and Calvinist theologians generally understand saving faith to be the dual act of trusting Christ *and embracing him as Lord.* Saving faith, they contend, is not only trusting Christ for salvation but a full *self-commitment* to God. However, such a view discounts what Paul taught, and it can be maintained only by misapplying some passages in the Gospels that have to do with discipleship rather than with salvation. Paul's teaching is clear. Romans 4 describes the faith of Abraham as a primary example of saving faith. Abraham was "fully convinced that God was able to do what he had promised. That is why his faith was counted to him as righteousness" (Rom. 4:21-22). Here is the biblical definition of saving faith. It is total trust. It is being fully convinced of the reliability of God's promise. When God says that He loves us and that Jesus is the Christ (the Messiah), the Son of God, and someone confidently believes that declaration, believes that it includes him or her, that one exercises saving faith.

The question comes, Is not Christ the Lord? Is he not deity incarnate? Can one be saved when denying this fact? Jesus Christ most certainly is deity incarnate, and saving faith includes receiving this fact. Otherwise He could not have suffered on the cross for the whole world. This, however, is not what Lordship theologians understand by self-commitment to the Lordship of Jesus. By self-commitment to the Lordship of Jesus, they mean that every facet of life must be placed under His control, not just at the beginning but throughout life. But who has ever done that?

Of course God earnestly desires that a very particular kind of life will follow the initial step of faith. Immediately following the receipt of salvation is the question of who is in control of the believer's life: self or God? Paul clearly states in Romans 12:1-2 that God expects to be in control. This is the subject of Ephesians 4-6, where we are taught what it is to make Christ the Lord, the Master, of our life. But a life of complete commitment to the will of God is not something to be added to faith as a condition of salvation.

(2.) *The purpose of the sealing.* This is a divine provision guaranteeing that from the moment a person becomes one of the redeemed, that person will receive his or her full inheritance.

When does the inheritance become a reality? Ephesians 4:30 states, "you were sealed for the day of redemption." It is the day when all of God's purposes of providing our redemption will have been completed. It is the day of the Lord's return and of our resurrection. Is the believer's salvation forever secure? There scarcely could be a more direct way of saying so than this! Some Christians live in fear that some misdeed of theirs has cut them off from heaven and consigned them to perdition. Yet every Christian can rest in confidence, for the moment a person understands the gospel and receives it in faith, the sealing of the Holy Spirit is fully completed. The sealing with its guarantee of eternal life and a coming resurrection does not wait on some condition the born-again Christian has yet to fulfill or on waiting to make sure through a life of continuing sanctification that a person is one of the elect.

Verse 14 reads. "which is the guarantee of our inheritance until we acquire possession of it." The Greek word translated "guarantee" (*arrabōn*) further reinforces the believer's security. Greeks used the word for a down payment. The gift of the indwelling Holy Spirit and His sealing ministry is the down payment on the future inheritance God has for every believer.

Not all evangelical expositors are willing to accept this simple truth. One commentator explained that the aorist "having believed" (as it is translated in the AV) "implies that the sealing was not concurrent with the initial believing but followed it as a distinct experience." In other words a Christian is not sealed until he or she has experienced God in the deepest way. This is to say that most believers can never be sure of an eternal inheritance, only those who in a second step of grace have totally allowed Christ to become the Lord of their lives.

What verses 13-14 assure us is that the newest and most immature believer, one who has yet to understand the least of God's claims on the Christian's life, is sealed with the Holy Spirit and has a lasting guarantee of the inheritance. This should be clear from three facts. First, is the point that that the aorist participle translated "have believed" can refer to nothing other than the initial point of faith in Christ. There is no evidence in the text that the sealing is not concurrent with initial believing. Second, the structure of verses 3-14 shows that everything listed is a work of God on behalf of every believer. Since verses 3-14 in the Greek comprise a single sentence, it is wrong to conclude with one commentator that verses 4-6 have to do with one topic, "salvation enacted before time," and verses 7-14 with a separate topic, "salvation realized in time." Third, the series of aorist tense verbs in 3-14, which describe things done by God with finality, lead inescapably to the conclusion that whoever was blessed with every spiritual blessing, whoever received sonship, whoever is redeemed and forgiven, and whoever is appointed for His glory, is also one who is sealed.

It should be evident that the sealing is for every believer, for it is the individual who believes and who is redeemed. Some translations, whether on purpose or inadvertently, have watered down the teaching that each individual believer is sealed. The NRSV, for example, makes verse 14 read, "this is the pledge of our inheritance toward redemption as God's own people." The wholly gratuitous addition of the words "as God's own people" injects a misleading note, as though the sealing is something we do not have individually but only have collectively. If it is collective, then the individual has no personal assurance. Amazingly, Snodgrass states that the NIV "correctly translates 1:14 so that the possession is seen as God's possession of his people, not their possession of salvation."[27] But the NIV, just as the NRSV, adds words which are not in the original. The Greek simply has "for the redemption of the possession," *not* "until the redemption of those who are God's possession."

3. *The agent of the sealing.* In what sense is the Holy Spirit a seal? The way the verb "to seal" is used in the New Testament, the meaning is plain enough. It is to indelibly

---

27 Snodgrass, *Ephesians*, 55.

mark something (by one means or another). It means to confirm or place something beyond doubt. In a metaphorical sense the believer has been marked, guaranteeing the authenticity of his or her salvation. This is the meaning given in verse 14. It is the "guarantee of our inheritance until we acquire possession of it." The possession of the seal is not something the Christian feels or experiences. It is a work of God that takes place the moment a person comes to faith. It will be fully experienced at the return of Christ. If a believer never knows about the sealing, it is nonetheless true. It is something that happens in the counsels of God. Some expositors teach that the sealing becomes valid as a Christian experiences a life of love, forgiveness, dedication, and worship. Presumably this follows from 2 Corinthians 1:22, where Paul writes of God "who has put his seal upon us and given us his spirit in our hearts as a guarantee." The phrase "in our hearts" is thought to imply something experiential. Yet a reading of 1 Corinthians 1:22 shows that it teaches no doctrine different from what we have here. Everything in Ephesians 1:3-14 is about what God has done, not about what we experience. These verses 3 to 14 refer to our standing, our position in Christ, not our experiences.

As the Christian walks by faith, he or she is *filled* by the Spirit. This is a ministry of the Spirit distinct from the sealing of the Spirit. A Spirit-filled Christian is one who experiences both a victory over sin and love for even the most unlovable of people. The sealing and the filling should not be confused.

4. *The effect of the sealing.* The primary purpose of the Holy Spirit's sealing is that God might receive glory from what is done for His child. This is the third time in verses

3-14 that we read the expression, "to the praise of his glory." Interestingly it is found first in verse 6, where the subject is the Father. Then it is found in verse 12, where Christ is in view. In verse 14 the Holy Spirit is in front of the reader. Is it the Father, or Christ, or the Holy Spirit whose glory is praised? There can be no distinction. It is the one Trinitarian God who is praised, while recognizing the responsibility of each member of the Godhead for the salvation of the believer. Significantly, only in verse 6, speaking of the Father, is the word *grace* added: "to the praise of his glorious grace." It is only the Father who bestows grace. That grace is made possible by the sacrifice of his Son and made effective by the ministry of the Spirit.

The editors of the *New Living Translation*, trying to produce the most readable and understandable version, failed in their effort to interpret the last part of verse 14 correctly when they translated, "This is just one more reason for us to praise our glorious God." No, the verses that go before establish just the converse. It is what God has done for the believer that *in itself* brings him praise. These 12 verses are *not* about the Christians duty to praise God. They are about what God has done and how his unconstrained gifts manifest his enduring grace. Unquestionably this ought to lead the Christian to an unceasing paean of praise--and the apostle voices such praise himself, but not until in 3:20-21.

Conclusion

Is Division A_1, Identified with Christ, nothing more than dull theological facts devoid of practical significance, nothing more than a bag of theological nuts and bolts? If one is tempted to think so, he or she should consider the deep inner problems with which many Christians struggle. Some are wrestling with a poor self-image, an image no doubt based on awful reality. God answers this need in verse 4: every believer is holy and blameless in the eyes of God. The Christian's proper "image," the one always to be kept in mind, is what one is in Christ, not what one is through human skill and achievement.

Is another Christian lonely, alienated, feeling no one cares? Think of verses 5-6, which declare that in bestowing sonship God cares far more intimately than any human ever could. God in his genuine concern is continually acting on the Christians behalf.

Guilt feelings? Such feelings, however much grounded in fact, can be left out of mind in the knowledge that our forgiveness is absolutely total (vv. 7-8). There is no sin not covered by the Cross, none at all, so there is no sin for which the believer is not forgiven!

Possibly some readers lament their lack of knowledge. Their education has been limited, so they stand in awe of the understanding presumably stored in the brains of philosophers, physicians, professors, scientists, financial wizards, business manipulators, and the shakers and movers of the world. Yet the Christian possesses knowledge that outclasses all that is bound within the minds of the most highly educated. Every true believer knows or can know the ultimate purposes of God (vv. 9-10). This is infinitely more important than knowledge derived by human educational achievement.

Does one feel a sense of worthlessness, a lack of significance and meaning in life? Verses 11 and 12 tell us that God values each of us above the most beautiful, most

Ephesians: Identified with Christ

talented, wisest, most brilliant, and richest of this world's famous who lack faith in Christ. God considers each of us his special treasure.

Then there are those who are desperately afraid that somehow they have failed God. But haven't we all? Because of their failure, has God cast them aside? The testimony of verses 13-14 is that every believer is sealed and the outcome is certain. It is God's responsibility, not one's own. No one who has trusted the crucified and risen Christ for salvation can ever be lost.

Ephesians 1:3-14 is a message of unmatched joy. There is no gloom in the truth of God's great salvation. How can any fail to exclaim, "Blessed be the God and Father of our Lord Jesus Christ."

DIVISION B₁ BE SUBORDINATE IN AWE OF CHRIST
(1:15-23)

Paul did not stop praying for the Christians in Ephesus and neighboring communities, even though he was ministering in another city and had been away from Ephesus for some time. This division summarizes his prayer for them. It expresses the most basic things a Christian ought to ask in prayer when interceding for other Christians. The prayer builds up to a statement exalting our resurrected Savior and the power that is His to provide every resource needed by believers.

In typical Greek literary form, the statement is compact. The reader needs to think through the significance of each phrase, for the apostle included no explanatory comments. It is not easy to keep up with the thought of the long sentence (in the Greek) that begins with verse 15 and continues to the end of verse 21. As the sentence is read, it becomes apparent that what is of greatest importance is not merely that believers might have their eyes opened (v. 18) but what they are to see when their eyes are opened. The qualifiers in the sentence are of greater magnitude than what they qualify. To follow what Paul is getting at, we need to view the entire section as follows.

PAUL'S CONTINUAL THANKSGIVING
For this reason . . . I do not cease to give thanks for you

I. SHOWING APPRECIATION
because I have heard of your faith in the Lord Jesus and your love toward all the saints,

II. SHOWING CONCERN
remembering you in my prayers,

THAT THEY MIGHT ENJOY DIRECTED KNOWLEDGE
that the God of our Lord Jesus Christ, the Father of glory, may give you a spirit of wisdom and of revelation in the knowledge of him, having the eyes of your hearts enlightened,

    A. IN KNOWLEDGE OF GOD'S CALLING
    that you may know what is the hope to which he has called you,

    B. IN KNOWLEDGE OF GOD'S INHERITANCE
    what are the riches of his glorious inheritance in the saints,

    C. IN KNOWLEDGE OF GOD'S POWER
    and what is the immeasurable greatness of his power in us who believe, according to the working of his great might

        1. THAT GAVE CHRIST LIFE
        which he worked in Christ when he raised him from the dead

        2. THAT GAVE CHRIST PRECEDENCE
        and made him sit at his right hand in the heavenly places, far above all rule and authority and power and dominion, and above every name that is named, not only in this age but also in that which is to come;

3. THAT GAVE CHRIST DOMINION
   and he put all things under his feet

4. THAT GAVE CHRIST PURPOSE
   and gave him as head over all things to the church, which is his body, the fulness of him who fills all in all.

Paul's Thanksgiving (1:16a)
¹⁶ªI do not cease to give thanks for you . . .

Verse 16 is the second verse of Section B_1, but it is the verse with the subject and primary verb of the long sentence that begins with verse 15 and continues through verse 23. So we need to consider verse 16 first.

American Christians are reminded at least every Thanksgiving Day that we ought to be thankful. So most believers are. We thank God for our health, for our good circumstances, for our church, for our salvation, for our parents, for our children. Some even have enough faith to thank God for their unpleasant circumstances. These are excellent things to be thankful for. Paul, however, goes beyond many of us. He thanks God for other Christian people.

It is not easy to thank God for a prickly or ignorant Christian acquaintance. Nevertheless in all of Paul's letters, whether addressed to individuals, to a particular church, or to a geographically clustered group of churches, he took pains to express his thanksgiving for the people and for what they had become. His thanksgiving led him in two directions. First, he showed his appreciation and second, his concern. These two are correlatives; either is incomplete without the other.

I. Showing Appreciation (verse 15)

¹⁵For this reason, because I have heard of your faith in the Lord Jesus and your love toward all the saints,

The apostle consistently looked for good in fellow believers. Then he told them of the good he had found, or at least heard about. There was both faith and love among the believers to whom Ephesians is addressed. He found the same among the saints at Colossae, at Thessalonica, and at Philippi. When he wrote to the Romans, he found only faith, but he praised them for it. Although some among the Roman believers evidently practiced love (Rom. 16), Paul had to explain the meaning of love for the benefit of the majority (Rom. 14). Even with the carnal Corinthians, he voiced his appreciation for the fact they were "enriched" (1 Cor. 1:5) and "not lacking in any spiritual gift" (v. 7).

How essential for each of us to look for good among other Christians. When we are living "according to the flesh," we will find some Christians we simply do not like. It may be some mannerism that annoys us, an irritating attitude, some ineptitude, a bit of gossip that has prejudiced us, or something we may be at a loss to account for. Most of us are conscious of a few Christian people who affect us in some unsavory way. We are commanded to love the brethren. But how can we love those who seem so unlovable? One way is to consciously look for something to appreciate in other Christians. In places each of us is ugly. But each of us through the Holy Spirit has received strength and some spiritual gift through which God has supernaturally made us valuable. Now our responsibility is to look for that value in the other person. To do so is indeed to be walking by faith, believing what God has said about each born-again person.

II. Showing Concern (1:16b)
¹⁶ᵇ*remembering you in my prayers,*

Along with his expression of appreciation, Paul had a deep and genuine concern for the believers addressed in this letter. This in itself is not unusual, for even unbelievers find themselves gripped with concern for their loved ones. What is unusual is that Paul should have had a genuine concern for such a large number of people, even for people whom he had never met and whom he probably would never see in this life.

More remarkable is his resolution. He recognizes there is nothing he can do for them in his own strength. What he can do is what we so seldom do. We fret and worry over those whom we love. Usually the more helpless we are, the more we are torn with anxiety. but not the apostle. He fully understood the power of God, and with perfect confidence in God's willingness to answer prayer, he presented his concern to the heavenly Father.

That They Might Enjoy Directed Knowledge (1:17-18)
¹⁷*that the God of our Lord Jesus Christ, the Father of glory, may give you a spirit of wisdom and of revelation in the knowledge of him,* ¹⁸*having the eyes of your hearts enlightened,*

Before discussing the main purpose of this verse, we need to pause to correct a misunderstanding of the expression, "the God of our Lord Jesus Christ." Jehovah's Witnesses cite this expression (and similar expressions in Matt. 27:46 and John 20:17) as proof that Jesus worshiped God the Father but was not God himself. To use the passage in this way is to ignore a host of other passages attesting to the deity of Jesus. It is far more reasonable to see in this passage an acknowledgment that in His ministry to the saints Jesus was serving the will of the Father. In his functions, He is subordinate to the Father, but in his very essence He is one with God.

What Paul prayed for is amazing. Our lack of understanding is evident when we fail to ask for the best things from God. Not that it is wrong to ask God for trivial things. But after we have asked for small things, we often stop before coming to essential matters. We ask for health, for wisdom to carry out the tasks of the day, for protection for ourselves and our loved ones, and for God to prosper the work of our pastors and missionaries. All these are fully acceptable things to request. If we stop here, however, it is because we have not yet learned what God desires most in us. Paul asked, as unfamiliar and even as strange as his request might seem, for God to grant each believer "a spirit of wisdom and of revelation in the knowledge of him."

This prayer, however, is subject to certain misinterpretations. First, Paul did not pray that believers might receive God's Holy Spirit. All believers already have the Holy Spirit, for all are indwelt by him, and according to verse 13 all are sealed with the Holy Spirit. This is true of Christians living in the will of God and also of Christians living unsavory Christian lives. The Christians in Corinth were living low, unproductive, fleshly lives, yet Paul wrote them, "Do you not know that your body is a temple of the Holy Spirit within you, which you have from God?" (1 Cor. 6:19). Every believer is indwelt by the Holy Spirit.

The word "spirit" in this verse should not be capitalized as it is in most versions, for it does not refer to the Holy

Spirit. (The ESV correctly leaves it uncapitalized). Like our English word "spirit," the Greek word for spirit may be used in two senses. In English we speak of a spirit in the sense of a real but noncorporeal being. We read in Hebrews 1:14 that angels are "ministering spirits." But then we also use "spirit" to refer to an attitude of mind. Thus we may speak of "the old college spirit." Paul is using the Greek word in this latter sense of an attitude of mind. He wrote in Galatians 6:1 of "a spirit of gentleness," in 2 Corinthians 4:13 of a "spirit of faith," in 2 Timothy 1:7 of "a spirit of power, love, and self control." Similarly he is writing here of an attitude of mind, an influence, or temper through which "wisdom and revelation" flow into the Christian's life.

However, the Holy Spirit is the power behind a proper attitude of mind. He is ultimately necessary for any true understanding of God.

Second, Paul is not teaching that Christians might be given new revelations from God. Among certain religious communities, new "revelations" by prophets or leaders have been added to the Scriptures, changing, modifying, and even contradicting the received Word. This verse and a few other passages are offered in support of the contention that Christians should expect such continuing revelations. It is true that in this verse the word "revelation" is the same word used elsewhere in the Bible of the unveiling of divine truth through human instruments. By revelation God gave the Apostle Paul truths not previously known to God's people (Rom. 16:25-26; Gal. 1:12). But observe that Paul does not pray that the saints might be given "wisdom and revelation" but prays that they might be given "a *spirit* of wisdom and revelation." This is the attitude of mind, influence, or power through which the revelation of God becomes *operative* in the believer's life. It is not new revelations to which Paul is referring. Instead he is referring to the illumination of a believer with respect to existing revelations. It is informing the Christian how the truths of the Bible are to work out in his or her thoughts and experience. In the same way "a spirit of wisdom" is the attitude of mind, influence, or power through which God's wisdom becomes a reality in the Christian's life.

Confirming this and central to the thought of this division, the illumination of the human heart, the "spirit of wisdom and of revelation," comes only *in the knowledge of him*, that is, of the Father. The word for "knowledge" that Paul uses (*epignōsis*) points to the object of the knowledge[28]. The object is God, the "knowledge *of him*." The knowledge of God is the door to a "spirit of wisdom and of revelation."

Paul is writing about knowledge that *follows* the knowledge needed for salvation, for his prayer is that this knowledge might become a reality in the hearts of believers. Using the same word, Paul wrote in Philemon 6 that when this knowledge is full it conveys knowledge "of every good thing that is in us for the sake of Christ." The more the believer knows of God and His rich grace, the more the believer understands the rich benefits granted him or her by a loving God. One commentator called this phrase, "a limping

---

28 This does not mean enhanced or intensive knowledge as some understand the word. Douglas J. Moo, *The Epistle to the Romans*, New International Commentary on the New Testament, ed. Gordon D. Fee (Grand Rapids: Eerdmans), 117, n. 139, wrote, "Any such distinction simply does not hold in Paul." This seems to be the consensus of most recent scholars. See Hoehner, *Ephesians: An Exegetical Commentary*, 258.

and inconsequential adverbial phrase." [29] But it is not at all inconsequential when one sees its place in the apostle's argument. It is knowledge that leads to spiritual enlightenment. It is an understanding of things of God that would be wholly incomprehensible to the unbeliever.

The clause in verse 18, "having the eyes of your hearts enlightened," explains directed knowledge. It speaks of an inner illumination which is a special privilege of Christians who are growing in their knowledge of God.

As this knowledge becomes a reality, there are three major areas in which the believer will be illumined. There may be many things about which he or she would like illumination and there may be other issues about which God will choose to provide special understanding, but in the Ephesian letter these three come before all others.

A. In Knowledge of God's Calling (1:18b)
that you may know what is the hope to which he has called you,

The hope of God's calling is the first critical area where the Christian requires enlightenment. When we read the word *hope* in the Bible, we lose its real force because of the way we use the word in English. In our language *hope* carries with it an element of doubt. If a wife says, "I *hope* my husband will let me watch my favorite soap opera instead of that old ball game," she really means, "I would like to watch my favorite TV program, but I am not sure my husband will agree to it." In most places the biblical word would much

---

[29] John Muddiman, *The Epistle to the Ephesians*, Black's New Testament Commentaries, ed. Morna D. Hooker (Peabody, MA: Hendrickson, 2004), 85.

better be translated "expectation."[30] Hope based on confident faith is not a wish but a certainty!

There are many things included in our Christian expectation. Here the apostle is writing about one particular item of our expectation, our calling. Ministers and missionaries talk about being called. What kind of feelings did they have to know they were called? Why are a few so selected? We need not wonder. When we read 4:1-3 it is clear that Paul used "calling" to refer to the way every Christian should live. Some may be called to use one spiritual gift, some another, but all are called to the kind of life God expects. There is no uncalled Christian, although not all respond equally to God's call.

As the Apostle Paul uses the word *calling*, he does not think of it as an invitation to *become* a believer. What the Scriptures teach is that when one becomes a believer he or she is called to a certain kind of life. All of us who are born again are called into the fellowship of God's Son (1 Cor. 1:9), to peace (1 Cor. 7:15; Col. 3:15), to freedom (Gal. 5:13), and to sanctification (1 Thess. 4:7; 2 Tim. 1:9). Also we are called to those eternal benefits that are ours in salvation. Note especially 1 Timothy 6:12, "Take hold of the eternal life to which you were called and about which you made the good confession." Timothy was not called to eternal life before he made the good confession. On making his confession of faith, he was called to eternal life. That life he could "take hold of," living each day as one fully assured of glory.

Knowing Jesus is to understand the character of this

---

30 Hope (*elpis*), is "the looking forward to someth. with some reason for confidence respecting fulfillment, hope, expectation" (BAGD, 319-20).

new life to which we have been called. Knowing Jesus is to appreciate that we are not to be like other people. We are different from those who belong to this world. We are to be like Him, growing in his image. This is tremendously important. If there is illumination of our hearts, if we have allowed the Father of glory to speak to us, we will have our eyes open to his expectations.

B. In Knowledge of God's Inheritance (1:18c)
¹⁸ᵇwhat are the riches of his glorious inheritance in the saints,

Paul's concern is not with what we shall inherit in heaven but with the fact that we ourselves are God's inheritance. This is exactly what he taught in 1:11.³¹ Yet knowing our inner self, our weak, faltering faith, our propensity to self-aggrandizement and self-satisfaction, how can we help but think, "What junk God has inherited." But this is not what the Spirit says. He specifies that we are his *glorious* inheritance. Not only glorious, but *richly* glorious inheritance. Although almost incomprehensible, the Word plainly states that we are God's treasure. Together with the Lord Jesus and other believers, any of us can assert, "I am the Father's richest, most valued possession." God does not value us for our sins and mistakes. He treasures us for what his grace has accomplished. We do not have to depend on vacillating human reactions for a sense of value. God values each of us; His Word declares it.

On the other hand, if any of us is inclined, as at times most of us unfortunately are, to despise some weaker brother

---

31 In 1:11 the word was heritage (*eklērōthēmen*); here it is inheritance (*klēronomias*)."The possessive pronoun *autou* shows that it is God's inheritance."(Hoehner, *Ephesians: An Exegetical Commentary*, 266).

or sister or to disparage some Christian for his or her ignorance or stupidity, we must remember that that person is also God's treasure. God deeply and fully values that one. So should we.

C. In Knowledge of God's Power (1:19)
[19]*and what is the immeasurable greatness of his power in us who believe, according to the working of his great might*

The word "love" does not occur in this division. Nonetheless the division continues the thought of the benefits available through the love of God, a cardinal benefit being "the immeasurable greatness of his power toward us who believe."

This is the climax of the three ways in which the believer should experience enlightenment. If we have become personally acquainted with Jesus Christ, if we know him with the knowledge Paul is writing about, then we will also experience the power of God in our lives. In the verses that follow Paul looks specifically at four aspects of this power.

1. Power that gave Christ life (1:20a)
[20a]*that he worked in Christ when he raised him from the dead*

There is a finality about death. Loved ones who stand about a bedside watching the sad shake of the physician's head as he straightens up after ceasing his vain efforts at external heart massage, who watch the nurse turn off the oxygen, disconnect the tube, busy herself putting things away, know in their hearts that acceptance of death is necessary. Only a crazed person would stand by that bed day after day, hoping something might change. The death of Jesus was every bit as final. Those hands that took him down from the cross had dealt with death before. There could have been no failure to recognize the absolute end.

But God raised Him! Here is power and authority beyond all imagination. Astoundingly this same immeasurably great power is available to the believer! (We shall deal particularly with this truth in some of the pages to follow.)

2. Power that gave Christ precedence (1:20b-21)

²⁰ᵇand made him sit at his right hand in the heavenly places, ²¹far above all rule and authority and power and dominion, and above every name that is named, not only in this age but also in that which is to come;

God's great power not only resurrected Jesus but gave him the greatest place of prominence in the universe. It seated him at the right hand of the Father. Miraculously God's power is available to the believer.

Two questions are raised by the words of this verse and a half. The first is whether they imply that Jesus is less than fully God. If at the present time Jesus is far above all rule and authority and power and dominion, could this mean these things did not belong to Him *prior* to his coming into the world? The answer to the question is not difficult. Paul is concerned with the obvious contrast between the Galilean peasant crucified as a malefactor and the glory He now shares with the Father. Since Paul is writing of the limitless might of God, he wants to exhibit in the strongest possible way the contrast between what Jesus was here on earth and what God has now made Him. It is God's power that Paul is demonstrating., not the question of the preexistent status of Christ. In his other letters the apostle amplified his position on the deity of Christ. Philippians 2:7 notes that He "emptied himself" of His prior exalted status in order to become the suffering servant. Colossians 1:15 says that He is the "visible representation of the invisible God," the Creator of everything that exists in the universe. Philippians 2:9 speaks of the exaltation of Jesus that placed Him far above everything else. For any today to think that he is less than God is not to think as Paul thought or as other apostolic writers thought.

A second question is, What is "all (or every) rule and authority and power and dominion" over which Jesus has been exalted? Some expositors take them to be spiritual powers of evil working against God. Others think the reference is primarily to angels. More likely both are in view. Colossians 2:15 says that God "disarmed the rulers and authorities and put them to an open shame, by triumphing over them" in Christ. These are certainly evil beings, probably demonic powers. Yet in Colossians 1:16 Paul wrote of "thrones or dominions or rulers or authorities" that were created through Christ and for Christ. This would seem to include angelic beings and no doubt also the angels who fell (Jude 6). What is important to Paul is not precisely who they are, but his awareness that certain teachers were concentrating on angels, placing them into special categories whereby they might assist in salvation and making them objects of worship. Christ is above all angelic beings, good or bad, any already named by these teachers and any who may exist, whatever their names and whenever they exist or function, whether in this age or in the age to come. Prayer to angels, worship or adoration of anyone other than Christ is futile, since Christ is Lord of all. Paul taught the identical truth in Philippians 2:9. God has exalted the Lord Jesus Christ to the highest place in the universe. This being true, every believer should have the utmost regard for His Word, for His counsel, for His instructions. For a Christian to look to any other source for spiritual help, whether self-help books, newspaper columnists, learned tomes on psychology or philosophy, exploration of internet opinions, consultation of mediums, or studying astrology is absolutely unthinkable.

3. Power that gave Christ dominion (verse 22a)
22a And he put all things under his feet

This short clause is a quotation from the last half of Psalm 8:6. The psalmist uses it to express his wonder at the dominion God has given mankind over all of nature. When Paul quoted it, he was doubtlessly thinking that what is applicable to man is all the more applicable to Christ in all His glory. In writing that all things are under the feet of Christ, he declared that in an even greater sense all of nature is under Christ's dominion. This is not a reference to Christ's sovereignty over the Church. Rather, it states that the infinite, almighty power and rule belonging to God the Father belongs as well to Christ. His power is over every other power or pretense to power. Power that gave Jesus this authority is power available to the believer!

The ESV places a period after verse 21. It would have been better if the editors had not ended the sentence at verse 21 but ended it with a comma, since verse 22 begins with the word "and." That would have retained the four distinct parallel thoughts (vv. 20-23) describing how God's power was manifested in our Lord. Then a comma should have followed the word "feet." Verse 22a is the third item and is followed by a fourth clearly separable item.[32]

---

32   In verse 22a the Nestle-Aland New Testament Greek Text places a

The mighty power of Jesus should lead us to constant worship with the deepest astonishment, admiration, and awe. How amazing that we should be privileged to stand united to the One who has dominion over all and yet one with whom we enjoy a loving, personal relationship.

One might think this is the climax of the sentence: the elevation of Jesus to a position of absolute lordship over all. Yet verses 22b-23 constitute the absolute climax!

4. Power that gave Christ purpose (1:22b-23)

^{22b}and gave him as head over all things to the church, ^{23}which is his body, the fullness of him who fills all in all.

Did not the Lord Jesus have an unimaginably great purpose in coming to earth and dying on the cross for our redemption? Without question. Yet His purpose did not end with His great sacrifice. With the resurrection His purpose continues. The power of God gave the ascended Christ something he previously did not have, a special purpose in filling the Church with His glory.

This Person, who is so great that he has authority over everything in the universe is a gift to the Church. This is a truly surprising way of stating the relationship of Christ to the Church. The Church was manifested at Pentecost through the work of the Holy Spirit, yet filling the Church with glory was not receiving the visible manifestation of tongues, but the Father's gift of Christ to the Church. The Church is more than a collection of people going through the form of worshiping a distant deity, but a body of people in actual spiritual union with the One they worship.

To understand this revelation of Christ's personal re-

---

semicolon after verse 21 and a comma after "feet"

lationship to the Church we need to make certain we understand what, in Paul's thinking, constitutes the Church.[33] This is the first time the word occurs in the epistle. The writer does not explain the word but assumes that the primary facts are known to his readers, even though this letter, more than any other of Paul's, is devoted to an exposition of the Church as an institution of God.

The word "church" is frequently invested by English-speaking readers with meanings that it never had in the New Testament. The Greek original (*ekklēsia*) has the simple meaning of "assembly." If we were to read "assembly" everywhere our translators have used "church," we would save ourselves some confusion.[34] The word is used in many places for local assemblies of God's people, such as "the assembly of God which is at Corinth" (I Cor. 1:2), "the assemblies [plural] of Galatia" (Gal. 1:2), and so forth. In most instances these were more or less organized groups of believers meeting regularly for fellowship, instruction, and worship. In a large city such as Rome, there were probably a number of assemblies. At least this seems implied by the designation of one specific Roman assembly that met in the house of Prisca and Aquila (Rom. 16:5).

It is just as certain that the word is sometimes used for the larger, comprehensive assembly that includes all Christians. How else are we to understand Hebrews 12:23,

---

33 "Church" is capitalized in the commentary when it refers to a universal assembly of believers; it is left with a lower case initial when referring to a local assembly.
34 See Earl D. Radmacher, *The Nature of the Church* (Havesville, NC: Schoettle Publishing Co., 1996), 115-76, for a study of the use of the word as applied to the Church in the New Testament.

which refers to "the assembly of the firstborn who are enrolled in heaven?" Paul quite obviously had the same larger assembly in view when he wrote to the Colossians that Jesus "is the head of the body, the church [assembly]" (Col. 1:18). When he qualified *church* with the term *body*, he wrote of this greater assembly. This is his meaning when he wrote of the body in 1 Corinthians 12:12-13: "For just as the body is one and has many members, and all the members of the body, though many, are one body, so it is with Christ. For by one Spirit we were all baptized into one body--Jews or Greeks, slaves or free--and all were made to drink of one Spirit." In this passage the body is a spiritual union rather than an earthly organization of Christians. Paul declared himself a part of the same body as the Corinthian believers, although when he wrote, he was ministering in Ephesus and probably had been separated from the Corinthians for a year and a half.

This body is a true corporate body from which no member will ever be excluded. All those who are *in him* are individually the elect and belong to one another by virtue of their union with Christ. Hence the Church, made up of those who are elect in union with the Lord, is an elect body (James 2:5; I Pet. 2:9; Rev. 17:14).

Could it be that God established one true earthly organization that alone deserves to be recognized as the Church? This is the conviction of many, based on their reading of Jesus' statement in Matthew 16:18, "And I tell you, you are Peter, and on this rock I will build my church." Such an understanding is doubtful, since Christ spoke to Peter as *petros*, a stone, but spoke of the foundation of the Church as *petra*, a related but different word meaning a rock suitable as a foundation for building a house. The rock is not Peter but Christ Himself. Furthermore in Paul's writings there is no hint of an ecclesiastical organization joining the earliest churches, and Paul never arrogated to himself any powers other than those of someone with a knowledge of God's revelation and a deep love for others.

Some teachers assert that each local assembly is a body of Christ. Such a doctrine would surprise the Apostle Paul, for in Romans 12:4-5 he included himself in the body of Christ along with Christians in Rome, although he had not yet visited Rome. His statement in Romans 12:5, "so we, though many, are one body in Christ," is not an editorial "we," since in verse 3 he writes to "you." If any doubt remains regarding the biblical concept of an assembly that embraces every Christian, whatever his or her denominational affiliation or lack thereof, it should be dispelled by the statement in Ephesians 4:4-6, "There is one body and one Spirit, just as you were called to the one hope that belongs to your call, one Lord, one faith, one baptism, one God and Father of us all, who is above all and through all in all." Thus there is a body that can be called the "one" body, a body as unitary as God Himself.

A puzzle in connection with the body of Christ, one that has evoked an enormous amount of scholarly speculation and writing, is what Paul meant by "the fullness of him who fills all in all." An understanding that does no violence to the grammar, the context, or to other doctrines of Scripture perceives *fullness* as a reference to the totality of Christ's ministry to and on behalf of the Church. Just as God completely fills Christ, so Christ in every way fills the Church. His bestowal of gifts for service and worship, his guidance, his empowerment through the Spirit for holiness, and his enabling through the Spirit for believers to live in love, all that Christ does for and with the Church is His fullness on behalf of the body. Salmond, commenting on this verse, wrote most appropriately,

> The relation between Christ and the Church, therefore . . . is not . . . one simply of Superior and inferior, Sovereign or subject, but one of life and incorporation. The Church is not merely an institution ruled by Him as President, a Kingdom in which He is the Supreme Authority, or a vast company of men in moral sympathy with Him, but a Society which is in vital connection with Him, having the source of its life in Him, sustained and directed by His power, the instrument also by which He works.[35]

There are several interpretations of fullness that cannot be maintained. One is that the Church fills and completes Christ. This interpretation ignores the context, which details the power God has exercised on behalf of Christ. The passage is not about what the Church has done for Christ, as if the Church were his complement, but what God the Father Himself has done in glorifying Christ. In other New Testament passages referring to fullness, it is never God who is filled, but it is God who fills Christ, and God or Christ who fills the Church. The interpretation that the Church fills or completes the risen Christ implies that he is less than deity, or that somehow His deity is incomplete apart from the Church. Another erroneous interpretation is that Christ fills the Church and through the Church God is filling the world. The Church is considered to be the messianic king-

---

35 Salmond, *The Epistle of Paul to the Ephesians*, 3:281-282.

dom, and through the Church God is building His kingdom in the world. Some advocates of this view consider fullness a synonym of the *shekinah* glory that went before and led the Israelites in the wilderness and that stood over the tabernacle when it was at rest, the visible emblem of God's presence. To answer this interpretation adequately would take us far afield, but it can be stated categorically that Paul never uses "the kingdom of God" as a synonym for "the Church." Neither is the *shekinah* equivalent to the presence of God in the Church. The *shekinah* represented the presence of God as the divine ruler of Israel when Israel was a true theocracy. Briefly the kingdom of God is the future reign of Christ on earth. (See Observation IV: The Church and Israel, p. 282).

How should we understand the qualifier, "who fills all in all?" In other passages where Paul uses the expression "all in all" he is emphasizing the comprehensive extent of Christ's fullness. There is no least member of the body who does not have the full benefit of Christ's ministry. Two passages support this view. In 1 Corinthians 12:6 the expression refers to the work of the Godhead collectively, and in Colossians 3:11 it refers specifically to Christ. In both these passages the thought is that Christ's ministry fully reaches every part of the body. This thought fits the context of "all in all" in Ephesians 1:23.

How significant that the risen Savior, the one "who fills all in all," has at His total command all the resources needed by the Church. God's people too often forget this. If it were believed, would any segment of the Church need to support its mission with appeals to the unbelieving of this world? Does an all-sufficient Christ need bingo games, bake sales, employment of professional fund-raising teams, and the like? If we cannot fulfill our mission without depending wholly on the resources He supplies, the question must be asked whether our mission is the one He has assigned, or at least ask whether our plan of attack is the one He has ordained.

What the Holy Spirit is saying in this division of the book is that the power of God that did all these things for the Lord Jesus Christ is available to each of us who comes in humble faith. Why then do we not see Christians today exercising the powers that Christ demonstrated in his earthly ministry? There is no restoring eyesight to those blind from birth. Children with spastic paralysis are not granted new motion. No one raises the clinically dead to life. Is this power a delusion, a fantasy?

Of course, the astounding powers given by our Lord to His disciples to heal the sick, raise the dead, cleanse lepers, and cast out demons were real, not mythic (Matt. 10:8). Because the disciples were granted these powers does not authorize Christians today to suppose they have the same. These commands were specifically given to the twelve, and they are named! The disciples had a message that Christians have not been given today, a command to proclaim that the kingdom of heaven was *at hand.* (See Observation IV, The Church and Israel, p. 282)

As we consider the epistle further, we discover that this power provides what God so emphatically wants in our lives: negatively, victory over sin, and positively, power to love others. A part of the message of Ephesians is that no Christian is under obligation to sin. If a true believer does sin, it is because he or she chooses to do so. The believer has power to resist sin and resist sin successfully. The Christian has power to do good without expectation of return, even to love and minister to the unlovable. He or she can find joy in the midst of trials, experience inner calm when all about is in turmoil, be patient in the most exasperating of circumstances, exercise self-control, be gentle with the weak without sacrificing the toughness of faith, and be faithful to every task granted through the providence of God.

Are these inconsequential powers? Viewed from God's perspective these are vastly more important than bringing a deceased person back to life or performing other visible miracles. We learn from 1 Corinthians 13 that the power to love is more important than the gift of speaking in tongues, than having the gift of prophecy and understanding mysteries, than having all ordinary knowledge. It is more important than even mountain-moving faith itself.

Handwritten notes:

5 →

1. mankind – Pg 69
2. mercy – Pg 79
3. purpose – Pg 82
4. method – Pg 83
5. product – Pg 89

DIVISION C₁. MADE ALIVE IN CHRIST
(Ephesians 2:1-10)

A widely used gospel tract is entitled, "Four Things God Wants You to Know." Campus Crusade, a Christian missionary work begun on college campuses, teaches students to win others to Christ by explaining the "Four Spiritual Laws." These are good approaches for introducing people to God's plan of salvation. In Ephesians 2:1-10, however, the Apostle Paul gives us *five things God wants you to know*. In this short division Paul explains what it means to be "made alive in Christ." He takes us through five steps God uses to bring it about.

I. God's evaluation of mankind (2:1-3)

God's diagnosis of our condition is brutally direct. Every human without exception is spiritually helpless, hopelessly self-gratifying, and as a consequence, condemned by an unwaveringly righteous God.

A. Helpless (2:1-2)
¹And you were dead in the trespasses and sins ²in which you once walked, following the course of this world, following the prince of the power of the air, the spirit that is now at work in the sons of disobedience.

The ESV has not included the words, "he made alive," in verse 1, although they are found in many English versions. The editors of the ESV made a good choice, since these are lacking in the Greek text. Translators of many other versions have arbitrarily included them, following ancient texts that copied them from verse 5.

The apostles' teaching in verse 1 is designed to tear down the good self-image that every well-adjusted person supposedly enjoys. He states that some people, supposing themselves physically and happily alive, are nevertheless dead because of the sinful path they have chosen. In the category of those who once were dead the apostle included all those to whom he was writing. Is everyone dead who is not a Christian? Yes, verse 3 clearly states the diagnosis is intended for all unbelieving humanity.

Death is always a baleful thought. But we have to ask, what kind of death? What does it mean? It has been interpreted in different ways. For a good understanding we might consider various possibilities the apostle conceivably had in mind.

1. Paul thought of physical death, simply foreshadowed by the infirmities to which all are subject. "You are living now, but you are as good as dead, for your death is coming." Yet something other than the bare thought of physical death must have been in Paul's mind. Christians, those once but no longer dead, must still experience the pain and infirmities that foreshadow physical death, and they will experience physical death, unless they are among those fortunates still living when the Lord returns. Yet verse 5 says that the death that once belonged to Christians is no longer theirs, so this is not about anticipated physical death.

2. Others suggest Paul was thinking of a life consigned to futility. This interpretation would seem to follow from the words, "following the course of this world." Is it not death when someone is molded by the world and governed by Satan? The selfishness of sin can have as its re-

ward a life without genuine meaning, no matter how much applause that life receives from society. We might think of the voluptuous widow in 1 Timothy 5:6. Such a person can well be called dead even while he or she lives physically. The prodigal son living a dissolute life was said to be dead, although physically he was alive (Luke 15:24).

Nevertheless, death in the Pauline Epistles does not consist of living in trespasses and sins but is the *consequence* of such living. Romans 6:23 speaks of the *wages* of sin being death. Whatever death is, it comes because all humans sin.

3. Death in this passage is commonly thought to mean a sinner's ultimate and final separation from God. This is the consignment of a soul to hell following physical death, the dread sequel of a life lived without true faith. This understanding acknowledges the fact that death is the consequence of trespasses and sins. Furthermore, it is a doctrine taught elsewhere in Scripture. Nevertheless death in this passage refers to an existing state, not to a state after the final judgment. Death is something true of everyone now living, with the exception of believers--and believers themselves were once in the state of death.

4. Complete exclusion from the life of God is the only reasonable interpretation. Jesus used death in this sense when he replied to a certain disciple, "Follow me and leave the dead to bury their own dead" (Matt. 8:22). This is Paul's sense in Colossians 1:21, where in a similar vein he wrote, "And you, who once were estranged and hostile in mind, doing evil deeds." One who is estranged from God is separated from him. This is death--to be without any relationship to God, the horrible consequence of being hostile and practicing evil.

Trespasses and sins brought about the state of death. Trespasses are acts of deliberate disobedience. The word *sins* is the plural of the common New Testament Greek word *hamartia*. An older Greek meaning of the word was "missing the mark" or "failing when trying." In popular Christian literature this is the way the meaning of sin is often explained. If this is the meaning, sinning would not seem to be so terribly serious. After all, an archer cannot hit the mark without a great deal of practice, and practice includes missing the mark much of the time. If this is what the author had in mind, sin is simply a matter of getting practice in right living. By New Testament times, however, the meaning of the word had changed. The idea of "missing the mark" is completely absent. In the first century the word always had an ethical sense of not conforming to a standard.[36]

Trespasses and sins together, each stating the same thing in a different way, emphasize the frightful gravity of human behavior in opposition to God. For anyone to gloss over his or her misdeeds as simple human frailty is to miss seeing reality as God sees it.

People practice trespasses and sins, first because they "follow the course of this world." In this verse the word *world* is the Greek word *kosmos*. There are different words translated "world" in the Bible. In Greek literature *kosmos* commonly refers to the inhabited world. In the New Testament it is commonly used in a metaphorical sense, designating the world of unbelieving, Christ-rejecting society (e.g., John 14:30-31; 15:18-25; 1 Cor. 3:19). This is the way it is used here. "Following the course of this world" is saying that someone's behavior is the consequence of seeking to

---

36 BAGD, 50-51.

conform to the dictates of society rather than by consciously seeking to do the will of God. Each person comes into the world with a batch of different inherited abilities and predispositions. These abilities and predispositions are profoundly modified by the individual's culture. Social groups differ in their cultural expectations in many obvious ways. To take a trivial example, in Navajo culture it is impolite to look someone directly in the eyes. In Anglo-American culture it is impolite--or at least suggestive of deviousness or a bad conscience--should someone converse with another and *not* look him or her directly in the eyes. Whatever the kinds of expectations, the pressure to conform to a peer group is enormous. A gang member is accepted for violence and law-breaking. In a different peer group one is applauded for civic cooperation. The simple fact is that people are willingly shaped by their particular society in both small and extensive ways. To conform is to satisfy a desire for society's approval. When feeling approved, self-esteem and self-glorying follow. The New Testament does not teach that there are "natural" good deeds and virtues that of themselves are acceptable to God. All "natural" good proceeds from a desire to conform and be accepted. Such are ultimately selfish motives, however socially laudable the outcome.

Behavior is also shaped by "the prince of the power of the air" (2 Cor. 4:3-4). This is unquestionably a reference to Satan, an expression explained in the following words, "the spirit that is now at work in the sons of disobedience." The word "spirit" is best understood as an influence rather than a reference to the person of Satan. Andrew T. Lincoln translated the expression, "of the spirit that is now at work."[37]

---

37 Andrew T. Lincoln, *Ephesians*, Word Biblical Commentary, ed.

The meaning is that Satan (a real person) is a spiritual force working among humans.

Why the peculiar expression "prince of the power of the air"? Some suppose Paul thought wind is activated by demonic power. A more likely explanation is that in Jewish thinking the atmosphere, the lowest of the heavenly realms, is peopled by demons. Whether Paul agreed with these metaphysics, he used a dramatic figure of speech, one well understood by people of his day. He is declaring that unbelievers are dominated by the very lord of all demonic power.

This does not say how Satan dominates, only that he does. His power, of course, is limited to what God permits. Nevertheless Satan's influence spreads to all humans. He can control an individual directly, as when Satan entered into Judas (John 13:27). Also, working through people who are under his domination, he can control the minds of others. Think of the way so many millions of German people succumbed to the influence of Adolph Hitler and readily assented to his satanic pogrom against Jews and other minorities.

What is asserted in Paul's terse statement is that humans are mastered by both interior and exterior forces that deter them from doing right. He does not state that each human is directly influenced by Satan; he states only that his influence is pervasive. Since humans practice evil, they have no contact or relationship with God and are wholly unacceptable to him.

What is so difficult for most people to understand is how Paul could cast every human into the same pit. It is more than evident that among the non-Christians of society some indeed are confirmed reprobates, yet the lives of others

---

Ralph P. Martin (Dallas: Word Books, 1990), 96.

are marked by probity and positive contributions to the welfare of mankind. The answer comes only when we recognize what actually constitutes sin, teaching found in the words that follow.

B. Self-gratifying

³Among whom we all once lived in the passions of our flesh, carrying out the desires of the body and the mind,

    The verb "lived" is not the more commonly used word for to live. This verb really means to walk about, but it has the implication of acting with complete involvement. Involved in what? Lived in "passions of the flesh" is a short way of saying that humans have a mouth-watering commitment to the same kind of passions that govern animal life. The word "flesh" (when used in the New Testament in an ethical sense) is a term equivalent to total selfishness. An animal is incapable of living any way other than selfishly. Even a dog that seems to act unselfishly toward its master is doing so instinctively (that is, through its genes), because it is in the selfish interest of the dog's livelihood. "Flesh" is a convenient word for self-interest, self-aggrandizement, self-promotion, self-glorying. The unbeliever is passionately interested in what will promote his or her welfare without regard to the welfare of others, except insofar as the welfare of others is in some way linked to his or her own ultimate interest and good.

    Modern thinkers are fond of pointing out that animals such as honey bees, ants, termites, and naked mole rats are, after all, altruistic. Many individuals in a colony forgo reproduction in order to enable the queen or queens to reproduce. This seems to be an example of genuine self-sacrifice, but it is part of a complex system that enables their genes to be propagated through their sisters. It is a colony of individuals acting collectively for selfish ends, namely, its own survival and reproduction. Nothing in the animal world is capable of altruism in the biblical sense of *agapē*.

Flesh is explained as "following the desires of body and mind." Unquestionably gratification of bodily appetites is the only goal of millions, and to some extent of everyone. There are, however, those who disdain base physical interests and live in the rarefied world of the intellect, pursuing science, literature, art, computer science, business, or the practiced skill of climbing over others to get to the top. But whether of body or mind, self-interest is king. There is, of course, nothing wrong with satisfying bodily appetites. One must eat in order to be of service to others. Sex in a marriage relationship is wholesome and has the approval of God (Heb. 13:4). Engaging in business or a professional field is not wrong. Neither are the arts nor intellectual pursuits. None of these are sinful in and of themselves. These activities become the "flesh" when any of them become the selfish goal of life. Bodily exercise is of value (1 Tim. 4:8), but exercise for the sake of personal admiration or for appearing muscular or svelte in the eyes of others, thus exciting their admiration, constitutes the "flesh." It is the "flesh" when, by whatever means, a person lives and acts *for the sake of* physical, aesthetic, or mental gratification.

Why are all unbelievers *equally* and basically selfish? Some people are selfish in such socially disruptive ways they obviously fit the category of the spiritually dead. They range from common thugs, panderers, and child sex-abusers to those who, like Hitler, Pol Pot, and Osama bin Laden have been responsible for the deaths of thousands. On the other hand, there are many people who are selfish, to be sure, but who advance their interests in ways entirely acceptable to society. They may present themselves as promoters of democracy, liberty, and social progress and may indeed contribute to such ends. Nevertheless, inside all drink from one common well. The branches grow in one direction or another, but every branch springs from a root of self-centered motives. Thus, whether at odds with society or conforming to the best expectations of society, all are equally sinners. God looks not at the branch but at the root motives of men and women. Because some have learned to channel their selfishness in a socially approved way does not mean that their motives are any less selfish. All are separated from God because all are fundamentally selfish. Every manifestation of selfishness is sin and those guilty of sin are dead, disconnected from the life of God.

C. Condemned (2:3b)

3b and were by nature children of wrath, like the rest of mankind.

What is meant by the words "by nature"? Here we could easily get entangled in a theological jungle, but it is best to take the expression in its most obvious meaning. Humans are unable to do other than sin, that is, to live for self. Put another way, humans are unable to do good, when doing good is defined as living in unrecompensed love toward others. In this passage there is no implication of humans carrying the blame for Adam's act of sin, although having descended from Adam, humans are the way they are. They have inherited an inability to live other than self-centeredly.

What is strongly implied is that humans are under condemnation, not because a succession of sins brought death, but because of what they are. God is not weighing some factual degree of their sin. He is seeing them as wrong at heart.

If people are sinful by nature, how can God be righteous in bringing wrath on them when they cannot help being what they are? The answer is that humans are not what God made them to be and they do not allow Him to make them what they could be. Until they come humbly to Him, their very sinful condition is odious to God.

Does wrath simply mean "deserving of wrath"? No, it means far more. It is *settled indignation*. It is a present wrath, for it is the lot of those who are excluded from the life of God. It is a wrath that will continue after physical death, since those who are unbelievers are never raised to life with God. It is exactly what is stated in John 3:36: "He who does not obey the son shall not see life, but the wrath of God rests upon him." It is what the apostle affirmed in Romans 1:18, where the context shows it refers to present wrath. It is also wrath to come, as seen in Romans 2:5.

Yet at present it does not appear that God's wrath is being experienced by all unbelievers, obviously not by all to an equal degree. Some who are conspicuously wicked and some who are blatant and scoffing blasphemers but socially approved seem to fare well in this life. Is God's wrath imaginary or selective? Neither. God in His mercy can and often does temporarily withhold wrath in the hope that the wicked will be led to repentance (Rom. 2:4). His wrath is on them, even though its full fury may be suspended for a time.

II. God's mercy (2:4-6)

After the gloom of the foregoing three verses, the apostle asserts four wonderfully positive things about God, things providing for someone's new life. The first (vvs. 4-6) is the mercy of God. This is followed by God's purpose, God's method, and God's product.

⁴But God, being rich in mercy, because of the great love with which he loved us, ⁵even when we were dead in our trespasses, made us alive together with Christ – by grace you have been saved – ⁶and raised us up with him and seated us with him in the heavenly places in Christ Jesus,

"But God." Two magnificent words! They introduce us to a different side of God's character. Verses 1-3 tell us He is a God of justice. His righteous character demands judgment of every act of disobedience. If He were not absolutely just, He could not be God. Yet in amazing contrast, He is equally a God of mercy, not merely adequate mercy but abundant, overflowing mercy.

The words, "even when we were dead," emphasize the hopelessness of our position. Dead people cannot bring themselves back to life. Being made alive in every respect has to be a powerful act of God.

How can God act toward wicked, judgment-deserving sinners in mercy, when His righteousness obligates Him to act in justice? The answer, of course, was given in 1:7. Because of the redemption provided by the Lord Jesus, God is now absolutely free to act toward us in mercy. His love is the ground, the basis, of His mercy. Because of the sacrifice of Christ, there are no moral impediments standing in His way. He can bestow the benefits of His love on any who come to Him in faith. C. I. Scofield felicitously termed him "our unshackled God."

What does it mean for a believer to be "made alive?" This cannot be a reference to resurrection from physical death, for that is a benefit that follows. It must be life in one's present state on earth. Unbelievers, according to 4:18, are "alienated from the life of God." To have the life of God is precisely the opposite. It means to be indissolubly united with Him. One who is alive is no longer separated from God and under a curse because of sin but is now capable of experiencing and enjoying the life and love of Christ.

At what point do believers enjoy this new life? There must be some specific time. The verb "made alive" does not tell when. It only states that it is an existing fact for every believer. Did this state of being alive with Christ begin at the moment of faith? Was it at the point of water baptism? Is it at the time of physical death, when all issues will have been settled? Each position has its advocates. The last notion, that the new life begins at the time of physical death and entrance into heaven, is quite unacceptable. If a Christian only anticipates receiving eternal life, everything guaranteed by God's grace in 1:3-14 amounts to a beautiful package enclosing nothing. Then it is difficult to think that new life waits until the moment of baptism. The only mention of baptism in Ephesians is in 4:5, where it is *not* connected with the granting of spiritual life but with the unity of Christians. In the earliest apostolic days, baptism took place as soon after a person's reception of the gospel as possible (Acts 2:41; 8:36, 38; 16:31-33). The question differentiating the time of salvation between the moment of faith and the act of baptism would not have come up. In any event the only term

Ephesians: Made Alive in Christ

given for receiving salvation is "faith." There are many who through circumstances not of their own making have been quite unable to go through water baptism, at least not until some period after first coming to faith. If their reception of life had to wait for baptism, God's promise of the sealing of the Spirit through faith (1:13) is made null, and salvation to some degree is made dependent on a human work. The only possible answer is that the new life begins at the moment one turns in faith to the Lord Jesus and His saving grace.

Abruptly at the end of verse 5, the thought is interrupted by a parenthetical statement. Paul is overcome with his realization of God's grand provision of grace and wants to emphasize the truth that salvation is all of grace, even though he previously wrote of God's grace in 1:6-7 and will discuss it again in 2:8-9. Grace is a sheer favor, which means that release from judgment and the granting of divine blessings come not as a result of what anyone does. After all, what can a dead person offer of worth to God in exchange for God canceling his or her frightful debt?

It might be noted that neither this verse nor any other states that grace is "irresistible," although those following the Calvinist tradition insist that it is. The notion that God irresistibly bestows grace on the elect but on no others comes from a system of theology, not from a careful analysis of the Scriptures.

In verse 6, two additional benefits of grace are given. First, as believers we have been raised. Raised, but in what sense? Obviously we are still living in our mortal bodies. Yet the verb speaks of what God has already accomplished. Our future resurrection is so certain that God (speaking through his apostle) can vouch that it is already done. Paul taught exactly this in Romans 6:5; Colossians 2:12; and 3:1. "Raised us up" is the translation of a single Greek verb. The meaning is "raised us up together," that is, raised us "in Christ Jesus."

The believer also has been made to sit with Christ in the heavenly places. The three terms, "made alive," "raised up," and "seated," picture the great span of God's grace. The intimate grouping of the verbs indicate that whenever the first is accomplished, the following are equally accomplished. This moment is the point of saving faith.

"Seated us with him in the heavenly places." In our study of 1:3, we considered what is meant by the heavenly places. It is a reference to the present spiritual world of the believer, threatened as it is by the forces of evil. It is where both God's Spirit and Satan are struggling for the soul of the Christian. And it is here that the believer will emerge victoriously, because as the battle rages, he or she is seated with Christ. The Christian cannot finally become Satan's victim, which is God's enduring promise.

III. God's purpose (2:7)

7so that in the coming ages he might show the immeasurable riches of his grace in kindness toward us in Christ Jesus.

Behind all actions are motives. God's primary motive in His kindness was that in the coming ages His grace might be displayed. To whom will God exhibit us as trophies of His grace? We can only speculate, for there are no pointers in Scripture we know of. Will it be to angelic beings? Perhaps to mortals born during the millennium? Will we be exhibited to sentient beings on a planet in some distant galaxy? Will it be to one another throughout eternity? Could it even be to ourselves as we witness the outworking of His purposes? This last may be the most likely, since it will be accomplished through union with Christ, emphasized again by the formula "in Christ Jesus." What is not speculation is that God in truth has acted toward us in grace, and no one realizes that more than the person who has seen his or her own monstrous unrighteousness in the light of God's Word and been willing to receive the glorious status granted by a loving God.

In showing us off now and through the coming ages, it sounds if God is motivated by self-interest. Some critics have contended that self-interest would be unworthy of God. Quite the contrary. God is the only one in the universe who can afford to speak well of Himself. He is the Almighty who has the right to speak of Himself, since His person is seamless in its perfect mercy and unblemished with the least taint of unrighteousness. By contrast, no human can boast of his or her qualities, since none is perfect.

IV. God's method (2:8-9)

⁸*For by grace you have been saved through faith. And this is not your own doing; it is the gift of God,* ⁹*not a result of works, so that no one may boast.*

Grace is God's unconstrained favor toward those who deserve nothing and who are wholly incapable of achieving any good. If there is the least human good required for salvation, then salvation is no longer by grace. If there is the least human good required to keep one saved, it is no longer by grace. If there is the least human good required to reimburse God for salvation, it is no longer by grace. If a worthy life is required to validate salvation, then it is no longer by grace. Human devices and efforts cannot bring life to an individual who is dead. C. S. Lewis aptly wrote, "No clever arrangement of bad eggs will make a good omelet." Salvation is God's gift, but astoundingly, it is granted to any who will offer a genuine Yes to God's provision through Christ.

What is meant by being saved? People of widely different Christian beliefs speak glibly of being saved. What did the apostle mean? The preceding verses provide the basic information. It is being made alive to God through union with the Lord Jesus. This includes a host of other benefits. The immediate context assures the believer of a coming resurrection like that of Christ's resurrection and the possibility of victory over sin (being seated with Christ in the heavenly places). Other immediate but lasting benefits are listed in Division A_1 (1:3-14).

Several misconceptions have been read into these two straightforward verses (2:8-9), and we must deal with them. The first has to do with an understanding of grace. According to some systems God's grace is what gives a Christian with the *ability* to do good works. In turn these good works lead to salvation. This is definitely wrong. If Paul's words to the Ephesians are not plain enough, Romans 11:6 states the principle clearly: "But if it is by grace, it is no longer on the basis of works; otherwise grace would no longer be grace." Salvation has nothing to do with human effort, even though it is true that a believer's strength to carry out good works is supplied by God.

A different problem is posed by those who insist that faith itself is the gift of God. Has God chosen to give not all but only some the ability to believe? This verse presumably supports this point of view, for allegedly it states that faith itself is a gift. The truth or falsity of the argument hinges on some Greek grammar. Greek nouns and pronouns, like those in German, Russian, Latin, and other inflected languages, are in a masculine, feminine, or neuter gender. "Faith" is a feminine (genitive singular) noun. "This" is a *neuter* demonstrative pronoun. A rule of Greek grammar is that a demonstrative pronoun should agree with the gender of its antecedent. So if Paul intended to say that faith is the gift of God, he should have used the feminine form of "this." But he did not, so "this" seems to refer to a different antecedent than "faith."

Yet neither can "this" refer to "grace," for "grace" also is feminine. It seemingly cannot refer to the verbal expression, "you have been saved," for this is the verb "you are" plus the *masculine* plural participle, "having been saved." To what then does "this" refer? Possibly it could refer back to the whole concept of salvation by grace through faith, just what is stated in verse 8a.

Nevertheless some commentators are adamant in their contention that "this" refers to "faith." They point out that sometimes in Greek literature a pronoun is in a different gender from its obvious antecedent. Quite true, and there are reasons for it. Sometimes it is simply a grammatical mistake, the kind any of us might carelessly make. In other instances it is a figure of speech used to heighten an effect by calling attention to itself. Or it can be a situation where the pronoun is caught between two nouns of different genders, but this is not the case in this verse. Could Paul have been using an unusual, even ungrammatical expression to call attention to the thought that faith itself is a gift of God? It does not seem that in this sentence an ungrammatical expression would accomplish that end. In the absence of some compelling, contextual reason, it is most unlikely.[38]

Paul's statement, "So faith comes from hearing, and hearing through the word of Christ" (Rom. 10:17), should put to rest any argument about the source of faith. It is the Word of God, the Scriptures, that brings faith.

The whole issue, so far as Ephesians 2:8 is concerned, has a very simple resolution, if we follow the suggestion made by the Greek grammarian Daniel B. Wallace.[39] It is possible that "this" is an adverbial expression, not a demonstrative pronoun at all. It would be a term highlighting and intensifying the verb. It could be translated, "And *especially*, it is not of your own doing." This takes out of the picture the whole question of where faith comes from while emphatically emphasizing that human works have no part.

An important question is "faith in what?" Faith is never something that stands by itself. It must have an object. Almost everyone has faith. Some have faith in their own ability. Some have faith that God will accept their church obligations. Others have faith that God is so loving He simply will not send anyone to hell. Yet in Ephesians we read in 1:13 and in 3:12 it is faith in the Lord Jesus Christ as He is revealed in Scripture. It is faith in the Christ who was deity come in the flesh, who died in our stead, and who was raised from the dead. This is exactly what the apostle taught in his

---

38 For a detailed study of the question see René A. Lopez, "Is Faith a Gift from God or a Human Exercise?" *Bibliotheca Sacra* 164 (July-September, 2007): 259-76.

39 Daniel B. Wallace, *Greek Grammar Beyond the Basics: An Exegetical Syntax of the New Testament* (Grand Rapids: Zondervan, 1996), 334-35.

other epistles and precisely what Jesus Himself taught when he declared, "No one comes to the Father except through me" (John 14:6).

Another important question is, What do the Scriptures mean by faith? Faith is complete trust in something. (For scriptural evidence for this definition, see comments under 1:13.) Saving faith is trust or confidence in the Lord Jesus Christ. The question is not fully answered until we understand what it means to believe in Christ. To believe in Christ with saving faith is to believe the testimony of Scripture regarding His person. He was not merely a wise human. He was more. He was the Son of God, deity residing in a human body. He lived a sinless life. He was crucified by sinful men in the stead of sinful men. Then God raised him from the dead. If any of these is denied, can a person be said to truly believe in the Jesus of Scripture?

A subtle error, one that has gained great popularity, is that saving faith is "active faith." Right actions certainly speak to the validity of someone's faith, but actions are never a required element of faith. Otherwise grace would no longer be grace (Rom. 11:6).

A wrong notion about faith in this passage is that Paul is not writing about our faith but about Christ's faith. Supposedly the passage should be understood, "For by grace are you saved through Christ's faithfulness." Hebrews 12:2, speaking of "Jesus the pioneer and perfecter of our faith," presents the great importance of our Lord's faith. Unquestionably His faith is a divine example for our need to exercise continuing trust in God. Nevertheless the antecedent to Ephesians 2:8 is the redemption we have "through his blood" (1:7)[40]. Nowhere in the context is there a suggestion that Christ's personal life of faith is the source of our salvation.[41]

Could faith itself be so valuable that its exercise is the very thing God rewards? Alfred Martin insightfully commented on the words "through faith:" "Paul never says *on account of* faith, for faith is not the cause, only the channel through which salvation comes."[42] Should a person be saved "on account of faith," it would follow that faith is a virtue. That is to say, its exercise is a kind of good work which God must recognize and which in some measure contributes to salvation. This is the very thing the Apostle is strenuously opposing, for any human credit detracts from the credit properly belonging to the Lord Jesus.

An important conclusion is set forth in the words, "not because of works, lest any man should boast." The first part is redundant, but deliberately so. If salvation is a gift, obviously it is not purchased by anyone's efforts. But the Apostle wants to leave his readers in no doubt. His proscription against human boasting clinches the argument. There is

---

40   Daniel H. Bell Jr., Associate Professor of Theological Ethics at Lutheran Theological Southern Seminary, wrote, "But as Paul points out, it is not a blood sacrifice that saves us, but Jesus' obedience and fidelity." "God Does Not Demand Blood," *Christian Century* (Feb. 10, 2009) 126:22-26. This makes one wonder what Bible Dr. Bell reads.

41   A fine discussion of whether faith is a meritorious work is included in the study by Anthony B. Badger, "TULIP, A Free Grace Perspective, Part I: Total Depravity," *Journal of the Grace Evangelical Soc*iety 16 (Spring 2003): 35-61.

42   Alfred Martin, "Ephesians," in the *Wycliffe Bible Commentary*, ed. Charles F. Pfeiffer and Everett F. Harrison, ed. (Chicago: Moody Press, 1962), 1306.

nothing, absolutely nothing, for which any person can take credit, because the entire credit belongs to the God of grace.

V. God's product (2:10)
¹⁰For we are his workmanship, created in Christ Jesus for good works, which God prepared beforehand, that we should walk in them.

"For we are his workmanship" is a shorthand for "He himself is responsible for everything that belongs to our standing before him and our ability to live a life pleasing to him." This is yet another way of saying that our efforts have nothing to do with our salvation.

"Created in Christ Jesus" carries the same idea as the expression "in Christ" that we considered in 1:3. It refers to the believer's total spiritual union with Christ. Apart from Him there is no new creation. United with him the believer has every spiritual blessing, including the power to live a new kind of life, a life built on good works. "Created" is significant, for it reiterates the truth that good works do not lead to salvation. There is no personal merit that accrues from doing good works. It is all of grace.

Surprisingly, Rotherham's *Emphasized Bible*,[43] which the writer has found to be a most useful work for understanding the Scriptures, translated here, "Created in Christ Jesus upon a footing of good works." Clearly this is wrong, for although the preposition "for" (*epi* followed by the dative) can be translated "on" or "upon," to understand it this way would be to deny all that has been said in the preceding two verses. The word "footing" is not in the Greek, a

---

43   Joseph B. Rotherham, The Emphasized Bible (Cincinnati: Standard Publ. Co, 1897), 4:197.

departure from Rotherham's usual effort to make his translation as literal as possible. The Christian is not created on his or her good works but for the purpose of doing good works. Hence there is no reason to boast of one's good deeds or faithful devotion.

Did God prepare specific good works long in advance for each Christian, for example, that one should drop a twenty-dollar bill in a Salvation Army kettle at Christmas time or that one should become a missionary to Afghanistan? There is no indication in Scripture that such is the case. The good works prepared by God and designated for every believer are truth and love. These are works corresponding to God's moral character of righteousness and mercy, the kind of good works God has intended for His people since their creation. The specific ways these good works are expressed depends on the believer's growth in understanding, experience in walking with the Lord, and the circumstances through which one is led by the providence of God. Beyond all question, the path of good works prepared by God will be marked by graciousness in every human relationship, a graciousness reflecting the grace of God.

"Walk" is a favorite word of the Apostle Paul. Here is the beautiful rhetorical climax to Division C_1. The division began with people walking about in trespasses and sins (v. 2) and ends with the believer walking about in good works (v. 10). The emphasis is notable. Just as we lived in unrelieved sinfulness before coming to Christ, so now, as believers, we are to live day by day, moment by moment in a life that pleases him.

DIVISION D₁. UNITED IN CHRIST
(2:11-3:13)

This division of the epistle has two parts. Plainly both parts are concerned with the same topic, the unity of Jews and Gentiles in the body of Christ. The first part declares the fact. The second justifies Paul as the human vehicle through whom God made this fact known. The second part continues the subject of unity but explains how Paul was a divinely chosen vehicle to reveal this unity.

Underscoring the doctrines in this division is the inescapable implication that God provides blessings through His love. In 2:13 we are told that those of us who once were far off from God have been brought near by the blood of Christ. This is stating plainly that our acceptance by God was not purchased ourselves but was granted by God who in love gave his Son for our redemption.

What value does this topic of unity of believing Jews and Gentiles have for Christians today? For one, it surely teaches the truth that each Christian should be accepting of other Christians regardless of their sex, racial origins, or social status. More importantly, the topic develops foundational truth about the nature of the Church, the body of Christ. Everyone who belongs to Christ belongs to every other believer. Belonging to one another, believers collectively are the Church. Christians need to know what this means. In turn, this foundation paves the way for the practical matters developed in the corresponding division, D₂ (4:1-16).

I. The Unity of the Body (2:11-22)

If we can put ourselves in the place of the Gentile

Christians in Asia Minor, we may be able to get some feeling for the significance of this passage. Those Christians represented only a very small minority of the total population. Previously they had been ordinary members of the community, accepted within their society, living and following the same pattern of behavior as all the rest. Now almost overnight they became devotees of a new religion. They renounced many of the customs and practices that identified them with their society. To make matters much worse, so far as their relationship within society was concerned, the religion they now espoused was one promulgated by a particular sect of Jews. The Jews were a people notorious for discrimination against non-Jews and in turn were hated by the Gentiles. To the ordinary Ephesian of that day, the strange new ways of the Christians were doubtlessly just as inexplicable as when in our day a neighbor suddenly decides to shave his head, don the saffron robe of a Buddhist sect, and spend his days standing in a park ringing a bell and handing out literature.

What the Gentile Christians of Ephesus and other communities of Asia Minor needed was a powerful reinforcement of the faith they had accepted. They believed in Christ. Yet the scoffing that followed their decision to align themselves with certain despicable Jews was bound to erode that faith. It was imperative that they have a strong undergirding of doctrinal truth. Here Paul answers their questions, explains their status, and fortifies their souls against onslaughts of ridicule and doubt.

The scenario of the first section (2:11-22) develops in three parts: (A) what the Ephesians were, (B) what Christ has done, and (C) what they have become in Him. As we read the section, we realize that Paul was not writing of

Christians in Asia Minor alone. Paul wrote a three-fold spiritual biography of every believer. The climax comes with the revelation in part C that every believer is built with all others into "a dwelling place for God in the Spirit."

A. What You Gentiles Were (verses 11-13)
11Therefore remember that at one time you Gentiles in the flesh, called the uncircumcision by what is called the circumcision, which is made in the flesh by hands . . .

The Gentiles were despised, despised by Jews who themselves did not understand. God gave a promise to Abraham, the forefather of the Jews, that he, Abraham, would be blessed personally, that he would be the father of many nations, and that his posterity would become a great nation. With specific reference to that nation, God promised to give them the land of Canaan as a permanent possession, promised that they would possess the gate of their enemies, promised that the ones blessing them would themselves be blessed and the ones cursing them would be cursed, and above all He promised that in a unique sense He would be a God to them. This covenant was unconditional. God guaranteed that it would be fulfilled. The first two announcements of this covenant (Gen. 12:1-3; 15:4-21) made no mention of circumcision. With the third announcement (Gen. 17:1-14) God added the stipulation that the covenant must be ratified by circumcision of each male descendant. The ultimate fulfillment of the promise was not dependent on circumcision. Nevertheless no descendant could be in the line of promise-recipients without the sign in his body.

Understandably the Jews were proud of the sign. It signified their great expectation as a nation. Apart from it, any male and his family would be denied participation in the promise. But with it a Jew could say, "I am in the sacred line. I have the promises made to Abraham, just as Abraham had them." Every national or religious honor that belonged to a Jew had its value only in the covenant which that circumcision represented.

There was nothing wrong with the sign. What went wrong was that the sign replaced the significance of the promise. The sign became a matter of pride, and that pride blinded the Jews to the very reason God had separated them as a nation. From the beginning it had been stated that "in you all the families of the earth shall be blessed" (Gen. 12:3). God did not tell Abraham how this should be done. Nevertheless the people at the foot of Mount Sinai were carefully advised that they had been separated to become "a kingdom of priests and a holy nation" (Exodus 19:6). They were not to serve themselves but to bring to the world the truth of Yahweh (the LORD). Isaiah understood their mission in this sense, for looking forward to the time when Israel truly shall be functioning as priests to the nations, he sees them receiving a double portion for their service. Aliens and foreigners shall speak of them as "the ministers of our God" (Isa. 61:5-7). The sign was to mark the nation assigned this holy calling.

Separation from the sins of the Gentiles was of course mandatory for the Jews. That in turn demanded social separation from those who would lead them astray from God. In Solomon's old age his foreign wives turned his heart to idolatry. But separation from union with idolaters did not warrant separation from a spiritual concern for Gentiles. The prophecy of Jonah should have been a continual reminder of this. The Jews should have been and could have been the priests of God to the rest of the world, even while living in separated holiness.

Ignoring their calling, the Jews hatefully flung the name "uncircumcised!" at the Gentiles, something they considered a terrible shame. Yet they were totally heedless that their circumcision, without the obligation it represented, was no more significant than any other operation performed on the body by human hands. Apart from faith in the meaning of the covenant, the sign was nothing.

[12]remember that you were at that time separated from Christ, alienated from the commonwealth of Israel and strangers to the covenants of promise, having no hope and without God in the world.

The pagan Gentiles were removed from God and the things of God. Once again these early Christians had to be reminded where and what they were before becoming Christians. In this verse the apostle points out their lack of a *standing* before God. In five distinct respects the Ephesians had been removed. First, they *lacked a relationship with Christ*. Most humans feel a need for established relationships. Many find a relationship in some fraternal organization. Some even join a church, not out of wanting to enter into a relationship with God but because church membership provides the relationship they crave. Paul's declaration is that the Ephesians were without the one eternally significant relationship in all the universe: union with the risen Lord. In view of all he has written about the Christian being "in Christ," the words, "separated from Christ" can mean only this.

Second, they were *left out of the action*. They were

alienated from the commonwealth of Israel. Or as in the HCSB, "excluded from the citizenship of Israel." Looking at the history of Israel, someone may disdainfully exclaim, "Big deal! What is so great about that?" What indeed is the advantage of being a citizen of Israel? The answer is that God chose Israel as his special people and became intimately involved in their affairs. When they lacked water in their wilderness wanderings, God instructed Moses to strike a rock, which cracked open to pour forth a life-giving stream. When they needed direction, God spoke to them either through the high priest or their leader Moses. Did they hunger? God provided manna. Did enemies block their way? It was nothing for God to shatter the walls of Jericho. On the other hand, when they were disobedient, God brought enemies or famine or pestilence upon them. From the founding of their nation, God never let them alone. The history of Israel is the history of a personal God intimately involved with his own people.

It is a great frustration to be always a spectator, never a participant. A man in a business organization who sees his colleagues invited to the president's office to help arrive at policy decisions but who himself is never invited will feel deep resentment. To be outside the realm of God's working, to feel ignored by God, is the greatest frustration of all. Paul's meaning is just this: to be outside Israel is to be outside a nationality where God constantly worked on behalf of its members.

Third, they were *unacquainted with God's great plan* and hence without real significance. They were "strangers to the covenants of promise." They were ignorant of the compacts God had made with the nation. The promises had to do with the future of Israel and through Israel with the future of the whole world. In the Gentile's case, ignorance was not bliss. The Jews, unlike the Gentiles, had a certain supreme self-confidence borne of the assurance they were God's chosen people. Where did this confidence come from? It was based on the unconditional character of the Abrahamic and Davidic covenants. The Gentiles were part of nothing except the shifting political system under which they happened to be living, certainly nothing of significance.

Fourth, they were *severed from any future*. They had no hope. Educated Greeks did not doubt the existence of God. They saw him as a philosophical necessity. He was, however, a God unconcerned with human beings, a God who could promise them nothing after death. Aristotle, one of the greatest of the Greek philosophers, tutor of Alexander the Great, idol of the learned, called death "the most to be feared of all things . . . for it appears to be the end of everything; and for the deceased there appears to be no longer either any good or any evil."[44] How futile life without hope beyond the grave. We are conscious of an Abraham Lincoln, a Madame Currie, a Jonas Salk, or a Winston Churchill having modified the course of human affairs for better, but this is small consolation for most humans, who come to the end realizing with Solomon the depressing vanity of life.

Fifth, they lived in a *directionless world*. They were "without God in the world." They had their mystery religions and their superstitious dependence upon oracles, clairvoyants, predictions of the future by observing the flight of birds, the movement of oil on water, and the markings of a liver, but no sense of stability or reliability in the world. Their universe was governed by the irrational whims of their

---

44   Aristotle, Nichomachean Ethics, 3.9.

deities who could, however, be induced to act favorably by certain incantations and sacrifices. The pointlessness of their lives must have been felt by all of them.

In contrast, how significant is the Christian's confidence. Although the world may have a superficial appearance of being controlled by nothing more than chance, behind everything is the God whose providence guarantees that for the one who loves God, "all things work together for good" (Rom. 8:28). The believer can experience and know this and can know that God has a plan that goes beyond this life.

Having shown the emptiness of their lives before they came to faith in Christ, Paul turns to the wonder of what Christ is.

[13]But now in Christ Jesus you who once were far off have been brought near in the blood of Christ.

Verse 13 is the happy conclusion to the darkness of verses 11 and 12. It is also the transition sentence to part B of this section.

There is no proclamation of the Christian message apart from the proclamation of the Cross. One might repent of sin, preach the necessity of faith, discuss the value of total commitment, minister to the needy, glorify the functions of the Church, yet without the Cross remain completely pagan. God's purposes for mankind revolve around the death of Christ as the sole and sufficient ground of salvation. Only in His death on the cross is anyone "brought near."

Verses 14 to 17 explain how believers are brought to God, to His life, and to peace. Although these verses list benefits belonging to believers, the primary emphasis is on what Christ accomplished.

B. What Christ Has Done (2:14-18)

[14]For he himself is our peace, who has made us both one and has broken down in his flesh the dividing wall of hostility [15]by abolishing the law of commandments and ordinances, that he might create in himself one new man in place of the two, so making peace, [16]and might reconcile us both to God in one body through the cross, thereby killing the hostility. [17]And he came and preached peace to you who were far off and peace to those who were near. [18]For through him we both have access in one Spirit to the Father.

Christ is our peace, but how? From these four verses six essential facts emerge explaining how He is our peace. (In the following comments we discuss them a little out of the sequence in which they occur in the verses but in a sequence that shows their logical relationships.)

One overriding fact underlies all the others. Peace is achieved only through the work of the Lord Jesus Christ Himself. Verse 14 begins with the words, "For he himself" (placed first in the ESV, correctly translating the emphasis found in the Greek). He alone has done what is necessary to unite the alienated in one body. How has He done this? In verse 15 the words "in himself" have the meaning "united to him." Here is the same "in him" phrase that we examined in Division A_1. Believers, regardless of race, belong to each other through being placed "in Christ." In God's reckoning they are all part of the same spiritual body, for they are all in union with Christ.

1. *His purpose was that of making believing Jews and Gentiles one.* Verse 16 says that he came that he "might

reconcile us both to God in one body." It was predicted in the Old Testament (e.g., Isa. 11:10; Mic. 4:2, Mal. 1:11) that at some time to come the Gentiles would worship the Lord, but there was no intimation that they would be equal to the Jews and united with them. Here is a new revelation: God was committed to bringing both together with equal status in a unified body. Verse 15 says that out of believing Jews and Gentiles, Christ has created "in himself one new man." The unity forms a completely new entity entirely different from either of the previous two.

    2. *The obstacle to unification was the Mosaic law, the law containing both commandments and ordinances.* The obstacle is stated to be the "dividing wall of hostility." Some commentators opine that the wall of hostility is a reference to a fence and enclosure around the temple in Jerusalem that kept Gentiles from entering. But a reference to a physical wall around the temple would have little significance for Gentiles living in Asia Minor. Best thinks the wall is simply a "separating factor" that lacks specificity.[45] This is also quite inadequate. There is only one explanation that fits the context. The reference to "commandments and ordinances" in the following verse makes no sense unless the dividing wall is the Mosaic Law.

    What was it about the Mosaic Law that made it a dividing wall between Jews and Gentiles? The commandments by themselves did not create hostility. The Israelites were commanded to love the Gentile strangers (Deut. 10:19). The Gentiles had the right of asylum in the cities of refuge, the same as the Israelites (Num. 35:15). Most unexpectedly,

---

45   Best, *A Critical and Exegetical Commentary on Ephesians*, 256-57.

a wealthy Gentile might even possess Israelite slaves (Lev. 25:47). A different explanation has to be found. Three factors working together altered the attitude of the Jews toward Gentiles so that by New Testament times the Jews manifested the most extreme aversion, scorn, and hatred toward the Gentiles. The first was the exclusivity of being the only people to whom the Law was given (Deut. 4:8). The pride of having the divine law engendered an attitude of haughtiness toward Gentiles who did not enjoy this superior privilege. A section in a letter written sometime between 250 B.C. and A.D. 100 reflects the attitude of Jews in New Testament times.

> In his wisdom the legislator . . . being endowed by God for the knowledge of universal truths, surrounded us with unbroken palisades and iron walls to prevent our mixing with any of the other peoples in any matter, being thus kept pure in body and soul, preserved from false beliefs, and worshiping the only God omnipotent over all creations . . . So, to prevent our being perverted by contact with others or by mixing with bad influences, he hedged us in on all sides with strict observances connected with meat and drink and touch and hearing and sight, after the manner of the Law.[46]

Second, their idiosyncrasy was reinforced by Ezra's deep grief over the Jews' mixed marriages after the Exile and the Jews' subsequent covenant to put away their foreign wives. The Law had not prohibited marriage with any Gentiles, only with women of one of the seven outrageously corrupt Canaanite nations (Deut. 7:1-5). Yet by New Testament

---

46 "Letter of Aristeas," trans. R. J. H. Shutt, *The Old Testament Pseudepigrapha*, ed. J. H. Charlesworth (Garden City, NY: Doubleday, 1983), 2:7-34.

times the Law had been interpreted as a prohibition against social or conjugal relationships with all Gentiles. The Law did not demand the extreme exclusivity practiced by the Jews, but its interpretation did.

Third, the terrible suffering of the Jews at the hands of the Greek rulers of Syria beginning with Antiochus Epiphanes and the Jews' continuing conflicts with the Syrians for many generations afterward could not help but sour their outlook on Gentiles. They saw Gentiles as people cruel and unjust because they knew not the Law. Midst all their oppression and trials, the Law was their anchor. It was the one great bastion of truth to which they could cling. The Gentiles, on the other hand, saw the Jews as prideful and stubborn.

3. *God's solution to unification was the nullification of the Law.* It would have been better if instead of "abolishing" the ESV had translated, "by *annulling*"[47] in his flesh the law of commandments and ordinances. The Greek verb *katargeo* carries the broad sense of both "make ineffective," that is, "nullify," and "abolish." Which sense should be selected to translate the word in this passage? It is not clearly indicated in Ephesians, but it is plain enough from Paul's other writings. There is a fine difference between the ideas. Something abolished is made nonexistent. Paul never wrote that the Law has been abolished. Quite the contrary. In Romans 3:31 he wrote, "Do we then overthrow the law by this faith? By no means! On the contrary, we uphold the law." What the apostle said is not that the Law has been removed from existence or that the Law has no value. It is nullified so

---

47 Adopting for *katargeo* sense 2 in BAGD. 525.

that it no longer has any force for the believer.⁴⁸

Making this wholly legitimate change, the words are straightforward. The Law is nullified, since for every infraction of the Law Christ satisfied the justice of God by taking the penalty upon Himself (Gal. 3:13; I Pet. 2:24). Hence, although the Law is still in existence and has a purpose, for the Christian it is neither a means to salvation nor is any part of it a rule by which to live.⁴⁹ The fact that Paul never thought obedience to the Law brought or helped bring salvation is obvious from the following representative passages:

> For by works of the law no human being will be justified in his sight, since through the law comes knowledge of sin (Rom. 3:20).
>
> Yet we know that a person is not justified by works of the law but through faith in Jesus Christ, . . . and not by works of the law because by works of the law no one will be justified (Gal. 2:16).

The following representative passages show that in the view of the apostle, the Law is not a rule by which the Christian is to live.

> For sin will have no dominion over you, since you are not under law but under grace (Rom. 6:14)

---

48 Snodgrass, *Ephesians*, 133, wrote, "What is abolished is the law as a set of regulations that excludes Gentiles." This is a complete misunderstanding. The Law, of course, is still part of the Word of God and is a witness to God's righteousness, His compassion, and His constancy. When it becomes the Christian's guide it can only stimulate sin, as Romans 7:8 asserts.

49 Reformed theologians generally refer to the moral aspects of the Law which Christians are expected to follow as the "third use of the Law." This includes the Ten Commandments and other moral teachings of the Law by which Christians are to direct their lives.

> But now we are released from the law, having died to that which held us captive, so that we serve not under the old written code but in the new life of the Spirit (Rom. 7:6).
> God, who has made us competent to be ministers of a new covenant, not of the letter but of the Spirit. For the letter kills, but the Spirit gives life (2 Cor. 3:6). But if you are led by the Spirit, you are not under the law. (Gal. 5:18).

Nevertheless few commentators and theologians have been willing to accept the words of Ephesians 2:15 as they are written. In large part this goes back to the theology of John Calvin. To be sure, he taught that no one could be justified by the Law, but he maintained that the moral laws of the Old Testament, as distinguished from the ceremonial and civil laws, are obligatory for the believer. He asserted that the moral law as a rule by which to live is the "principal use" of the Law."[50] Most evangelical commentators have followed this pattern. There is, however, absolutely no textual evidence here or anywhere else that Paul distinguished between the moral law and the ceremonial law. Markus Barth correctly pointed out that "the distinction between moral and ceremonial laws cannot be upheld. Neither the Bible, nor the history of religions, nor sound theological reasons support it."[51]

---

50 John Calvin, *Institutes of the Christian Religion* 2.7.12.
51 M. Barth, *Ephesians: Introduction, Translation, and Commentary on Chapters 1-3:288.* Yet astonishingly Barth places the believer under the Law as a rule by which to live, arguing, "Christ has abrogated the divisive functions of the law and therefore not God's holy law itself"

To justify the concept that the Ten Commandments define the Christian's rule for living, expositors resort among other passages to Romans 13:8-10. Verse 8 reads, "Owe no one anything, except to love each other; for the one who loves another has fulfilled the law." Verse 10 concludes, "Love does no wrong to a neighbor; therefore love is the fulfilling of the law." Many read this passage as if Law-keeping fulfills an obligation to love. But Paul does not say, "If you keep the Law, you practice love to your neighbor." Rather he says in effect, "If you love your neighbor, you will do all the Law intended." The emphasis in the passage is not on Law, but on love, an emphasis that continues through Romans 14. The same truth is taught in Galatians 5:14, "For the whole law is fulfilled in one word, 'You shall love your neighbor as yourself.'" Douglas J. Moo well stated: "Fulfilling the law . . . denotes that complete satisfaction of the laws demands that comes only through Christians identification with Christ and their submission to that commandment that Christ put at the heart of his new covenant teaching: love. It is the love of others, first made possible by Christ, that completely satisfies the demand of the law.[52] This is the precise point. In finding salvation through the deep love of Christ, the Christian is given a compelling motive for love. Love achieves the end for which the law was designed and thus fulfills the intent

---

(ibid., 291).The position taken here is developed in the study by Wayne G. Strickland in *Five Views on Law and Gospel*, ed. Wayne G. Strickland (Grand Rapids: Zondervan, 1993), 229-79, and in the careful analysis by J. Daniel Hays, "Applying the Old Testament Law Today," *Bibliotheca Sacra* 158 (January-March, 2001):21-35.

52 Douglas J. Moo, in *Five Views on the Law and Gospel*, 360. Also see excellent comments by Richard N. Longnecker, *Galatians* (Dallas: Word, 1990), 242-43.

of the law unrestricted by rules. (See Observation V: The Church and the Law, 287).

Not a few writers have argued that since nine of the Ten Commandments are repeated in the New Testament, those nine are Christian obligations. They are the Christian's rules. This is exegesis at its worst! When the context for each citation of a commandment is considered, the argument crumbles. Many of the citations are included in commandments given to Israel before the Cross at the time when the Law was still in force. Others, especially in the Pauline Epistles, need to be examined with something other than a prejudiced eye.

If a Christian refrains from violating the Law against murder, it is not because the Law said, "Thou shalt not kill." It is because no believer acting in love would ever want to take the life of another. The Law said, "Thou shalt not covet," but this rule is not why the Christian should refrain from coveting. The Christian refrains because in love he or she would not want what another possesses but is glad that someone has possessions to enjoy. Love goes even further and seeks to bestow one's goods on someone in need.

Someone protests, "If love is the only rule, isn't this moral relativism?" No. Moral relativism says that what is right is what is dictated by the circumstances. Without the Law and with only love as a guide, it would seem as though the Christian is limited to moral decisions based on nothing more than circumstances. This would mean, the protester says, there are no absolutes for the Christian. Wrong! There is a very clear absolute for the Christian. The absolute is to have the best interests, the welfare, the rights, and the feelings of the other person at heart rather than his or her own. It is the absolute of *agapē* To be sure, *agapē* looks at circumstances. This requires, of course, that the believer is sensitive to the circumstances of other believers. Paul prayed that the Philippians might have love that abounds "more and more, with knowledge and all discernment" (Phil. 1:9). Effective love requires a knowledge of the other person's true circumstances and responds to them with genuine understanding. This way of thinking is not moral relativism. It is Christian radicalism! It is totally contrary to the world's way of thinking and acting.

4. *The condition for union in one body was reconciliation.* Someone who is reconciled is someone who has come to a totally opposite view of another person from that held previously. In Ephesians there are three parties who need to have a totally new view of one another. Believing Jews are to be reconciled to believing Gentiles. Believing Gentiles are to be reconciled to Jews. Both have entertained only distrust and anger toward each other. The third party is God. According to verse 3, everyone, including both Jews and Gentiles, are objects of God's wrath. God is justly angry at both. God must be reconciled to both.

Some theologians argue that God does not need to be reconciled and that the Scriptures do not say that He is reconciled; it is only humans who need to be reconciled to Him. However, Ephesians 2:3 should put that notion to rest. The works of men made God their enemy, so God needed to be reconciled. Colossians 1:20 looks at reconciliation from God's standpoint. He needed to be reconciled to a rebellious world, something he made possible "by the blood of his cross." On the other hand, humans at enmity with God definitely need to be reconciled to him. Second Corinthians 5:20

urges men and women, "We implore you on behalf of Christ, be reconciled to God." Reconciliation between heaven and earth was accomplished by the Cross. With the realization that God is reconciled, Jews and Gentiles willing to come by faith can be reconciled to one another through the Cross.

5. *The result following reconciliation is peace.* Verse 15 reads, "that he might create in himself one new man." The "one new man" is the Church, the assembly that includes both believing Jews and believing Gentiles. The last part of verse 16 is translated in the ESV, "thereby killing the hostility." This is a striking expression. Normally it is an enemy that does the killing. Here it is the Cross that kills the enemy, the hostility. The union of believing Jews and Gentiles can come only through an intimate union with Christ, yet there is no union with Christ and no peace apart from the Cross. As believers understand what they have become, being united with Christ, superficial racial distinctions, so important to the unregenerate, become of absolutely no importance.

6. *The proclamation through Christ's preaching is peace.* Verse 17 states that this peace is for Israel (those near at hand) and for the Gentiles (those far off), peace that should reign between believers of both groups.[53] Yet the statement seems contradicted by the words of Jesus, for He said, "I was sent only to the lost sheep of the house of Israel" (Matt. 15:24). The words of Jesus have to be taken at face value.

---

53   Verse 17 is a quotation from the last half of Isaiah 57:19, except that the Isaiah passage is addressed "to him" whereas Paul makes it an address "to you." In the Isaiah verse those who "are near" refers to the people of Israel who mourn for their sins. The context, particularly Isaiah 56:7-8, suggests that those "far off" must be the Gentiles, who, as followers of Yahweh, will be gathered to Israel.

His preaching was in truth limited to Israel, although a few Gentiles benefited from His ministry.

For those who read the Synoptic Gospels in the light of the natural meaning of the Abrahamic, Mosaic, and Davidic covenants and in the obvious sense of the Old Testament prophets, the reason Jesus primarily preached to Israel is not difficult to find. Jesus came to offer the promised earthly kingdom to Israel. It was a bona fide offer. So far as Old Testament prophecies were concerned, the kingdom could have been received by Israel when Christ offered it, had the people genuinely met the conditions. This does not mean that Jesus would not have gone to the Cross. And it does not mean that the time of "distress for Jacob" (Jer. 30:7, Israel's tribulation) would not have followed. But Christ's resurrection glory could shortly have been glory for Israel. When it became clear that the nation rejected Christ and His offer of the kingdom, Christ predicted they would be set aside and God would turn to the Gentiles (Matt. 21:33-43; 22:1-14; 23:37-39; etc.). How then can Paul write that Christ preached to those far off? The answer has to be that the proclamation was made through His viceregents, the apostles and their successors. He delegated them with His authority (Matt. 28:18-20). Christ's preaching is proclaimed today through every believer who witnesses to the authentic gospel.

Ephesians 2:18 adds a new emphasis to what has gone before. Through Christ, free access to God the Father is available to believing Jews and Gentiles. The word "both" emphasizes that in the sight of God, believing Jews and believing Gentiles stand together as one people with the previous distinctions no longer having significance. That it is access "in one Spirit" implies that coming to God in prayer does not require the worshipers' presence in a temple or church building, but a worshiper can pray to God anywhere and anytime. The Holy Spirit, who indwells every believer, makes prayer possible wherever that believer happens to be and whatever his or her circumstances. Significantly the verse reinforces Paul's statement in 1 Timothy 2:5 that no go-between other than the Lord Jesus Christ is needed or is possible. The Christian can come to the Father directly without going through Mary, some departed saint, or an earthly priest.

C. What You Are (2:19-22)
19So then you are no longer strangers and aliens, but you are fellow citizens with the saints and members of the household of God, 20built on the foundation of the apostles and prophets, Christ Jesus himself being the cornerstone, 21in whom the whole structure, being joined together, grows into a holy temple in the Lord. 22In him you also are being built together into a dwelling place for God by the Spirit.

    1. *"Fellow citizens"* speaks of the believer's privileges. The Christian is privileged to be a fellow citizen with the saints, but who are these? The word "saints" is literally "holy ones." As we have seen, sainthood is the status of every believer. At times the word "saints" is used by Paul to refer to angels, and a few commentators have taken "saints" in this verse to be the angels. The word, however, is used of believers a number of times elsewhere in Ephesians (1:1, 15, 18; 3:8; 4:12; 5:3, 6:18), so it is a bit rash to propose any other meaning here.

    What seems odd is that Paul did not write, "you

are now saints" but seems to have implied, in our English translations at least, that "saints" are a class to which not all Christians belong. But in the Greek, Paul actually wrote, "you are fellow citizens in association with the saints." As separate words, "in association" is not there. But the idea is indicated by the particular Greek structure.[54]

2. *"Members of the household of God"* speaks of the Christians responsibilities. Everyone in a household, immediate family members, more remote relatives living in the same home, and servants in more well-to-do households have chores and tasks necessary to keep the household on an even keel. So it is in the household of God. Each believer has a gift to be used for the benefit of other believers (Rom. 12:4-8; I Cor. 12:4-30). Each Christian is responsible to use his or her gift for others.

Suggesting that we have responsibilities as Christians does not imply a burden. Responsibilities point to the family intimacy that each of us should feel with every other believer. A responsibility is a decided privilege when it is connected to a family to which one has given his or her life. Our Christian responsibilities are joyful tasks when we see ourselves in union with the Lord of glory and other believers.

3. *"Built into a temple"* in verses 20-22 speaks of our relationships. Before addressing the question of relationships, we need to clarify the identity of "the apostles and prophets." They are those apostles and prophets whose initial ministry made the church a reality. With respect to apostles, this would include Peter and John to whom special

---

54   This is a genitive of association. Wallace, *Greek Grammar beyond the Basics*, 128-29.

revelations were given, other members of the Twelve, Paul, and a few others. (See 4:11 for a discussion of apostles and prophets.) They were those who preached the gospel and vouched for it.

Who were the prophets? Many expositors consider these to be the Old Testament prophets. The tradition comes from assuming that the Church, the body of Christ, is an extension of Israel, the "Old Testament Church." The tradition is an error. Some of the evidence for this conclusion follows from the fact that "apostles" precedes "prophets," and from the fact that the two are linked together in 3:5. The prophets considered here were prophets in the earliest days of the Church. The gift was essential at a time when the revelation of the New Testament was far from complete. The gift of prophecy often included foretelling (Acts 11:28; 21:10-11), but not necessarily. Prophecy in the Old Testament consisted of preaching the will of God as well as foretelling the future. Judas (called Barsabbas) and Silas are termed prophets (Acts 15:32), but they seem primarily to have been preachers. Here Paul is undoubtedly referring to those gifted with a ministry of instructing and fortifying the early Church with oral records of the words of Christ and subsequent revelations of the Spirit that had yet to be committed to writing. In due course the written Word would become a reality and the role of a prophet limited to that of setting forth the truths of the Word.

Verse 20, which states that *Christ Jesus himself* is the *cornerstone,* and verses 21 and 22, which speak of the growing structure of a *holy temple,* direct our minds to our relationships with Christ and also with one another. The word "cornerstone" refers to a foundation stone, not to the keystone of an arch over a gate or to the capstone on a building, as many expositors suppose. Psalm 118:22 likely suggested the illustration to Paul, a verse that is quoted in several other New Testament passages. The Hebrew of this verse does not clearly indicate whether the psalmist was referring to a foundation stone or to a keystone, so we have to see how Paul used it. Those who take the word to refer to a stone that completes the top of a building have missed the dynamic imagery Paul is projecting. The temple is being built but its growth is far from complete. Paul's teaching is not about the relationship of Christ to the completed Church but to the development of the Church. The temple is being built and will continue to grow until the Lord returns. The Church began with the apostles, prophets, and above all with Christ. To make Christ the topmost stone is to separate the apostles and prophets from the Lord, whereas together they are the supporting base.

The message of the three verses is this: Christ is the cornerstone, on which is built the foundation of the apostles and prophets,[55] into whom all others are spiritually mortised. Since he is the corner stone, he determines the lay of the walls and crosswalls throughout. All the other stones are obligated to adjust themselves to him. It is Christ and not some human authority who gives the temple its needed direction. It is not a temple made up of static rules and traditions but a temple of living saints who together are growing in union with the Lord. This growth comes, as Paul explains in the corresponding division, as each believer ministers to

---

55 For a discussion of what seems to be a contradiction between this passage and I Cor. 3:11, in which Christ is the foundation, see Radmacher, *The Nature of the Church*, 265-74.

other believers. The growth the apostle is writing about is not growth in numbers but in spiritual power and maturity. This growth is possible because God dwells in this temple. In the days of ancient Israel, God's presence with humans was specifically in the Holy of Holies, first in the tabernacle and then in Solomon's temple. Following the resurrection of Christ and his ascension into heaven, the temple of God's choice is Christ's body, the Church. God's presence in this temple is through the indwelling union of the Holy Spirit with every believer.

II. Paul the minister of God's mystery (3:1-13)

At first glance verses 1-13 seem rather barren of spiritual profit. Few sermons are developed from these verses compared to the numbers preached from chapters 4-6. Yet here are some fundamental truths relating to the Church, the body of Christ. Those who place their faith in Christ are members of this body. Surely then, each one should have a vital interest in what it means to be a member. More importantly the verses show the cosmic importance of the Church. It is vastly more than an organized group of people getting together for moral instruction. It is God's witness of His infinite wisdom to "rulers and authorities," evil beings beyond human comprehension.

The foundational theme of Division D_1 is God's plan to unite believing Jews and Gentiles in one body. This plan, however, was a mystery. The Apostle Paul and his fellow apostles and prophets were given an understanding of the mystery, and Paul was assigned to make it known everywhere possible.

In some English translations the verses are broken

into as many as eight sentences. As Paul wrote these verses they consist of one incomplete sentence followed by two long sentences. It is quite unlike our English style of writing. Nevertheless it is not difficult to follow his thinking.

A. Entrusted with a Plan (3:1-7)

Before coming to the plan, Paul tells his readers of his circumstances. From the perspective of the saints in Ephesus, his circumstances are very much related to the plan God gave him to deliver to the Gentiles.

1. Paul a prisoner (3:1)

¹For this reason I, Paul, a prisoner for Christ Jesus on behalf of you Gentiles –

The verse is not a complete sentence. Did Paul start out to write a complete sentence, then half way through, because some parenthetical material popped into his head, decide to break it off? Many commentators think so. However, Paul was using a deliberate figure of speech to emphasize a point. Such a usage was not unknown to Greek rhetoricians, who even had a name for it: *aposiopesis* (literally, "becoming silent"). It is an abrupt and calculated failure to complete a sentence. But if so, what was Paul trying to emphasize? It is a reminder that he had a powerful message, a message that above all his imprisonment was for them, the Gentile believers.

The introductory phrase, "For this reason," ties 2:11-22 and 3:1-13 together as part of the same literary unit. This includes the immediately preceding truth that believing Jews and Gentiles are brought to God on the same terms of grace and are united in one body.

The authorities in Rome kept Paul in prison, quite unjustly. Why? They left no written record, but undoubtedly Paul was considered a traitor to the official worship of the emperor and the Roman gods. Paul obviously believed he was in prison because of his Christian faith. So he answered, in essence, "I'm here on your behalf!"

Why should Paul have told his readers this? The explanation given in verse 13 is that newly converted Gentile Christians would tend to lose heart over his imprisonment. They might well question the reality of the faith he preached, especially if God was unable to give him freedom to continue his missionary labors. A God of limitless power would surely deliver his faithful servant from the hands of pagan rulers. If not, could it be that such a God does not exist, or could it be that Paul was not a true apostle? Paul knew, of course, that being in Rome was part of God's providential design, even if it required his long detention in Caesarea and his journey to Rome as a prisoner. What primarily mattered was that God was using Paul's imprisonment to reach Gentiles who otherwise would not have known the gospel. In 3:7-9 he explained that he was made a minister and empowered by the grace of God to preach to the Gentiles. The implication is that his personal circumstances were of no concern as long as he was an effective tool for Christ.

Paul refused to accept the feeling that people or events were in control of his life. Wonderful liberation from any circumstance comes as we who are believers recognize that we are never a prisoner of some miserable circumstance but, as with Paul, a prisoner of Jesus Christ!

Although not stated in Ephesians Paul explained in Philippians 1:28-30 that his strength under the conditions of his imprisonment was a witness to the validity of his faith. There Paul wrote that those who courageously suffer for the sake of Christ become an omen of judgment to unbelievers and a confirmation of salvation to other believers. In the same way our fortitude in a difficult and trying circumstance may well be the crucial witness God truly needs for someone close by or some group of people.

2. Paul entrusted with a secret previously unknown (3:2-3)
²assuming that you have heard of the stewardship of God's grace that was given to me for you, ³how the mystery was made known to me by revelation, as I have written briefly.

Paul does not tell us when he was given this revelation or how, although he may have received it in the vision described in 2 Corinthians 12:1-6. What the apostle's statement tells us is that he knew his understanding of the mystery had been supernaturally imparted. It did not have its source in reasoned thinking, it was not a deep intuition that came to him, it was not the consequence of an extraordinary imagination. From God alone he received the Word.

The word "stewardship" is translated "administration" in the NIV and the HCSB and "dispensation" in the NKJV. An equally legitimate translation is "plan." The ESV translates the word by "plan" in 1:10 and 3:9. This is the translation it should have here. God's grace is the foundation of an extensive plan that provides eternal spiritual benefits and a new way of life for the believer. Paul's mission was to spread the good news of this plan. If we take the word in the sense of "stewardship" or "dispensation," it implies that Paul's mission was to dispense God's grace, as if he could dole out God's grace as he went about ministering. But no; Paul was sent not to dispense the grace but to share the knowledge of God's grace.

Looking at the last clause of verse 3, we need not try to make Paul say that he wrote a previous letter to the Ephesians, one unknown to us, or that he had in mind some previously written epistle, a letter that is now lost, or the notion advanced by some that Romans 16 was originally addressed to the Ephesians. The words "I have written briefly" are frequently found in the correspondence of that time period (on papyri) with the sense "as I have written above." Where did he write this? In 2:13-22. He did not use the word "mystery" in 2:13-22, but these verses certainly must be, at least in part, an expansion of the "mystery of his will," a term which he introduced in 1:9.

3. The secret (3:4-7)

⁴When you read this, you can perceive my insight into the mystery of Christ, ⁵which was not made known to the sons of men in other generations as it has now been revealed to his holy apostles and prophets by the Spirit. ⁶This mystery is that the Gentiles are fellow heirs, members of the same body, and partakers of the promise in Christ Jesus through the gospel.

⁷Of this gospel I was made a minister according to the gift of God's grace, which was given me by the working of his power.

Why did Paul write, "When you read," when they had already read (or had read to them) chapters 1 and 2 of Ephesians? The correct answer is not difficult to come by. As Hoehner points out, the introductory words (*pros ho*) translated "when" in the ESV are difficult to put into exact English. "Basically, the expression directs ones attention back to what was just stated."[56] Paul was reminding them that by reading the preceding discourse they were able to perceive his insight into the mystery of Christ.

We ordinarily think of a mystery as something beyond human comprehension, or else a secret that a special class of people want to keep others from knowing. A major feature of almost all pagan religions are secrets reserved for a priestly caste or special initiates. God gave Paul and other apostles and prophets access to a mystery. It was a mystery because it was beyond comprehension until it was revealed. God did not reveal a secret that was reserved for a select group only, but gave it that it might be disclosed to everyone. What distinguishes the faith of the Bible from many other religions is that it keeps no secrets. (A religion that has its secret initiations and ceremonies, even if professing to be Christian, is certainly to be shunned.) The now unveiled mystery is that the gospel is available to everyone equally on the simple condition of faith in the Lord Jesus Christ.

Here we run headlong into an area of major disagreement in interpreting what the apostle meant when he wrote that the mystery was not made known to previous generations. Did Paul mean that the Church, the body of Christ, existed through the centuries before Christ? Did he consider that the Church is organically one with believing Israel? Did God grant Paul *additional* truth about the Church, namely, that it will include Gentiles as well as Jews? Or did Paul intend us to understand that the Church is a wholly new entity, something not even imagined by the Old Testament prophets?

---

56   Hoehner, *Ephesians: An Exegetical Commentary*, 424. Hoehner prefers the translation "whereby", which is found in the AV and the ASV.

Those who take the former point of view generally hold that God has no plan to redeem the Jews as a nation and restore them to the land, although He promised as much in such passages as 2 Samuel 7:10 and Isaiah 60:21. They consider that in any literal sense the promises were forfeited by the Jews through their continued unfaithfulness. Nevertheless, they say, the promises are being fulfilled in a spiritual sense in and through the Church. The Church is the heir of the promises and hence an extension of true, faithful Israel. This is a position taken by most theologians and expositors who follow the amillennial system that traces back to Saint Augustine, the fifth-century Bishop of Hippo. (Amillennialists hold that at Christ's return, He will not come to reign over a literal earthly kingdom but that the kingdom of God is in some sense or other entirely spiritual.)

The second point of view is that the Church is an altogether new structure that began on the Day of Pentecost and is organically distinct from Israel. This includes the view that ethnic Israel will continue in its national distinctiveness but with the conversion of its survivors at the return of Christ will be redeemed and will receive the promise of the land (Rom. 11:25-28). Consequently during the present age there are three distinct entities: unredeemed Jews as a people who still have the promises made to Abraham and David (Israel "after the flesh"), unredeemed Gentiles, and the Church of God (1 Cor. 10:32). Most commonly this position is advocated by Bible students who are premillennialists. (Premillennialists believe Christ will establish His kingdom on earth at the time of His return.)

Which understanding should we follow? The following four paragraphs explore the issue in some detail.

First, Ephesians 3:4-6 does not teach that the Church is an extension of Israel. Some suppose it does by placing an emphasis on the word "as" in verse 5. They explain, "The doctrine was not formerly revealed *as*, that is, not so fully or so clearly as under the Gospel."[57] Yet if this had been Paul's meaning, one would have expected him to add the word "fully" before "revealed." The word "as" (*hōs*) does not necessarily indicate a relative difference or difference of degree. It is a word indicating a comparison, so it just as well may mark the occurrence of something new. It also can have the meaning of "but," and this is the way it was translated in verse 5 by the editors of the NEB, a translation bringing out the sense of the Church as a wholly new institution: "In former generations this was not disclosed to the human race; but now it has been revealed by inspiration to his dedicated apostles and prophets." Furthermore the contrast is between "not made known" in verse 5 and "was made known" in verse 3, so the apostle evidently considered that the Church was unknown in the Old Testament.

Verse 6, referring to the Gentiles, includes three expressions (actually just three words in the Greek), "fellow heirs, members of the same body, partakers of the promise." These direct our attention to unity within the Church rather than with Israel and her past. As Lincoln has well noted, "The Gentiles have not been added to an already existing en-

---

57 So Charles Hodge, *Ephesians* (1856, reprint, Wheaton, IL: Crossway Books, 1994) 163, and Hendriksen, *Exposition of Ephesians*, 154. Both cite as proof a number of Old Testament verses, such as Genesis 22:18, which states that by Abraham's descendants all the nations of the earth shall bless themselves. This and similar promises are a far cry from a prediction of the Church.

tity; they are fully equal joint members, totally necessary for the life of the body, which without them would not exist."[58]

Added to this, 2:15 speaks of the Church as "one new man." indicating its novelty. Colossians 1:26 almost certainly caps the argument, for here Paul wrote of "the mystery hidden for ages and generations but now made manifest to his saints." The Church, the body of Christ, was simply unknown in any respect until after the ascension of the Lord.[59]

Will agreement ever be reached among evangelical Bible scholars (those who accept Ephesians as the inspired Word of God) that Paul meant to teach that the Church is a new institution and not an extension of ancient Israel? Probably not, for evangelical interpretations of Paul are almost always governed by convictions that come from outside a study of Paul's Epistles. At root, those convictions are drawn from theological conclusions about the interpretation of the Old Testament. On one side are those who take the covenants and promises in a spiritual sense, meaning that they will not be fulfilled in any literal sense but that they are to be

---

58   Lincoln, *Ephesians*, 180 (See also p. 177). Lincoln is a modern commentator who seems to have written without a particular philosophical bias. He understands the epistle to teach that the Church is a new institution. In contrast, the NIV in verse 6, after "heirs together" ("fellow heirs" in the ESV), adds the words, "together with Israel." These added words are totally without textual warrant and come from a mistaken understanding of Paul's meaning. Paul is not writing of a relationship of Gentiles with Israel and her past, but he is directing attention to unity within the Church.

59   For a thorough exposition of the Church as a novel institution, see Radmacher, *The Nature of the Church*, 201-19, in which he discusses whether Jesus' statement in Matthew 16:18 confirms the existence of the Church or predicts the formation of the Church.

fulfilled spiritually in the Church. On the other side are those who interpret the Old Testament covenants and promises to Israel in their normal historical and literary sense, that is, the sense the covenants and promises had for those who first received them.

Does it make a practical difference whether the Church is an extension of Israel or a new institution that began with Pentecost? Yes, for it makes a great deal of difference in deciding which Scriptures are to be taken as normative for the Church. Are policies for the earthly churches to be gathered not only from the Epistles but also from directions given to Israel in the Old Testament and from passages in the Gospels addressed to Israel? Or are church policies to be drawn primarily from the Epistles? This question has had a long and turbulent history. Both the Roman Church and those Reformers who held that the Church was an extension of Israel logically reasoned that just as the civil government in ancient Israel was inseparable from the priesthood, so human governments since the time of Christ should be controlled by the Church, Israel's supposed successor. This led to years of frightful wars and the ghastly persecution of nonconformists, including the wholesale slaughter of Anabaptists.

That the Church is distinct from Israel also follows from Paul's instructions for the church. Ephesians 2:15 is a case in point. If Israel and the Church are organically one, and God gave the Mosaic Law to Israel as a rule of life, then God gave the Law to the Church as a rule of life. Thus, the thinking goes, it must be that only a part of the Law was annulled, not the entire Law. Following such reasoning, people in our churches are placed under the "moral core" of the

Law. Yet in the teaching of Paul, Christians are free from *every* part of the Law, both as a means of salvation and as a rule by which to live.

How are we to understand the *promise* in 3:6? Paul doubtlessly intended something he had already mentioned, and that leaves two possibilities. In 1:13 he wrote of the "promised Holy Spirit." In 2:12 he wrote of "the covenants [plural] of promise." Here he was likely referring only to the promised Holy Spirit. Believing Jews and Gentiles are joint possessors of the one promised Holy Spirit and equally sealed by him.

Verse 7 is the beginning of a new paragraph in the ESV. Some Greek texts end the sentence after verse 7, not after verse 6. This is not an important matter. What is important is the truth of verse 7. Paul's ministry was a gift of God's grace, a theme that will be repeated in verse 8.

B. Purpose of the Plan (3:8-10)

The heart of these verses is the apostle's statement of the ultimate marvel of the Church. Verse 8 rehearses the apostle's commission to proclaim the glories of Christ, and it adds his lack of personal worthiness for the task.

⁸To me, though I am the very least of all the saints, this grace was given, to preach to the Gentiles the unsearchable riches of Christ, ⁹and to bring to light for everyone what is the plan of the mystery hidden for ages in God who created all things, ¹⁰so that through the church the manifold wisdom of God might now be made known to the rulers and authorities in the heavenly places.

Paul's task was to bring the truth of the riches of Christ to the Gentiles. In verse 8 two phrases are strongly emphasized in the Greek by the word order. One is "To me." Was Paul emphasizing "To me" to defend his special right to proclaim the truth of the Church? More likely it is expressing his amazement that one so unworthy, one who is "the very least of all the saints" (v. 3), should be granted such an enormous task. In the same way each believer should feel amazed that God has called him or her to be a witness for Christ and to exercise the spiritual gift God has given.

The words "to the Gentiles" receive the second strong emphasis. This indicates the nature of the specific task Paul received, one not given to all the apostles, for Peter was commissioned to go to the Jews. The implication is that Paul was to bring the truth to *all* Gentiles, so it was a task with borders no human could possibly traverse. Yet Paul sought with every ounce of his strength to fulfill the task.

How are we to think of Paul's startling statement that he is "the very least of all the saints?"[60] Is he parading his humility? Some writers think these words support the position that Paul was not the actual author of Ephesians. They say these words sound like false modesty, artificial and exaggerated, more easily understood as words written by a later disciple who wished to make his master appear as excelling in penitence and humility as well as insight. But no, these are the genuine words of the apostle, words that are unfathomable to unbelievers and to Christians not yet fully touched by the truths of Scripture. The words may be unfathomable even to one who is a highly educated and brilliant biblical scholar. To the extent that a Christian fully accepts God's expectation of holiness (1 Pet. 1:16; Lev. 11:44), who seeks

---

60 More precisely, the Greek reads "less than the least," as in the AV, the NEB, and the NET, thus expressing a comparative of the superlative.

to love as Christ loved and commanded His followers to love (John 15:12), and who is correspondingly sensitive to his or her own failures, to that extent that person will grasp the genuineness of Paul's statement. Indeed, the sensitive Christian will do no less than echo Paul's confession deep within.

In the clause, *this grace was given.* to what specific grace was Paul referring? The grace of responsibility. Some Christians fret when called on to exercise themselves in God's service beyond certain self-imposed limits. Paul's example is that of a saint who understands that God's grant of responsibility is a gift of grace. *The greater the responsibility the greater the grace.* He and his companions ministered to others when, he testified, "our bodies had no rest, but we were afflicted at every turn--fighting without and fear within" (2 Cor. 7:5). They had no "personal" time, for their whole lives belonged to the Lord.

Plainly Paul had two goals, both hopelessly out of full reach. One was announcing the gospel to all the nations. Another was what Paul continued to find overwhelming, that of discovering the fathomless, the inscrutable, the ultimately incomprehensible riches of the Lord Jesus Christ. He continued to find this overwhelming, yet this is what he was determined to preach. We too can begin to grasp, yet we can never fully probe, the depths of Christ's wonder and His glory.

The verse builds up to the declaration of God's great purpose, namely, that His wisdom be made known through the Church to "rulers and authorities." "Principalities and powers" is the translation found in many versions. The question is, Who are these? This translation in the ESV implies they are human rulers and political structures, a point of view held by some New Testament scholars. Some suppose they are beneficent angelic beings. Yet in 6:12 Paul links them with "the cosmic powers over this present darkness" and "the spiritual forces of evil." They most certainly are not beneficent beings. If in any sense they are human rulers or human authorities, the primary reference is to the demonic forces that often control human rulers and authorities.

To modern Christians the assertion that the Church is to make God's wisdom known to demonic forces may seem far-fetched. Nevertheless the assertion would impact the Ephesian readers whether Gentiles or Jews. Those ancients believed in a world peopled by demons. Our contemporary opinions regarding demons stem, no doubt, from a modern worldview that has been informed and molded by science. We understand the movements of the earth and planets about the sun, we know what causes earthquakes and volcanoes, we find logical explanations for meteorological events. Birth defects, sad as they are, can be explained through genetics, infectious organisms, or the influence of environmental toxins. In none of these is there any suspicion of demons at work. Accepting the truth of Scripture, we probably believe in demonic and angelic beings, but we do not ordinarily think of the world as densely populated by them or consider them creatures of enormous power and influence.

Yet if we reflect, the purpose of Satan and the spirit powers he controls is to oppose all that honors God and overthrow all that is good and right and true. How better can Satan and his minions achieve their purposes than to lead the civilized masses to deny their existence and to trust in a system of metaphysics that exalts science, a science that by its very nature can never discover any evidence for or against the reality of demons? Yet science has never provided a satisfactory account for pervasive evil in the world, evil that leads people to abuse, cheat, and murder not only strangers but frequently members of their own families, evil that led to the many horrifying genocides of the "enlightened" twentieth century, evil that prompts people to lie when there is neither immediate nor long-term advantage in doing so, evil that produces a constant stream of profanity and blasphemy heard on every hand and glorified by the entertainment industry. The answer of Scripture is that beyond the imagination of any of us there are enormous unseen powers at large. It is to these wicked powers that the Church bears witness. The witness of the Church is to a world in need of a Savior, but beyond human society the Church has a far-reaching *cosmic* witness. We do not observe the effect of this cosmic witness, but it serves God's righteous purpose.

C. Outworking of the Plan (3:11-12)
¹¹This was according to the eternal purpose that he has realized in Christ Jesus our Lord, ¹²in whom we have boldness and access with confidence through our faith in him.

How does an often weak and vacillating Church bear witness to demonic beings, including their lord, the devil? Verse 11 says that it is "according to the eternal purpose realized in Christ Jesus our Lord." Ages ago God had a plan that was brought to fruition only through sending to the earth, clothed as a human, His eternal Son. The Church consists of people who through the Cross have been united to the Son of God and stand holy and blameless before the Father, being fully redeemed and wholly forgiven. Here is the answer to every demonic being. The Church by its very existence is an exhibition and proof of the manifold wisdom of God. In the

Cross the wisdom of God solved the problem of sin so that the Church might be brought into existence. In the Cross the reality of the Church becomes the condemnation of Satan and all demonic powers.

Because the Church is the great cosmic witness, the wonderful consequence and power of verse 11 follow in verse 12. Every believer, from neophyte to veteran, can come to God boldly. None need fear that their petitions, voiced in faith, are not thoughtfully considered by a loving and omniscient God. Every Christian has access to the ear of God, since each belongs to the exclusive inner circle of those embraced in God's plan.

4. Suffering for the Plan (3:13)
¹³*So I ask you not to lose heart over what I am suffering for you, which is your glory.*

In discussing verse 1, we considered why the subjects of the letter might have been losing heart, knowing that Paul was a prisoner. The conclusion is this. Paul's suffering was to achieve God's purpose through bringing the greatest number into the Church. Instead of being disheartened by the seeming defeat of God's purpose--after all, Paul was in the hands of evil men--the Ephesians should have recognized that it was no defeat at all.

How could Paul's suffering be *their* glory? It was *his*, because he was the chosen messenger whose suffering enabled men and women to be reached who otherwise would not have heard the message. At the same time it was *their* glory, because they were united to him as fellow members of the body. What was his was also theirs. All believers share in the glory and honor of participating in the Church with its cosmic witness.

The apostle's suffering is *our* glory as well. We also are one with him. We are not one because of our common, deep admiration for the apostle. We are one because we have been placed "in Christ." Our union is a reality beyond human discovery but a reality as certain as the most fundamental of any biblical truth. We are one with missionaries who suffer to bring the message of truth to people in troubled lands. We are one with believers imprisoned for their faith and those martyred for their faith, of whom there have been many in the centuries gone by but many more in our day.

What is grievous is that so many Christians have little vision beyond their local and immediate problems. The unity of the body ought to bring every believer to a deep consciousness of sharing in the sacrificial suffering of others who are serving Christ across the world. This should be all the more true as modern means of communication make it possible to become aware of the persecution of many Christians almost as it happens and to communicate instantly by e-mail with most of our missionaries.

FOCUS: THE FERVENT CENTRAL PRAYER
(3:14-21)

Located at the center of the epistle's structure, these eight short verses enjoy particular prominence. They direct the readers' attention to the primary message and purpose of the epistle. Chiastic structures are unknown in most English literature. If in a document today an author wants to state his or her purpose, it is ordinarily given in an introductory paragraph or occasionally delayed to the end where the author summarizes what was written. In contrast, a chiastic structure carries the reader to a deliberate summary of its contents at its climactic middle. Accordingly it is here we find the theme of the epistle. As Dorsey observed, "In nonnarrative compositions with a symmetric structure, the central unit often represents the highlight, centerpiece, or most important point, much like the center of a symmetrically arranged work of art."[61] Accordingly it is here we find the theme of the epistle. This theme, the subject of the apostle's deepest prayer, is for believers to be filled with all the fullness of God. This is accomplished through the Holy Spirit producing the habitual practice of love in every believer. This practice of love is experienced as the believer, living by faith, thoroughly apprehends the surpassing love of Christ Himself.

The prayer consists of two brief paragraphs, each of one sentence in the original. The first paragraph (vv. 14-19) expresses Paul's fervent desire that every Christian might know the surpassing and well-nigh inconceivable love of

---

61 See Dorsey, *Literary Structure of the Old Testament*, 41, and references under Observation I: Literary Structure in Ephesians page 270.

Christ. The second (vv. 20-21) is a glorious paean to God and the Lord Jesus Christ, in whom alone can be found grace for living.

I. Prayer for the saints (3:14-19)

Paul's life was one of constant prayer. His prayer life is opened to us twice in Ephesians, first in 1:15-21 and again here. The verses that follow lay bare the spiritual heights to which his soul ascended in prayer. Yet God has made it possible for every believer to have a prayer life equally rich and far-reaching.

A. An Introductory Clause (3:14-15)
14For this reason I bow my knees before the Father, 15from whom every family in heaven and on earth is named,[62]

To what does "for this reason" refer? Does it mean "for the following reason," referring to every family being named from the Father? This is quite unlikely, since it would constitute an anticlimax. Much more likely it refers to verses 11-12, the nearest antecedent. Verses 11-12 state that every Christian can come boldly and confidently to God in prayer because of the "eternal purpose" that God "has realized in Christ Jesus our Lord." The eternal purpose includes all that the apostle has unfolded in the previous chapters about the gifts of God's grace. Anyone glimpsing but a corner of the

---

62   The translation, "from whom the whole family," found in the NIV, is erroneous. See M. Barth, *Ephesians: Introduction, Translation, and Commentary on Chapters 1-3*, 381; Hoehner, *Ephesians An Exegetical Commentary*, 474; Lincoln, *Ephesians*, 202; and O'Brien, *The Letter to the Ephesians*, 255-6.

immense and magnificent grace of God can do nothing other than humbly bow before him, as did Paul.

As a prelude to the apostle's climactic prayer, he writes about every family in heaven and on earth being named for the Father. Assigning someone a name is commonly used in Scripture with the sense of giving someone power and conveying authority to that person (as in Gen. 11:4; 12:2; Exod. 5:23; 1 Kings 21:8; Luke 6:13-14; Matt. 16:18-19). Every family of beings in the universe, both those with and those without physical bodies, has power to exist, because that power is derived from the Father Himself. With this statement the Paul extols the greatness of God the Father. He is the one who is the Creator of all and apart from Him no one could continue to exist.

As Paul wrote these words, most likely the Abrahamic Covenant was in the forefront of his thinking. The first expression of the covenant is in Genesis 12, where in verse 3 "all the families of the earth" has reference to all the nations of the earth springing from families. Paul likely thought of this expression, and then expanded it to include beings in heaven as well as on earth. Which beings? Believers who are living together with those who have died and are now in heaven, or angelic beings? Possibly both were in the apostle's mind.

After explaining the relationship that everyone has to the Father, the apostle voices three prayer requests. In the Greek each one begins with "in order that" (*hina*). This threefold division is not apparent from the ESV. Nevertheless the three "in order that's" define the outline.[63] The third request depends on the second, and the second depends on the first.

---

63 Larkin, *Ephesians: A Handbook on the Greek Text*, 59.

B. First Request: For Strength (3:16-17)

¹⁶[in order] that according to the riches of his glory he may grant you to be strengthened with power through his Spirit in the inner being, ¹⁷so that Christ may dwell in your hearts through faith---that you, being rooted and grounded in love,

Since "In order" is not in the ESV, it is put in brackets above. This first "in order that" follows from verse 14: "I bow my knees before the Father. . . in order that." Paul prayed *in order that* believers in Ephesus might be strengthened. His prayer is effective for us as well. God has limitless resources to answer Paul's prayer. His resources are expressed by "the riches of his glory." If any of us feels we have never experienced the wealth of God, it is not because His riches are lacking or for some reason are unavailable. It is because we have not yet learned to appropriate them.

This first request is that each believer might be strengthened "in the inner being." How remarkably different is this from the prayer most of us would offer. To many Christians there could be no greater good than to win ten million dollars in the lottery (with the mental promise, of course, of making a liberal contribution to Christian work!). To others the greatest good would be unbroken physical health. To God, in contrast, inner strength surmounts any other sort of good. A believer who has an effective walk with the Lord, even though impoverished or chronically ill, is far ahead of the most famous or richest or longest-lived Christian who suffers a spiritually marginal life.

How is God's strength communicated to the Christian? It can be accomplished only through supernatural means. It comes through the work of the Spirit of God in the life of the believer. The American psyche is quite confident that anything can be accomplished through logical planning, appropriate techniques, or almighty effort. If a Christian lacks maturity, then most certainly psychological counseling, life-management through the educational program of the church, or a determined struggle to do right can remedy the lack. But the message of Ephesians is that none of these can ever achieve what God wants. This is not to denigrate a proper role for counseling and education, but these do not lead to true inner strength.

What releases the power of the Holy Spirit? The next clause tells us, although additional words inserted in the ESV are misleading. In the ESV the next clause begins with "so that." The sense becomes that having Christ dwelling in the believer's heart through faith is the *result* of the Spirits work. Yet in Paul's original language the two clauses are connected by neither "so that" nor "and that." It is best to consider "may dwell in your hearts through faith" a statement in *apposition* to the preceding clause.[64] *It provides extra facts about the preceding clause.* If a connecting word is needed, "namely" might be supplied. Then the apostle's request would read, "That . . . he may grant you to be strengthened with power through his Spirit in the inner being, *namely*, that Christ may dwell in your hearts through faith."

Here is an altogether wonderful and amazing truth. Spiritual strength for the believer comes as he or she walks by faith. No other condition is given.

What is puzzling in the passage is the consequence of walking by faith. The passage explains that the one walking by faith will have Christ dwelling in his or her heart. Paul

---

64   O'Brien, *The Letter to the Ephesians*, 258, n.151.

prays for the redeemed because they may very well *not* have Christ dwelling in their hearts. Does this mean the Christian *not* walking by faith will *not* have Christ dwelling within? The word for "dwell" in verse 17 is not the more common word for dwell (*oikeō*). It is the ordinary word with a prefix that intensifies it (*katoikeō*). It has the meaning "to be at home in," that is, "at the very center of the believer's life."[65] A person truly may be born again with the Spirit permanently within, yet, not have Christ at the center of that person's heart.

What is the consequence of the Christian having Christ dwelling within? The Greek, literally translated, reads, "in love being rooted and being grounded." The Greek lacks "that you." The words, "being rooted and grounded in love" simply explain the preceding clause, telling what happens when the believer has Christ dwelling in his or her heart through faith. The believer apprehends the remarkable meaning of love and understands how to make it personally applicable.[66] How is true *agapē* love possible? It is a consequence of Christ fully occupying the believer's heart.

Here the apostle introduces what will become a major theme of the chapters that follow. God's desire is that the whole Christian life be "rooted and grounded in love."

The person who in any spiritual sense is strong is the person who lives victoriously over the selfish demands of the flesh and is able to love others, not only the favorable but also the unfavorable. A Christian who habitually gives in to self and who is incapable of exercising a genuine concern

---

65 Hoehner, *Ephesians: An Exegetical Commentary*, 481.
66 This is the sense found in the NRSV. Larkin disagrees, arguing that the indwelling Christ is a common theme equivalent to being "in Christ."

for the best good of others is one who, even if highly regarded by fellow church members, is living a useless, spiritually infantile life.

The question that follows is, How can we know that Christ is truly and fully dwelling within? The question is answered in the apostle's second request.

C. Second Request: For Knowledge of the Love of Christ (3:18-19a)

¹⁸[in order that you] may have strength to comprehend with all the saints what is the breadth and length and height and depth, ¹⁹and to know the love of Christ which surpasses knowledge,

The added words "In order that you" constitute the second "in order that" and mark the second prayer request. This prayer request depends on the Christian being rooted and grounded in love. This is truly wonderful, although the story is not yet complete. Paul earnestly desires that every believer will have strength to comprehend something incomprehensively vast: "the breadth and length and height and depth" of Christ's love.

The ESV begins verse 19 with "and," though this word is not in the Greek. What follows is not an addition to the dimensions, but an explanation of what they are about. They are about knowing the love of Christ. Paul is not thinking as a mathematician. He is not introducing a mysterious fourth dimension. He is saying most graphically, no matter which way you go, you can never finally probe the unimaginably great magnitude and glory of the love of our Lord. Then follows a fascinating oxymoron.

An oxymoron is a self-contradicting statement, one

all of us sometimes make, commonly through carelessness or ignorance. The Scriptures are not without oxymorons, but the question may be asked why the Holy Spirit would lead an author to use an absurd combination of opposites to get a point across. Verse 19 is such an instance. Here Paul used an oxymoron, "to know the love of Christ which surpasses knowledge." The one in whose heart Christ fully dwells is one who *is to know the unknowable!* What a grand contradiction! The oxymoron is the author's deliberate misconstruction of sense. It is intended, plainly enough, to arrest our minds with its significance.

How does the Holy Spirit, working from within the mind of the Christian, enable the Christian to *understand* that which can never be fully *understood*? It is a supernatural work beyond our comprehension. Nevertheless the Holy Spirit's strengthening with might enables the Christian to comprehend what is an opaque mystery to the unregenerate mind. To the unbeliever the Cross may be a fact of history, but without the Spirit's inner ministry the profound love it represents amounts to empty words.

In verse 18 we read, "may have power to comprehend with all the saints." Does this mean that every believer comprehends the unimaginable expanse of Christ's love? No, but every believer, walking by faith, can begin to comprehend it. For the believer, a growth in grace is always marked by a growing appreciation of the Savior's wondrous and finally incomprehensible love.

D. Third Request: For Filling (3:19b)
[in order] that you may be filled with all the fullness of God.
Here is the final and gratifying goal of what has gone

before: to experience the fullness of God. A person may be a true believer, yet not be filled with the fullness of God. Otherwise Paul would not have voiced this third petition for them. Nevertheless it can become a reality in the life of each willing Christian.

The question is, What is fullness like when it is received? How can it be recognized? What measure is there by which one can assuredly say he or she has obtained it, or at least is near to it? Here is the radical teaching of the apostle. One who has God's fullness is one who is rooted and grounded in *love*. Being God-like is loving, for "God is love" (I John 4:8). The filling is the unfailing practice of *agapē* in every human relationship. Without love, every religious thought and practice is empty (1 Cor. 13:1-3). Yet *with insightful, knowledgeable love, God's fullness in all its glory is present.*

How is fullness received? Many religiously minded people strive in some way or other to experience the fullness of God in their lives, but they miss the path God has mapped out. That path, as stated in verse 17 and taught in many other places in the New Testament, is faith. When a Christian lives by faith, then Christ will truly dwell in his or her heart and God's fullness will be realized not only in an apprehension of the love of Christ but also in a personal ministry of love toward others.

Were Paul's expectations for Christians unrealistic, thinking they might actually be filled with love equal to what Christ expressed in His earthly life? Answering this question, Bruce appropriately commented, "Has Paul sought too much from God for his fellow-believers--praying that they may be filled up to the level of the divine fullness? They might think so as they heard this letter read aloud, but Paul reassures them: it is impossible to ask God for too much. His capacity for giving far exceeds his people's capacity for asking--or even imagining."[67] May each of us discover the amazing scope of God's power to fill us for His glory, making us godly, that is, God-like!

II. Prayer of Praise (3:20-21)

[20]Now to him who is able to do far more abundantly than all that we ask or think, according to the power at work within us, [21]to him be glory in the church and in Christ Jesus throughout all generations, forever and ever. Amen.

This rich doxology is closely tied to the prayer for the saints which precedes it. In verse 16 Paul prays that Christians might be strengthened with *power*. Then the doxology begins by praising God for this *power* at work within them, power either implied or stated throughout the first three chapters. In Division A_1 (1:3-14), God's power clearly grants the believer the enormous spiritual blessings the apostle lists. Then the climax of Division B_1, stated in 1:19-20, is that his power in us who believe is immeasurably great, infinitely far above any other imaginable power, for it raised the Lord Jesus from the dead (1:21). An instance of this power is what made Paul minister of the good news (3:7). And herein lies the wonder, a wonder of which so many Christians seem woefully unaware. This power is available to accomplish what truly matters!

We commonly want God's power exercised for some improvement of our creature comforts and are disappointed when it seems to be withheld. Paul readily accepted the loss

---

67 Bruce, *Ephesians*, 330.

of all physical comfort but gloried in the power that enabled him "to make all men see what is the plan of the mystery hidden for ages in God" (3:9). The more we look toward the greatest height, the more we shall see God accomplishing the seemingly impossible, doing more than "all that we ask or think."

This power works *within us.* God's primary concern is not with changing the environment in which we live but in changing our innermost selves. It is a supernatural power and achieves what no amount of human effort could ever accomplish. As Paul wrote in Colossians, he was greatly concerned because word had come to him of Christians at Colossae seeking to curry God's favor through practices of self-abasement, adherence to legalistic restrictions, and pursuit of rigorous devotions. He declared that all such are "of no value in checking the indulgence of the flesh (Col. 2:16-23). What succeeds in checking fleshly self-indulgence is, first, self-judgment, expressed as putting "to death what is earthly in you" (Col. 3:5-6). Second, it is putting on "compassion, kindness, lowliness, meekness, and patience . . . and above all these put on love" (Col. 3:12, 14). The power to "put off" and "put on" comes through faith in all that the believer has and is through Christ, the unmistakable thought of Col. 3:1-4. A drastic change in the inner person is God's goal for every Christian.

This is God's desire, but why should God want to change the inner person? Cannot God accept and respect us for what we are, for the way we were born? No, for He has a special purpose, and that purpose cannot be realized apart from what the Holy Spirit can do in our innermost being. It is transformation leading to glory given to God. That is plainly stated in Ephesians 3:21.

How can it possibly be both glory "in the church" and "in Christ Jesus?" Are the two in any way to be considered on the same plane, bearing equal dignity? The NKJV tries to avoid the question by translating, "to Him be the glory in the church by Christ Jesus." The translators arrive at this through omitting the word "and," which is found in most but not all of the ancient Greek texts. The sense then becomes that Paul wants God to be glorified in the Church, and He will be, insofar as the Church magnifies Christ. But this interpretation diminishes the full scope of the glory belonging to God described in the preceding verses. It is better to go with the majority of ancient texts and to retain the translation, "in the church and in Christ Jesus." But then we have to ask, How do we put these together?

God received glory from the perfect obedience and faithfulness of Jesus, who willingly left his prior glory to become the humblest of men and to suffer the pain and ignominy of the cross (Phil. 2:5-8). As a God of perfect love, He continues to receive glory from the Lord Jesus wherever His love is known. Nevertheless it is more than surprising that the Church is listed in the same breath, a Church so marked with all manner of human flaws, so torn by internal discord, and so little practiced in the love to which God has appointed her. Yet God is glorified because in His immeasurable grace He has taken sinful men and women, granted them uncountable spiritual benefits, united them with the Lord Jesus, gathered them into a single body, and constantly and persistently ministers to their spiritual growth. The Church, a union of those deserving judgment, nevertheless abundantly glorifies God, inasmuch as Christ is her infinitely great Deliverer.

The total, loving servanthood of the Lord Jesus together with the Assembly of those united with Him and sealed for their future resurrection will throughout eternity bring praise and honor to the Father.

DIVISION D₂ LIVE IN UNITY
(4:1-16)

In D₁ the Apostle's message is that the believer has been reconciled to God in one body through the cross. In view of this comes the appeal in 4:1 to "walk in a manner worthy of the calling to which you have been called." Unity with other believers demands certain actions. If we genuinely accept this as true, we surely will want to live worthily of the grace that gave us this unity. Even though the practice of unity is detailed in but six verses, the verses are deep and far-reaching.

In two Bible versions (ESV and RSV), verses 1-16 are printed as a single paragraph. Yet most others (HCSB, NAB, NEB, NET, NIV, NKJV, NRSV) print verses 1-6 in one paragraph and 7-16 in a second paragraph. Along with the majority, there seems little question but that two distinct sections make up the division. The sections correspond to the two major sections of D₁ (2:11-3:13). The first section of D₁ develops the truth of the body, and the second explains that Paul was called to serve as minister of that truth. Similarly, in D₂ the first section (3:1-6) is an exhortation to walk in unity in accord with the truth of the single, united body. The second states a ministry of the risen Savior through whom the walk in unity is made possible (4:7-16).

The word "therefore" at the beginning of the second half of the epistle, looks back to the immediately preceding division D₁. Division A₁ (1:3-14) developed the believer's absolute unity with Christ.

Live in Unity
A. The Plan — worthy of life
B. " Prescription — Totally Unselfish
C. " Predisposition — Eagerness for unity
D. " Pattern — Unity in God

I. Live in Unity (4:1-6)

The doctrine that believers belong to a single body, whatever their race or social status, is a Christian truth, although our earthly experiences seem to belie it. The Church of the living God is fragmented into numerous denominations. Perhaps much more seriously, ill will frequently separates brothers and sisters within individual congregations. Christians may hold grudges toward other believers, may be unwilling to have fellowship with those whom they consider inferior, may be embittered toward others, may allow disagreements over trivial issues to balloon into major causes. Nevertheless, since unity is a fact in the eyes of God, an urgent priority of every Christian should be to make unity a genuine reality in practice. Unfortunately the practice of unity does not simply happen. To make it a reality, each believer needs to step through the following four important doors.

A. The Plan: A Worthy Life (4:1)

¹I therefore, a prisoner for the Lord, urge you to walk in a manner worthy of the calling to which you have been called,

The first door is recognizing that God has given each Christian a plan for living. The word "calling" may be understood in the sense of *vocation*. Vocation is the noble design that God has for each believer. His design is a plan that will make the Christian's future genuinely significant. Many Christian people find little meaning in life other than pride in their offspring or in the trade or profession through which they earn a living. The vocation designed by God is not equivalent to an occupation by which one earns a living, although for a few, such as pastors and missionaries, financial support may be incidental to the vocation. Plainly enough, from all that follows, the Holy Spirit is speaking here of that calling through which each believer serves other members of the body of Christ and witnesses of Christ to the world.

The calling is a high honor. When understood it cannot help but evoke a strong response. Paul *urges* each one to live a life worthy of the calling. A salesperson dressed in ragged blue jeans and a dirty T-shirt can hardly expect much success waiting on customers in a fine clothing store. The Christian life must also measure up, not by stylish clothing but by total honesty and genuine compassion.

The word "urge" can be translated by a number of different English words, *invite, request, beg, appeal to, implore, entreat, encourage,* collectively a kaleidoscope of what was in the apostle's mind. Why did the apostle not use a word of command such as "I order you"? Here is the freedom of grace. God has not placed the believer under legalistic restrictions. There is no threat here of disenfranchisement for failing to live up to one's spiritual station. God wants the believer's willing response in gratitude for what he or she has received.

B. The Prescription: Total Unselfishness (4:2)
²with all humility and gentleness, with patience, bearing with one another in love,

Is there a paradox here? How do we live up to our station in life, a station in which we are one with the Creator himself? Not by humility, surely! According to many psychologists, humility and gentleness are formulas for failure. The way to get ahead in life is to be pridefully assertive. The question is, What do we mean by "getting ahead?" Are we interested in getting where God wants us to be or where we ourselves want to be? God's plan is unselfishness that recognizes the value of others and puts their concerns and interests before our own. It is willingly being the servant of others (Mark. 10:43-44). Unselfishness, the very essence of love, constitutes a second door to practical unity.

Humility and gentleness should always be our attitude. But are there ever exceptions? Yes. When our personal interests are at stake, we should be humble and gentle. But when we are protecting the rights and welfare of some weaker person against a bully or an exploiter, then in all righteousness we can be firmly tough.

"Enduring" "tolerating," and "putting up with" are other possible translations in place of "bearing." The word sheds further light on what it means to love. It is easy enough to see how someone else can put up with our faults, which we think, after all, are but minor personality traits. But other people's faults are a different matter; they annoy and vex us. Nevertheless, if we live in true love, we can endure an offensive person by genuinely feeling and thinking what that person feels and thinks. How often most of us begin a word of advice by saying, "If I were you." What we usually mean is the converse, "If you were I." Because of our persistent self-occupation, it is exceptionally difficult to put ourselves in another person's shoes. But to the extent we do, we can be humble, gentle, patient, and able to bear with others.

C. The Predisposition: Eagerness for Unity (4:3)
³eager to maintain the unity of the Spirit in the bond of peace.

Paul does not say "inclined to maintain," or "willing to maintain," or "pleased to maintain, but *"eager* to maintain." The truth developed in the corresponding Division D$_1$ is that we are one with each other. Consequently fighting with other believers is fighting ourselves. A heartfelt eagerness to work for and maintain unity constitutes the third door.

If every born-again Christian is already one with every other, what then do we maintain? O'Brien stated, "To *keep* this unity must mean to maintain it *visibly.*"[68] Not only believers but outsiders as well are to picture each Christian assembly as a haven from the stress and turmoil of the world, a place where there is acceptance, understanding, and peace, where fighting and anger are altogether absent (John 13:35).

"In the bond of peace" is the *manner* in which unity is to be maintained. Some Christian leaders are willing to maintain unity by sacrificing doctrines, even basic ones, that anyone in the fellowship might find disturbing. This is furthest from the thought of Paul, for whom doctrines of Christ and of God's grace are the very foundations on which unity is built.

Paul is writing of the peace that follows a loving acceptance of others, not only of those in our circle of intimates but of believers whose culture or race or social level is different, of believers with rough edges that have not been smoothed off, of believers who are dependent on handouts to keep going, of believers who are chronic dyspeptics and complainers. Peace is linked to and bound by love.

D. The Pattern: The Unity that Is in God (4:4-6)

⁴There is one body and one Spirit--just as you were called to the one hope that belongs to your call--⁵one Lord, one faith, one baptism, ⁶one God and Father of all, who is over all and

---

68   O'Brien, *The Letter to the Ephesians*, 280 (italics his).

through all and in all.

There is no division in God. Here is an emphatic reminder of the unity in God Himself and His total plan. Recognition of this fundamental truth is the fourth door to the practical maintenance of unity. Since every believer is united to Christ, and Christ is one with the Father, believers surely ought to live in unity among themselves.

Every believer is called to the one hope, that is, the sure confidence described in 1:3-14. Although this hope includes many elements, it can be spoken of as single, since it is the one great salvation secured by the Lord Jesus.

Is the doctrine of the Trinity taught in Scripture? The word "Trinity" is not found in the Bible, yet the concept of the Trinity is unquestionably found in these words in 4:4-6. "One Spirit" is grammatically parallel to "one Lord," which is grammatically parallel to "one God and Father." The parallelism shows that each is a being of the same order. Each is equally personal, equally divine. Someone with Unitarian convictions might argue that just as "one faith" is not personal, so "one Spirit" need not be personal but should be written "one spirit." Yet this will not do, since each part of the confession is expressed in a triad of about equal length: "body-Spirit-hope," "Lord-faith-baptism," and God and Father of all, who is "over, in, and through all."

What does "one baptism" mean? The Greek literally says "one immersion." Is Paul arguing that only baptism by immersion is the correct way to be baptized? Quite unlikely. The question of the mode of baptism would not have come up in Paul's day, since pouring as a practice in Christian churches did not emerge until the second century and sprinkling came much later. What Paul was writing about is connected to "one faith." What results from that faith? An immersion into all that Christ is. The believer is *placed into* Christ, that is, united with Him. Paul was using the metaphor of immersion for identification with Christ. There is only one identification with Christ. No believer is partially identified or conditionally identified or on a probationary status waiting to be identified. Water baptism is a public testimony of a person's confidence in that identification. Through a symbolic immersion into water, a believer voices his or her assurance of having been placed into the death of Christ, and hence into unity with Him and the resurrection that is His.

Is theology important for the Christian to understand? It is downplayed in many of our contemporary churches as being impractical. Yet here in verse 6 the Apostle gives us a powerful, theological statement on the nature of God. First, He is over all. He is not part of the universe, he is not identified with it, but he is above it. He is transcendent to the universe and to every believer as well. This is in direct contradiction to all new age thinking that God is identical with the universe and that by meditation a person can become aware of his or her identification with God and the universe.

Second, God is in all. That is, he is the immanent God, intimately involved in every least aspect of the universe. The Scriptures teach that he is omnipresent. Being *in all* he not only is present but his knowledge is infinite. He knows us and all others intimately.

Third, He is through all. His presence is not only everywhere, but in His presence He exercises power. He maintains and controls even the very minutest of the subatomic particles, the very leptons and quarks of which subatomic particles are composed. Hence He can work all things out for the good of those who love him.

II. Christ the Minister of Gifts for the Body (4:7-16)

Ephesians 4:7-16 is the second section of this division. These verses state that the Lord's ministry is carried out through gifts he bestows on each member of the body.

The question follows, How is the meaning of this section connected to verses 1-6? Verses 1-3 speak of those practices that make for unity; verses 4-6 speak of the fact of unity. When we come to Section II, the conclusion in verse 16 speaks of "the whole body joined and knit together." Obviously, the section was written to explain God's design for putting unity into practice.

A. The Bestowal of God's Gifts (4:7-10)
⁷But grace was given to each one of us according to the measure of Christ's gift. ⁸Therefore it says,
   "When he ascended on high he led a host of captives,
   and he gave gifts to men."
⁹(In saying," He ascended," what does it mean but that he had also descended into the lower parts of the earth? ¹⁰He who descended is the one who also ascended far above all the heavens, that he might fill all things.)

Verse 7 is foundational. Each believer has been given a measure of Christ's gifts. In grace God supplies each one with everything necessary to carry out that gift.

The word "but" in verse 7, the translation found in most English versions, implies a continuation, a contrast, or an inference, none of which fit the context. The HCSB nicely translates the first clause of verse 7, "Now grace was given to each one of us," translating the Greek word (*de*) as "now," thereby defining a transition to a new topic. Verse 7 properly begins a new paragraph.

The words "to each one of us," placed in an emphatic position, state that God has granted every believer a special gift of grace. Further along in these verses we discover that the gifts are gifts for ministry. The gift is not some native ability, such as the gift of a fine singing voice, the capacity to make sound business decisions, or a brilliant intellect. Christ's gifts are spiritual gifts, although a spiritual gift may utilize one's native ability. There are a number of different gifts. A partial list is found in Romans 12:4-8, and another list is found in 1 Corinthians 12:27-31. Some of the gifts in the latter passage may have ceased, but that does not detract from the fact that every Christian has a gift. Can a believer enjoy the possession of more than one gift? Such is not impossible, although Paul's point in Romans 12:6-8 is that each one, living by faith, is to use his or her own gift, implying that the exercise of one gift is enough. Another question is, How can any Christian know what his or her gift is? Romans 12:1-2 has the answer. As someone is transformed by the renewal of his or her mind, that one may *by testing* discern the will of God. God leads the willing believer through experiences that demonstrate which gift for service God has in mind.

What is meant by "the measure of Christ's gift?" This is endlessly debated by commentators, but there seems to be a clear answer. The answer begins with the assumption that Christ has given every believer the gift of salvation. This excellent gift is of infinite value. *The same measure of excellence extends to the gift for service God has given each of us.* Is my gift for service of significance? Definitely! In the plan of God it has *infinite* significance. Is my gift one that can be effective? Yes! It is the measure of Christ's gift; therefore it can be as effective as God wants it to be. But then why are our gifts too often ineffective? It is because of unjudged sin in our lives. Sin blocks the use of our gift. When we live self-centeredly, the use of our gift languishes. But when we judge our sins and walk by faith, God is able to use our gifts in those precise ways that meet *His* particular goals.

Verse 8 is one of the problem verses in Scripture. Paul quoted Psalm 68:18, but the trouble is that he seems to have misquoted it. In most editions of the Hebrew Bible the passage reads, as in the ESV,
> You ascended on high,
> leading a host of captives in your train,
> and receiving gifts among men.

The last line is equally well translated, "receiving gifts consisting of men."

Paul understands that this passage refers to the Messiah, and for Him to have ascended He must have descended. Skipping over the question of whether the passage is an address *to* the Messiah or a statement *about* the Messiah, the big problem is that Psalm 68 says the Messiah *received* gifts, whereas Paul has the Messiah *bestowing* gifts. Fortunately, the apparent contradiction can be resolved by recognizing the problem consists in an accidental transposition in the Hebrew text. Paul probably quoted the original text accurately.[69] The passage in Psalm 68 is a prophecy of Christ returning to heaven. When Christ ascended, He did not go empty-handed. He took with Him, so to speak, people whom God had given Him. He received gifts from the Father, those gifts consisting of humans. Paul understands that he received these gifts *in order to give them as gifts*. In the Old Testa-

---

69 Larkin, *Ephesians: A Handbook on the Greek Text*, 74-75.

ment those who were victorious in battle and also righteous in character captured spoil but then divided the spoil as gifts. When Abraham defeated Chedorlaomer and his allies, he took booty with the intention of giving away to Lot what he had lost, to Aner, Eschcol, and Mamre their portion, and to Melchizedek a tithe. When David defeated the Amalekites at Ziklag, he recovered the booty the Amelekites had taken and a great deal more. All of this he then distributed throughout Israel. In the same way, believers are God's gifts to Christ. Christ distributes these people as gifts to his Church.[70]

In verses 9-10 Paul is simply explaining that this passage in the Psalms refers to the Lord Jesus, since for him to have ascended he must have descended. The Psalm does not use the word Messiah, but is about Yahweh, the LORD. Paul understood that Jesus, who descended to the earth, is indeed none other than the Yahweh of the Old Testament.

Verse 10 should read, "He who himself descended." The editors of the ESV omitted the pronoun "himself," probably because they imagined it added nothing to the thought. The pronoun does not carry the thought of "the same one" but is an emphasizing pronoun. "It emphasizes that the descent into death was entirely voluntary."[71] It is the identical thought that we find in John 10:18, where Jesus, speaking of his coming death, said, "No one takes it from me, but I lay it down of my own accord." Jesus was not an unfortunate martyr, but the one who freely gave his awful sufferings on the cross for our redemption.

---

70   Hendriksen, *Ephesians* 191. See Richard A. Taylor, "The Use of Psalm 68 in Ephesians 4:8 in Light of the Ancient Versions," *Bibliotheca Sacra* 148 (July-September), 1991, 319-336.
71   Muddiman, *The Epistle to the Ephesians*, 197.

Many fine New Testament scholars have argued that Christ's descent into "the lower parts of the earth" means that after His death he descended into hell. (This is included in the Apostles' Creed.) Christian writers have taken this in different ways, some teaching that He actually suffered the torments of hell. Nevertheless, the notion that "the lower parts of the earth" refers to hell (or *hades*) seems quite unnecessary, since the passage in Psalm 68 has to do with Yahweh's presence on the earth rather than in the place where spirits of the dead were sequestered, and Paul would have taken it this way.[72] It is true that *hades*, the New Testament equivalent of the Old Testament *sheol*, is the place to which the disembodied spirits of all the dead descended, both righteous and unrighteous. In the story of the rich man and the beggar in Luke 16:19-31 Jesus described *hades* as compartmentalized, as both a place of rest ("Abraham's bosom") and a place of torment, between which "a great chasm has been fixed." First Peter 3:19 teaches that Christ "preached to the spirits in prison." Then as Jesus hung on the cross he promised the penitent thief, "Truly, I say to you, today you will be with me in paradise." Putting these together, writers take paradise to be equivalent to Abraham's bosom. Then they conclude that from paradise Jesus preached to the wicked who were in the torment of *hades*. After He preached there, at His ascension all those in paradise itself were taken by Him to heaven. This doctrine, particularly the final conclusion, may or may not be

---

72 Wallace shows that the Greek most probably refers to Christ's descent to the earth rather than to a place within the earth (*Greek Grammar beyond the Basics*, 112). See also W. Hall Harris III, "The Spirit and Descent of Christ in Ephesians 4:9-10," *Bibliotheca Sacra* 151 (April-June 1994): 213

valid, but it is quite unlikely to be the teaching of Ephesians 4:9. After all, Paul did not write that Christ descended into the *lowest* part of the earth, but rather into the *lower parts*. Verses 9-10 are simply explaining the quotation in verse 8, which in turn verifies that it is Christ Himself who gives the Church spiritual gifts.

Paul taught elsewhere, just as he does here, that God gives his Church individuals who have particular gifts. In 1 Corinthians 12:4 it is "varieties of gifts, but the same Spirit." In 12:5, it is "varieties of service, but the same Lord." Although gifts are from the Spirit, the administration of the gifts is a ministry of Christ.

This has a modern application. As every believer serves, particularly those in public ministry, there needs to be the consciousness that the appointment, if genuine, is not from man but from the Lord. A board, a congregation, or a denomination does not decide on its own who should be appointed to serve in particular roles, not if acting scripturally. Rather, those who are served have the responsibility of recognizing those whom the Lord has called and to whom the Spirit has supplied an appropriate gift.

B. The Purpose of His Gifts (4:11-14)

¹¹And he gave the apostles, the prophets, the evangelists, the pastors and teachers, ¹²to equip the saints for the work of ministry, for building up the body of Christ, ¹³until we all attain to the unity of the faith and of the knowledge of the Son of God, to mature manhood, to the measure of the stature of the fulness of Christ, ¹⁴so that we may no longer be children, tossed to and fro by the waves and carried about by every wind of doctrine, by human cunning, by craftiness in deceit-

ful schemes.

These gifts are people, but people to whom God has given a specific gift or gifts by the Holy Spirit. Although the people listed here are by no means all those who are gifted, they are those who carry a greater degree of responsibility, because their gifts are exercised in public. Furthermore, each of these persons specializes in gifts of speaking. Along with the exercise of the gifts goes the public reputation of the Church. A brief explanation of the ministries of these individuals may serve to remove some confusion.

Who are the persons designated in these roles? The first two are apostles and prophets, which we are told in 2:20 are the foundation of the "household of God," a foundation laid in the first century.

What exactly are apostles? The Greek lexicographers Bauer, Arndt, Gingrich, and Danker define them as "believers with a special function as God's envoys."[73] Their number would include the original Twelve, with the exception of Judas, who was replaced by Matthias. Without question the Twelve are frequently referred to as the apostles in a specific and limited sense. Yet the number was increased by the recognition that James was included among the apostles (Gal. 1:19). Paul defended his addition to the apostleship through having seen the Lord at his conversion on the Damascus Road (1 Cor. 9:1). Nevertheless, as the work multiplied, the number of apostles seems to have been expanded beyond the Twelve, James, and Paul. It included some who undoubtedly were not among those who had seen Christ after His resurrection. Barnabas, a native of Cyprus, cousin of John Mark, and a companion of Paul on his missionary

---

73 BAGD, 122.

journeys. is termed an apostle in Acts 14:14. In Romans 16:7 Andronicus and Junias are termed "men of note" among the apostles. Then Silvanus and Timothy are designated apostles (cf. 1 Thess. 1:1 with 2:7). Furthermore Paul related that he had received a call to work as an apostle (Rom. 1:1; 1 Cor. 1:1; Gal. 2:7), but above all, Paul could point to his converts as the sign and seal of his apostleship (1 Cor. 9:2; 2 Cor. 12:12). In his day there were false, deceitful workmen cleverly disguised as apostles of Christ (2 Cor. 11:13). Such are not wanting in our time.

Prophets were those in the Church with the gift of publicly setting forth the mind of God, which might include foretelling the future. That meant they were given an understanding of the Word of God before it was fully committed to writing. Are there individuals today who have the gift of foretelling the future, as some people claim? No. This aspect of prophecy was of value in days before the completion of the New Testament, but it is fruitless to look for it among gifts given Christians today because the written Word is now complete (Rev. 22:18). There is no longer a need for prophets.

An especially interesting aside is the implication of Ephesians 2:20. If the apostles and prophets laid the foundation of the Church, this implies that their function is completed. Yet 4:11 states that all five gifted individuals are given "to equip the saints for the work of ministry for building up the body of Christ," a present activity. In a true sense, the ministry of apostles and prophets continues today, for it is the completed Word of God, the very foundation, which today is the blueprint for building up the body. Apart from them there would be no growth. If the work of the apostles and prophets is completed, this implies that the evangelists, pastors, and teachers are those who lead believers to "grow up in every way into him who is the head, into Christ (v. 15)."

Evangelists are ordinarily thought to include soul-winners who reach great numbers through public campaigns. Yet in verse 12 we read that their function is included among those who "equip the saints for the work of ministry for building up the body of Christ." It is *believers* to whom the evangelists are to minister. Could it be that these are individuals in the local church whose example of soul winning encourages and leads others in a church to witness effectively? Their ministry could well include verbal instruction. Along with pastors and teachers they are said to have the important function of building up the body, yet almost no church today places either evangelists or teachers on the same level as pastors. Tradition makes a single pastor the top gun and often the only gun.

Does the next expression refer to people belonging to two distinct categories of gifts, pastors *and* teachers, or does it refer to a single category, pastors who are expected to be teachers? Some expositors insist the Greek means that Christ's gift to the Church is "pastors, even teachers," but this is an error.[74] Although the Greek makes pastors separate individuals from teachers, the pastor is expected to be a teacher of the Word.

---

74 "Pastors and teachers" does not qualify under the Granville Sharp rule. See Wallace, *Greek Grammar Beyond the Basics*, 284. It is clear that two distinct persons are in view. Nevertheless, as Wallace concludes, "Eph. 4:11 seems to affirm that all pastors were to be teachers, though not all teachers were to be pastors."

Here we need to pause to note the relationship between the terms pastor and elder. In Acts 20:28 elders are guardians over the *flock*, a clear reference to elders functioning as shepherds, that is, pastors. In 1 Peter 5:1-5 elders are those who "tend the flock" under the Chief Pastor or Shepherd, that is, Christ. That elders are teachers follows from their role to "feed the church" (Acts 20:28), to instruct in doctrine (Titus 1:9), and to labor in teaching and preaching (1 Tim. 5:17). A pastor, on the other hand, is a person with a particular gift. Pastor is not a title for someone who is a church officer. In many congregations, people think of their pastor as an officer, but if they were to follow the Scriptures, they would note that the leading officers in a congregation are to be the elders. In preaching to a congregation, an effective elder ought certainly to be gifted by God. His gift could include that of being a pastor, an evangelist, or a teacher. Timothy seemingly had all three gifts (1 Tim. 4:13; 5:17; 2 Tim. 2:24; 4:2, 5).

The gifted individuals are given by Christ with three goals in view. Understanding the three goals and their relationships is essential for those using the gifts as well as for those who are benefited by the gifts. These goals include three ends: to equip the saints, to carry out the work of ministry, and to build up the body of Christ.

1. The gifts build (4:12)

"Building" is an unusual word to apply to a body. "Build" carries the idea of laying rocks or bricks, whereas bodies grow from within. The apostle is using the best available metaphors for growth both from within and from without.

At the same time all those who are part of the body need to mature spiritually, so they need teachers, and as verse 16 explains, they also need the ministry of other believers.

How do evangelists, pastors, and teachers equip the saints? The answer seems to be in verse 12, but the answer also depends on how we choose to punctuate the verse. Should there be commas after the words "saints" and "ministry" in verse 12? The AV and the RSV insert commas after both. The ESV, the NAB, the NIV, the NKJV and the NRSV place a comma only after "ministry." Which is correct? The Greek will not help us, for New Testament Greek was written without commas. It was written with all the words run together without even spaces between them. The translator or the reader determines where the commas go. It makes a big difference, however, whether in our minds we place a comma after "saints." If a comma is there, it implies that there are two classes of people in a church: a clerical class and a separate, distinct laity. The clerical class has the total responsibility for equipping, ministering, and building. (We are using "clergy" as a convenient term to stand for elders, although in most churches "clergy" refers to pastors.)

The diagram above represents one possible position an interpreter can take. This is the model in many traditions and congregations where the pastor is placed at a different level than the unsalaried members of the church. He or she and the professional staff, if any, feed the church through preaching and teaching, minister to the spiritual needs of the members through counseling, and organize and administer programs to increase the growth of the church. The church has no opportunity to minister to the pastor or the staff other than through financial support. In many instances any effort on the part of members to minister to the pastor(s) would be rebuffed. The equipping, the ministering, the building all come from the professionals. Ministry to the pastor and staff is presumably unnecessary, since they have been trained in seminary or other schools for the positions they hold. With this model, both the privilege and burden of building up the body rest exclusively with this omnicompotent, select class.

A second possible position places no comma after "saints" but places a comma after "ministry." This implies a model in which the pastor and his staff equip selected members of the congregation who in turn minister and build up others. It can be represented as follows.

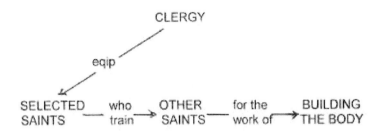

This pattern, popular in many evangelical churches, is adopted in recognition of the burden placed on a pastor who is expected to carry out the total program of equipping, ministering, and building. It avoids encumbering a pastor with numerous ministerial tasks. The inability of a pastor to perform all the duties expected of him keeps many evangelical churches from growing. In this second plan, the pastor (or pastor and staff) equips the more mature and willing saints with skills required to minister to others. These in turn organize and lead classes in counseling, soul-winning, small-group leadership, Christian education, and other types of ministry. The pastor is relieved of the large task of trying to minister to everyone. When a core of workers is trained to carry out the equipping tasks, the pastoral ministry is magnified many times. This pattern can be justified by omitting the comma after "saints."

Although this pattern succeeds in spiritually strengthening a much larger number of the congregation, it fails in significant respects, not the least of which is that it misses the understanding developed in Ephesians of the body of Christ. What are the reasons there should be no comma after *either* "saints" or "ministry"?

(a) The two patterns above both fail to provide for a reciprocal ministration from the saints to the clergy. Is the pastor one of the saints? One certainly expects as much. Does not this strongly imply that God's intention is for each member of the body to minister meaningfully to every other member, including the clergy? In their training in seminary or Bible institute, pastors, missionaries, and evangelists are provided with fundamentals of biblical theology and exegesis, biblical language tools, preaching methods, counseling methods, and a knowledge of how to organize and expand a church. But this is miles away from developing the spiritual maturity needed to use the training with Spirit-directed effectiveness. Many a well-trained minister has had to leave the ministry, having become discouraged, having wrestled unsuccessfully with inner conflicts, having found himself at odds with leading members of the congregation, or having fallen into egregious sin. None of these things need have come about, but when the pastor functions insulated from those gifted by God to help him grow in grace, disaster lurks just around the corner. The corrective is for evangelists, pastors and teachers, and others in public leadership to recognize that their gifts do not place them in a special class with special prerogatives. They are on the same level as all others in the congregation. Their gifts are for a specific purpose, but they are organs in a body with many diverse organs, each of which is necessary to the health of all the others (1 Cor. 12:14-26). Because a person is paid a salary by a congregation should not place him or her in a privileged class, even though that person, when serving well, should be accorded due respect and honor.

(b) An attitude expected of every member of the body is given in 5:21: the evangelists, pastors and teachers should subordinate themselves to one another as well as to other believers in the church. Patterns 1 and 2 inevitably tend to elevate a pastor in his own esteem. This makes it exceptionally difficult for a pastor to be truly subordinate to others in the flock. How can a pastor be expected to subordinate himself, when he is the spiritual leader? Did not Paul urge Christians "to respect those who labor among you and are over you in the Lord and admonish you" (1 Thess. 5:12). The words "are over you" are presumed to carry the thought, "who manage you."[75] If this is the correct meaning, it implies that these are persons to whom others should submit but who themselves are in an exempt category. Undoubtedly Paul thought of them as leaders. But spiritual leadership is not at all to be equated with being general of an army, manager of a corporation, head of a political entity, president of a university. *Spiritual leadership for the evangelists, pastors and teachers is living and exemplifying humility, loving concern for people, rectitude, sound judgment, devotion to the Lord, knowledge of the truths of the Word, and a gift for presenting the Word.* Spiritual leadership clearly does not mean that one is not to hearken to advice, to accept counsel, to be ministered to by others, to be released from admitting

---

75 There is a disagreement among scholars whether the verb translated "are over you"(*proistēmi*) in 1 Thessalonians 5:12 should be understood in the sense of "to be at the head of, to rule" or in the sense of "to be concerned about, to give aid." The latter seems most conformable to Paul's teaching.

mistakes or confessing wrong. If the words "are over you" mean management of others, it is not management by command but management by presentation of God's directions.

(c) Verse 13 tells what "building up" will achieve, something to which *we all* should attain. According to verse 7, it includes each of those to whom grace is given. It is worthy of note that the words "until we all attain" included the apostle himself. If it included the great apostle, surely building up intends to include every evangelist, pastor and teacher, and other believers. It is worth remembering that when Paul wrote to the Romans he said he wanted to come to Rome to impart "some spiritual gift" to strengthen them (Rom. 1:11). That is easy enough to accept, given Paul's demonstrated spiritual gifts. But then he acknowledged his personal need of the saints in Rome: "that is, that we may be mutually encouraged by each other's faith, both yours and mine." How astonishing that even Paul needed and valued encouragement from Christians who yet had much to learn of the gospel of grace!

This third possible interpretation holds that those gifted with public ministries are fully responsible for equipping the saints, not just a fraction but *all* in the congregation, yet everyone in the congregation is in turn responsible for the work of ministry. All are to share in building up the body of Christ. The terms "for the equipment of the saints for the work of ministry for building up the body of Christ" are *sequential*, not parallel.[76] How can one know that there is no comma after "saints" and that this third position is the one

---

76   This point is insightfully and powerfully developed by M. Barth in *Ephesians. Introduction, Translation, and Commentary on Chapters 4-6*, 477-84.

the Holy Spirit intends? It follows from verse 16. But first, note verse 13.

2. The gifts develop unity. (4:13)

If Christians in a local fellowship are following God's plan, there will be no divisions in the church. A local church filled with disharmony or a church that splits through discord is a church with a manifest failure to build up the saints in the plan of God. A goal of all ministry is that saints embrace one another in love. Christians who have genuine, perceptive concern for each other will be united in spite of differences of temperament, education, culture, possessions, status, or understanding. Someone reading verse 13 might miss this, for in it we do not find the word love. Instead Paul writes of ministry leading each Christian toward three goals: (a) unity of the faith and of the knowledge of the Son of God, (b) maturity, and (c) the measure of the stature of the fullness of Christ. What do these three concerns come to? Whatever they mean, they are goals toward which all should be moving, although the implication is that no one has yet fully attained the goals.

(a) "Unity of the faith" refers to faith in the Son of God. In this context unity-bringing faith does not refer to a specific creed to which all Christians must subscribe. It is the unity that comes from a common confidence in all that Jesus is and has done for the believer. This is a confidence that goes far beyond what can be expressed within the limitations of any written creedal or doctrinal statement. The word "knowledge" is the word for a growing, personal knowledge of God, that is, the directed knowledge that we saw in 1:17. Unity follows a deep, personal relationship with Christ that greatly exceeds simply knowing about Him. This exceptional grasp of the person of the Savior, according to 3:19, is to know the love of Christ, which surpasses knowledge. The Christian whose confidence (faith) in Christ is alive can move toward a surpassing knowledge of Christ that leads to love, which in turn guarantees true unity. Merely proclaiming the need for unity and encouraging Christians to practice it, if apart from love, becomes an exercise in futility (John 13:17).

(b) "Mature manhood" ("mature womanhood" is surely implied!) is another way of simply saying "mature," or "spiritually grown up." Paul uses the word mature (*teleios*) as his personal goal for every Christian (Col. 1:28), something that is God's will (Rom. 12:2; Col. 4:12). How is a spiritually mature person recognized? The spiritually mature person, as 1 Corinthians 13 declares, is the one who is practicing love.

(c) "The fullness of Christ," as pointed out in the discussion of Ephesians 1:23, is the totality of Christ's ministry to and on behalf of the Church. What then is "the measure of the stature of the fullness of Christ"? This is stating that the Christian has the power to move toward what Christ is in His ministry to and on behalf of the Church. Christ gave Himself for the Church (5:25), Christ gives gifts to the Church (4:7), Christ nourishes and cherishes the Church (5:29), in short, Christ acts toward the Church in total love. In 3:19 Paul prayed that believers might be filled with the fullness of God. (The fullness of Christ is, of course, identical to the fullness of God.) Saints enter into the fullness of God, according to 3:19, when they deeply know the love of Christ. The apostle is stating in a third way that God's goal is for believers to practice the love of Christ in all they do, divorcing themselves from self-interest, self-glory, self-gratification. The Church with its mutual ministries is critical to this goal, as will become clear in verse 16.

In three different but graphic ways, verse 13 tells us that the goal of all ministry is to develop lives that reach out to others with concern and compassion. Ministry exists to enable Christians to grow into lives expressing love as Christ loves. When the primary purpose of any ministry is the promotion of some organization, the achievement of a political goal, the construction of some edifice, the enhancement of a leader's personality, the entertainment of a congregation, or anything else that would be foreign to Christ were He ministering on earth today, true ministry is not taking place.

3. The gifts stabilize. (4:14)

Christ's gifts to the Church are productive because they build spiritual stability among God's people. Paul's concern was that corrupting forces might readily delude and confuse God's people. As the subsequent history of Christianity amply demonstrates, it was and is a valid concern for every generation. Every conceivable distortion at one time or another has been grafted onto the simple gospel of salvation by grace through faith. Plain biblical assertions about the person and character of God are twisted almost beyond imagination. False teaching within congregations is promoted not openly but by "human cunning." The word "cunning," as Marcus Barth points out, is derived from a word denoting dice used by players.[77] In this context it means "wicked dice-playing," that is, cheating. In Paul's day more formal and

---

77 Ibid., 443.

more or less organized perversions of the faith had not yet risen. What winds of doctrine did he have in mind? Doubtlessly doctrines of salvation by works such as those peddled among the believers in Galatia. The self-inflating attitudes of the Corinthian church may also have been at the front of his thinking. Possibly by the time he was composing Ephesians his heart was aching because of the counterfeit spirituality to which he heard the Colossians had fallen victim. In whatever way the ministries of the leaders function, a primary purpose for which God gave them was to establish stability of doctrine.

The question is, how does ministry by spiritual leaders promote growth so that other believers can think through false teaching with mature rather than infantile judgment? The answer is found in verse 15: "speaking the truth in love." In this verse we read how gifts to the body are expected to function in loving practice.

C. The Reciprocity of His Gifts (4:15-16)

15Rather, speaking the truth in love, we are to grow up in every way into him who is the head, into Christ, 16from whom the whole body, joined and held together by every joint with which it is equipped, when each part is working properly, makes the body grow so that it builds itself up in love.

Interestingly "speaking the truth" is a translation of but one Greek word, which simply means "being truthful." Does this refer to the spiritual leaders who are to be truthful in order to promote maturity? Or does it refer to members of the body as a whole who mature by telling the truth? Unquestionably both. To impart the truth concerning Christ and God the Father is the reason Christ gave gifts of apostles, prophets, evangelists, pastors, and teachers to the Church. When will the leaders' words of truth carry weight? When their listeners perceive their leaders' sincere and deep love for them. The spoken word is empty without love.

The same responsibility belongs to followers as well as leaders. None among us is personally exempt. Truth is absolutely essential for every Christian (4:25, 6:14a), and so is love (3:17; 5:2). Truth offered in a spiteful, contemptuous, or disdainful manner creates resentment rather than remediation. If concerned love is lacking, others cannot avoid a lurking suspicion of a Christian's sincerity and truthfulness.

Where verse 15 speaks of growing up into our *head*, the apostle is affirming that we are to grow up in our understanding of and closeness to the One who is supreme over all. The context does not suggest "authority" so much as Christ's capacity to direct the Church with all wisdom. The body will grow properly, as stated in verse 16, when each part, each believer, is working properly.

Verse 16 explains how each one in the body should minister to other members for effective growth. Here is the very heart of Paul's instructions for establishing unity. Each believer has his or her spiritual gift. Not all gifts are exercised in public. A gift such as doing acts of mercy with cheerfulness (Rom. 12:8) may be carried out unknown to anyone except the recipient of the mercy. Whatever the gift, someone uses his or her gift in ministering to another, with the result that the recipient grows in grace. Growing in grace, the recipient becomes more effective in the use of his own gift. Then as he uses his gift in ministering to another, that person grows in grace too. And growing, that one becomes more effective in ministering to the one who ministered to him. As each one's gifts improve in effectiveness, each is better able to minister to others. The body functions effectively when there is a true *reciprocal exchange* of ministries, just as the human body cannot grow from infancy without each organ contributing its function for the good of all the other organs and receiving benefits from all the others. For a personal growth in grace each one needs every gift God has supplied for a particular worshiping congregation. Each needs to value the gifts others bring for his or her personal benefit.[78] At the same time each must be willing in love to use his or her gift for the benefit of others (1 Pet. 4:10).

In the apostle's plan for reciprocal ministry, no one is so insignificant that he or she can be disregarded; no one is so superior to be exempt. Some will have gifts placing them in positions of greater organizational responsibility and priority. In the human body every organ has a value for all the other organs in the body, although when we meet a friend on the street, that person's public face gets our attention. The believer who may be little noticed is nevertheless someone who needs the ministry of others and to whom the Spirit has granted a gift of value to others. There is no question but that the ministry of public leaders is to enable all the members to minister. Yet by using their gifts to and on behalf of the leaders, the members enable the leaders to minister more effectively. O'Brien accurately commented, "If it is only the leaders of v.11 who perfect the saints, do the work of ministry, and edify the body of Christ, then this is a departure from Paul's usual insistence that every member is equipped

---

78 Earl D. Radmacher, *Mobilizing the Members for Maximum Ministry.* Five audiotapes (Portage, MI: Lake Center Media Resources, 2005).

for ministry."[79]

Will this plan of mutual growth work in a huge megachurch? This is an important question, since enormous local churches are the trend among evangelicals today. Obviously only a minuscule number, if any, of such a congregation will ever have an opportunity to minister to the senior pastor and few will have opportunity to minister to more than a small number of other members. Christians need to ask whether a megachurch is truly God's plan or a plan engendered by human ambition.

Some moderately large congregations have enabled members to minister to the senior pastor by appointing a five-to-ten member pastoral accountability group. The group consists not of officers of the church but people representing and acquainted with different segments of the congregation. The group meets with the pastor on a regular basis, reviewing his work and reporting to the pastor the members' concerns, commendations, and recommendations. This is an indirect way of allowing various members an opportunity of ministering to a pastor, but it does not fully replace personal contact between the pastor and each member.

In larger congregations adult Bible classes often become small congregations in themselves. If the members are taught to minister reciprocally to one another, many of the scriptural functions will have been solved.

Did Paul really write of joints, when the illustration would have been more pointed if he had mentioned heart, lungs, nerves, and bowels? Larkin explains that the word (*haphē*) should be used in the general sense of "connection."[80]

---

79 O'Brien, *The Letter to the Ephesians*, 303.
80 Larkin, *Ephesians: A Handbook on the Greek Text*, 83.

This is a much better understanding, since the passage is about the connection of each believer with others.

After writing of the functioning of the body, Paul now breaks into an obviously new topic, the behavior of individual believers who have come to know and trust their Lord.

DIVISION C_2, ARISE FROM THE DEAD
(4:17 - 5:21)

The whole manner of living and thinking among the Gentiles was utterly futile. It was then, and it is today. In contrast--here is the powerful thrust of this division--the Christian is no longer bound by human nature to squander life in selfish, profitless vanity but rather is able to live in fruitful love.

This division, "Arise from the dead," is an evident reflection of C_1, "Made alive in Christ," where the passions and desires of unregenerate mankind are contrasted with good works that ought always to follow salvation. Both sections begin with a characterization of unbelievers. In C_1 unbelievers are incapable before God of any good. Hence they are spiritually dead and condemned. In C_2 the Gentiles practice every kind of uncleanness.

Both divisions are also concerned with the daily behavior of the Christian. C_1 ends with an emphasis on the Christian's walk as the product of God's new creation (2:10). Correspondingly the major part of C_2 is an emphasis on the Christian's walk. In C_1 we read that we have been "raised up" with Christ (2:5, 6). This is what we are in our standing before God. In C_2 the Christian is to arise from among the dead *in practice* (5:14). In fact most of division C_2 has to do with the resurrection kind of life the believer should and can experience.

Since this is the longest of the divisions, the comparative length of this division might suggest that our analysis of the chiasmus is faulty. Nevertheless the thrust of Paul's argument requires a long discussion, for it is here that he explains in detail what he means by Christian love.

Salesmen know the excellent quality of a product is often best exhibited by contrasting it with the inferiority of its competitors. Paul shows the emptiness of a life without God. This directs the Ephesians' thoughts to the satisfying path of the life when it is truly lived for God.

I. Principles of the New Life (4:17-24)

A. A Caution (4:17-19)

17Now this I say and testify in the Lord, that you must no longer walk as the Gentiles do, in the futility of their minds. 18They are darkened in their understanding, alienated from the life of God because of the ignorance that is in them, due to their hardness of heart. 19They have become callous and have given themselves up to sensuality, greedy to practice every kind of impurity.

The empty thinking that characterizes the godless today is well illustrated in a Pulitzer Prize-winning book by Harvard University sociobiologist Edward O. Wilson. He believes in no God, at least no God who can lend direction to the world of nature or the affairs of mankind, but he has great faith in what science will yet achieve. He contends that once science has stripped away "blind ideologies and religious beliefs" and the brain is packed with the techniques of critical analysis and tested information, the brain will of itself reorder previous absurd and enfeebling beliefs into some form of morality, religion, and mythology. Get rid of God, he is saying, follow the shining light of science, and by some unspecified alchemy a marvelously superior code of morality will burst forth. Evolutionary thinking will be the new religion and mythology.[81] In its demonic direction, this differs little from the idolatrous thinking of the first century.

How did Gentile futility come to be? The passage lists a series of steps by which Gentiles came to this present state. The list begins with causes and moves to effects. The first step is that the hardness of their hearts led to their ignorance and darkened understanding. This in turn led to their alienation from the life of God. As a result (verse 19) *they have become callous and have given themselves up to sensuality, greedy to practice every kind of impurity.* "Sensuality" stands for every kind of sexual depravity. When "greedy" is connected to "impurity," the idea becomes insatiable sexual desire. In the Greek of verse 19, the word "themselves" is in an emphatic position. The emphasis shows that impure practices come through personal choices. People are individually and personally responsible for their practices.

Verse 18 states that they are alienated from the "life of God." This is a remarkable phrase found nowhere else in the New Testament. It is not a reference to the inner life of God, as some suppose. It means the spiritual life that originates with God and which by grace He bestows on those willing to come to Christ, but from which unbelieving people are willfully estranged.

The apostle explains that Gentile futility began with their ignorance, ignorance that is in them because of their "hardness of heart." As a result, they became callous and

---

81   Edward O. Wilson, *On Human Nature* (Cambridge, MA: Harvard University Press, 1978), especially 198-209. A more recent and much more confrontational book reaching the same conclusion that Darwinian natural selection refutes the necessity of God is Richard Dawkins, *The God Delusion* (Boston: Houghton Miflin, 2006).

gave themselves up to sensuality and were greedy to practice impurity. One can hardly watch television today without being aware that this is a description of our modern culture. Where did Gentile ignorance come from? In Ephesians Paul does not say, but in Romans 1 he explains that its source is the unwillingness of Gentiles to acknowledge the evidences that God has given them concerning His eternal power and divine nature, evidences available to everyone through creation. This is the beginning of the downward course of humankind, whether in the first or the present century, a course that leads to hardness of heart.

The word *alienated* in 4:18, just as the word *dead* in 2:1, carries an all-or-nothing force. One is dead or one is alive. One is alienated or one belongs. The word presents a clear dichotomy: No one belongs halfway to God, nor is there a step-by-step process by which one enters the life that is in God. When an individual comes to faith in the Savior, that very moment that person is declared righteous by God and *in Christ* and is no longer an alien but is an intimate part of the family. Prior to that crucial point, that person was a persisting enemy of God.

B. Learning Christ (4:20-24)
[20]*But that is not the way you learned Christ!* – [21]*assuming that you have heard about him and were taught in him, as the truth is in Jesus,* [22]*to put off your old self which belongs to your former manner of life and is corrupt through deceitful lusts,* [23]*and to be renewed in the spirit of your minds,* [24]*and to put on the new self, created after the likeness of God in true righteousness and holiness.*

The humble unpretentiousness of Jesus is the very

opposite of the self-centered, lust-gratifying practices of the unsaved. To be a disciple of Christ, a learner of Him, the believer adopts His way of thinking and living.

But why the words, "assuming that you have heard about him and were taught in him"? Two possibilities exist. One is that the letter was not first addressed to those Ephesians among whom he had lived and ministered, but was addressed to a circle of churches and included a great many people who knew very little of Christ, so Paul was wondering if they really knew anything about Him. The second possibility is that Paul was making his point with a bit of gentle sarcasm. The first view is less likely, since Paul doubtlessly would have written much more about the life of Jesus and His sacrifice on the cross had he for a minute thought they were basically ignorant of Him. The second is in character with some of Paul's writing in 2 Corinthians, and is more likely.

Here in the ESV, the infinitive to "put off" in verse 22 goes back to the verb "learned" in verse 20, a bit awkward for English readers. Nevertheless it correctly reflects the language Paul used.[82] This is also true for the infinitives "to be renewed" in verse 23 and "to put on" in verse 24. In effect, what Paul said in verses 20-24 is this: "The moment you put your faith in Jesus, you put off the old wicked self that you once were, you were renewed in your mind, and you put on a new righteous and holy self."

The only trouble is, this seems altogether contrary

---

82 Many other translations make commands out of "put off," "be renewed," and "put on. The reasons behind the translation in the ESV are involved but are thoroughly explained in Hoehner, *Ephesians: An Exegetical Commentary*, 596-604.

to our common experience, and it does not account for the verses that follow, where the apostle instructed Christians about what they need to do to live righteous and holy lives. We were converted because we recognized our sins and put our faith in Jesus Christ for forgiveness. Yet we still find ourselves a long way from being righteous and holy, at least when we measure our lives against the standard beginning with verse 25 and continuing through 5:21. How is this to be explained?

First, what is meant by the "old self" that we put off?[83] It is Paul's graphic way of referring to the flesh. The primary meaning of "flesh" stands for the physical stuff of ours as well as for animal bodies. It is more or less equivalent to meat. But in Paul's metaphorical use, it represents the actions and thoughts of a person whose only concern is the benefit of self. It is everything a person is before coming to faith in Christ. "Flesh" is explained in Romans 7:18-20, where Paul wrote, "For I know that nothing good dwells within me, that is, in my flesh . . . it is no longer I that do it but sin which dwells within me." And again in Romans 7:25, "with my flesh I serve the law of sin."

The old self is clearly equated with the flesh. The

---

83   Paul wrote "old man," not "old self." "Old man" is the translation found in the AV and a few other translations. Most modern translators interpret it for their readers by substituting some other term. It is puzzling, however, why translators suppose the ordinary English reader cannot understand the meaning of "old man" in this context. "Old nature" is found in some versions. This can be misleading. See Moo, *Romans*, 372-76 for a helpful discussion of the old man and the new man. Moo may be mistaken in taking the infinitives "put off" and "put on" in Eph. 4:22 and 24 as imperatives instead of indicatives, but we believe he clearly explains the meaning in Paul's use of the expressions

expression "old self" is used in only two other places, Romans 6:6 and Colossians 3:9. There should be no difficulty in understanding the expression if we follow Paul's thinking in the Epistle to the Romans. In Romans 6:6 the old self is equated with *sin*. When Paul uses *sin* (singular) he means the *principle* from which the practices of sin arise. When Paul uses *sins* (plural) he is referring to sinful *practices*. The *principle* from which practices of sin arise is pictured by both "the old self" and "the flesh."

It may be helpful to note that when Paul uses "flesh" in a metaphorical sense, he does not mean that activities of the body or the gratification of bodily or mental appetites are wrong of themselves. When Paul uses "old self" and "flesh," he is referring to the self-centered foundation that underlies all actions outside the control of Christ.

How can it be said that any of us have put on the new self, the new man? The HCSB makes it more explicit: "You took off your former manner of life." It does not say "You should take off" but describes something believers have done. Is there an inconsistency here? It would seem so, when so often Christians live according to the flesh. The inconsistency seems even more real, when we read that the Christian has had the old self crucified with Christ (Rom. 6:6). Paul stated the same thing in two other ways: the flesh is crucified for those who belong to Christ (Gal. 5:24), and the body of flesh is "put off" in the spiritual circumcision accomplished by Christ (Col. 2:11).

The explanation is that the Christian is no longer under any *compulsion* to sin. Whereas the unbeliever can live only in self-centered ways, the Christian has the *power* to practice love (*agapē*), which is the exact converse of self-centeredness. (The obvious sense of Romans 7:13-25 is that the unbeliever can do nothing other than practice sin, but that it is possible for the Christian to live victoriously over sin.) Paul wrote in Romans 6:6 that the believer is crucified with Christ "in order that the body of sin might be brought to nothing, so that we would no longer be enslaved to sin." Obviously the Christian is quite capable of living in the flesh and acting in the same self-centered ways as ordinary (unsaved) men and women (1 Cor. 3:1-4). Paul's epistles are filled with warnings against the manifestations of the flesh in a believer. When the old self was crucified, it was *killed*, rendered incapable of domination. Yet the flesh is still present and available to us. So now--what a wonderful and essential thing for every Christian to realize--is that *none of us has to give in to sin*. If we do, it is by our own choice.[84]

What is the meaning of the words "to be renewed in the spirit of your minds?" Humans are distinguished from animals not merely in degree of brain capacity but in possessing an indestructible spirit. Unbelievers have a spirit, but their spirit remains ineffective. On believing, a person is indwelt by the Spirit of God. The Holy Spirit establishes a union with the human spirit. Through this union the Holy Spirit is able to empower the believer so that he or she is capable of resisting temptation and able to live in love toward others. The human spirit, associated with the mind, is activated by the Holy Spirit, so that the believer can have a totally new outlook.

The "new self" refers to all the Christian has become

---

[84] See the interesting and valuable article by Robert A. Pyne and Matthew L. Blackman, "A Critique of the Exchanged Life," *Bibliotheca Sacra* 163 (April-June 2006):131-57.

through union with Christ. When a person "learned Christ," Paul is saying, he or she learned about the amazing new power that God granted. Having this relationship, believers can consider what it means to live accordingly. The following six actions teach what is to put off and put on in practice.

II. Actions of the New Life (4:25-31)

Ephesians 4:25-31 is not a set of commandments or rules but *instructions on what it means to practice love*. How does love act in operation? Here is Paul's answer. Each instruction is tied to a reason. In the Greek, each main verb is an imperative in the present tense, except for verse 31, where for a special reason there is an aorist imperative. The verbs have this thought: keep on doing this, practice it habitually. (This the believer can do, since he or she has "put on the new self.") Then the reason that follows is a fundamental principle associated with love.

A. Our Membership in the Body (4:25)

²⁵Therefore, having put away falsehood, let each one of you speak the truth with his neighbor, for we are members one of another.

"Speak the truth" is the instruction. As a present imperative it could well be translated, "Habitually speak the truth." The reason is, "we are members one of another."

Why do people lie? There are, of course, some apparently excusable reasons for not telling the truth. An espionage agent for the government must not tell the truth to those being spied on. A soldier captured by the enemy may tell a lie about troop dispositions and other valuable information to protect the lives of fellow soldiers. These are situations that may be covered by some other biblical principles, but in any event, they are the kind of circumstances few of us encounter. Why in ordinary situations do we lie? It is almost always to protect *ourselves* from embarrassment, disapproval, or personal liability. We lie out of self-interest, not out of interest for the other person.

A subtle but significant difference exists between the prohibition against bearing false witness in the ninth commandment and Paul's injunction against falsehood. In the Ten Commandments truthfulness is an absolute. The only reason to be considered is that it is God's order. In contrast in Ephesians 4:25 truthfulness arises out of concern for those to whom we belong: "we are members one of another." Loving concern as a basis for truthfulness does not soften the evil of falsehood. It changes the ground. Hansen's disease, popularly known as leprosy, is caused by a bacillus similar to the one responsible for tuberculosis. One effect of the disease is to anesthetize the nerve endings in parts of the body. A leprous, poverty-stricken unfortunate living in a rat-infested hut may have a finger chewed off by a rat during the night without being aware of it. The failure of the nerve to inform the brain of the truth leads to horrible mutilations of members of the body. Within the body of Christ, falsehood of any kind can only engender mistrust and lead others to act wrongly and thus lead to spiritual mutilations. The life of the believer must be characterized by complete honesty, openness, and transparency, for anything less is not of love.

B. The Opportunism of Satan (4:26-27)
²⁶*Be angry and do not sin; do not let the sun go down on your anger,* ²⁷*and give no opportunity to the devil.*

Jesus said in Matthew 5:22, "But I say to you that every one who is angry with his brother will be liable to judgment." But then Jesus became angry with the Pharisees, who were waiting to see if he would heal on the Sabbath so that they might accuse him (Mark 3:5). Is there inconsistency here? Paul himself seems inconsistent, since a few verses further down he wrote, "Let all . . . anger . . . be put away from you" (Eph. 4:31).

There is no inconsistency if the *source* of the anger is considered. When anger stems from a self-regarding, vindictive spirit, it is rightly to be condemned. When it arises from grief for another person's hard, unloving, legalistic attitude of heart, as with Jesus' anger toward the Pharisees, or from injustices done to the poor or helpless, as when Jesus drove the money-changers from the temple, it is worthy anger. It surely is more worthy than when crime and injustice are met with no more than an indifferent shrug.

What is Paul saying? Justifiable anger may arise in the Christian who is sensitive to hurts willfully inflicted on others. Nevertheless that anger should not be nursed lest it turns into an occasion for sin. Paul quotes the first two clauses from Psalm 4:4, nicely translated in the NIV: "In your anger do not sin; when you are on your beds, search your hearts and be silent." Cherished anger, anger that lasts over the night and into the day beyond, even if it is so-called "righteous indignation," will lead to intemperate and injudicious actions. Satan will get the advantage. Paul was mirroring the thought of the psalmist. Cool down and reflect on the situation. If action needs to be taken, plan for it, but let it be loving and carefully considered action rather than a fire that burns out of control.

C. The Needs of the Poor

²⁸*Let the thief no longer steal, but rather let him labor, doing honest work with his own hands, so that he may have something to share with anyone in need.*

The injunction against stealing worries some commentators, who think it unlikely that the Ephesian church (or churches) would include Christian thieves. On the contrary in churches filled with relatively new believers, it is easy for people who made a living of thievery to continue the practice after finding the Lord. For new believers in America, the prohibition is certainly relevant. Christians are not immune from temptations to pilfer from indifferent employers. It is easy to find justification for doing so. Church treasurers have been known to steal significant sums from their church. A close pastor friend of one of us (Beal) was justly dismissed from his position after the members discovered he was misappropriating church funds for his own use.

The eighth commandment said simply, "You shall not steal." The contrast in verse 28 vividly illustrates what it is to be under grace and not under law. Under the law a command was to be carried out because it was so ordered. In the present (post-Cross) age the Christian is on new ground. The believer refrains from stealing but not because the Law prohibited stealing. Under grace the rule of life is love, not law. Love does not take from others; love does not even want what others have. Love delights that others have valuable possessions. Instead of feeling resentful or covetous, what love does is think about those in need and work honestly to supply those needs.

In working to supply the needs of others, the Christian is not somehow making up for those times when he or she stole from others. If a Christian can recompense those from whom he or she stole, the Christian most certainly should. The leading example is Zachaeus, the tax collector who resolved after his personal encounter with Jesus to restore fourfold anyone whom he had defrauded (Luke 19:8). In most instances, however, a life of thievery leaves a trail of anonymous or forgotten victims. The apostle is insisting that the Christian's entire orientation is now to be totally different. This is not a matter of repayment by measure but of going far beyond. It is genuine concern for meeting the needs of the destitute.

The believer has been saved by God's exercise of grace. Correspondingly the Christian who gives to those in need is exercising grace. The Christian who acts in selfishness is acting in ungrace, action totally inconsistent with what he or she has become in Christ.

D. The Need to Edify (4:29)

29Let no corrupting talk come out of your mouths, but only such as is good for building up, as fits the occasion, that it may give grace to those who hear.

The third commandment of the Mosaic Law was an injunction against swearing. Paul's injunction goes much further. It includes all kinds of evil talk, whether four-letter expletives, dirty stories, or any kind of obscene or blasphemous language. All such are expressions of selfishness, because they are ways of saying to others, "Pay attention to me." They ask for attention at the moral expense of others.

Here again the injunction is the imperative of grace, not law. What should determine the speech of the believer?

The principle of love. Love helps others by building them up. It never leads others to immoral or faithless behavior. The Christian whose heart's concern is strengthening and encouraging others in their Christian walk (true edification) is reflecting the grace that God has already poured out on him or her.

Perhaps someone feels, "A little strong language here or there simply adds emphasis without hurting anyone." Yet we never know how our language affects others, and love does not take chances.

E. Not Grieving the Holy Spirit (4:30-31)

30And do not grieve the Holy Spirit of God, by whom you were sealed for the day of redemption. 31Let all bitterness and wrath and anger and clamor and slander be put away from you, along with all malice.

What did Paul mean by grieving the Holy Spirit? The expression is a quotation from Isaiah 63:10. The meaning is clear both from the context of the quotation in Isaiah and from Ephesians 4:31. Isaiah summarized Israel's history: "But they rebelled and grieved his Holy Spirit; therefore he turned to be their enemy, and himself fought against them." With few exceptions, the people of Isaiah's day engaged in idolatry, oppressed the poor and helpless, practiced violence, loved bribes, lived for pleasure, and above all rebelled against God by completely ignoring him. Their galling, rebellious sin was what grieved the Holy Spirit.

Most commentators think that 4:31 is a distinct topic without an immediate connection to 4:30. The commentator Rudolph Schnackenburg even takes verse 31 as the beginning of a new paragraph.⁸⁵ For the following reasons, it is better to view the two verses as intimately connected. (a) Each of the other imperatives in 4:17-32 consists of a command and a matching motive. Verse 31 is a command, but lacks the motive, unless indeed verse 30 is the motive. (b) The command in verse 31 is not parallel to the commands in the rest of the division. It does not have the sense, "You are to habitually avoid these things." Rather the sense is, "Let these things right now be taken away from you." The way to keep verse 31 parallel to the other commands is to connect it with verse 30, "Do not be grieving." Then verse 31 tells what it is to grieve the Holy Spirit. By connecting verses 30 and 31 into a single train of thought, we have first the command to avoid grieving the Holy Spirit followed by a reminder of what the Holy Spirit has done, and then a statement of conduct that grieves the Holy Spirit.

The motive for not grieving the Holy Spirit is that we believers are "sealed for the day of redemption." This brings us back to 1:13-14, which refers to the fact that the Spirit's sealing is a guarantee that we shall acquire possession of our inheritance. There is little question but that "sealing" in both passages guarantees the believer's safe arrival at the time when our redemption from the effects of sin is complete, that is, when we are raised from the dead. Then in truth we shall experience a total realization of all that is promised us in our salvation. How does this become a motive? Since the Christian has the guarantee of the Resurrection, and this is through a ministry of the Holy Spirit Himself, it is unthinkable that the Christian should thoughtlessly offend Him. It is the same

---

85 Rudolph Schnackenburg, *The Epistle to the Ephesians: A Commentary*, trans. Helen Heron (Edinburgh: T & T Clark, 1991), 210.

principle that Paul enunciated in Romans 6:1-11, where we learn that God considers Christ's death also the death of the believer. Because of this, the believer has the certainty that he or she will be raised and will live with Christ. Hence it is unthinkable that the believer should live in sin.

Each of the six specific attitudes that grieve the Holy Spirit is unmistakably self-centered. God's Spirit must sorrow when the Christian's thoughts and actions are directed toward self rather than in love toward others. Bitterness is first on the list. Why does one Christian become bitter toward another? A Christian is never bitter toward one he or she truly and deeply loves, even though that person may do things difficult to accept. When someone is genuinely loved, the lover tries to understand the reason for a displeasing act, and even if the reason is unacceptable, still makes allowances for it. When one is overcome with bitterness toward another, there is a failure to try to understand or make allowances. It is an emotion of arrogance, of self-glorying.

The word for bitterness (*pikria*) carries with it the thought of animosity and anger. The words that follow are more or less synonyms, but they are more than a simple list of evils. Paul clearly advances from a gentle simmer to a mighty explosion. Bitterness is the first, for which "resentment" would be a good translation. Bitterness unjudged will quickly eventuate in wrath (*thymos*). Some translations (the NET, for example) reverse the words, putting "anger" before "wrath." In either case the first refers to bitterness that does not go away; it is settled bitterness. The next (the third on the list) might better be thought of as "rage" (*orgē*) It is a loss of self-control through violent emotion. It implies an intent to get revenge. Rage leads to clamor (*kraugē*), which is an open shouting back and forth. The thought is that of people screaming at each other in a severe quarrel. The clamor of a screaming quarrel builds up to slander, every kind of abusive speech and defamation. The Greek word translated "slander" is *blasphēmia*, from which we derive our English word blasphemy. Our English word ordinarily carries the thought of cursing or reviling God or using words or signs impugning the dignity of God. The Greek word has the broader thought of all abusive language, not necessarily against God, although blasphemy against God cannot be discounted here. A Christian might even become bitter toward God. The danger is there for any Christian, whether beginning with bitterness toward God or toward fellow believers.

At the end, lest anyone should think that some level of anger is the only thing that might grieve the Holy Spirit, the apostle adds, "with all malice." The word translated malice (*kakia*) has a meaning that goes beyond mere malevolence. It is used for depravity, wickedness, and vice generally, although in certain contexts it may have the more limited sense of ill-will or malignity. In 4:31 it seems to be more than a summary of the preceding degrees of anger. It includes whatever might follow beyond these, such as doing bodily harm to the person who is the object of one's anger.

Most importantly the Christian need not slide from bitterness to slander or to any other evil. The words "put away" are instructive. As pointed out above, the verb has the thought of "let it be taken away from you." By our own effort or resolve we simply cannot avoid bitterness and wrath, because we still have sinful desires that react in selfish ways to the actions of others. Significantly, the instruction to put away sin is associated with the Holy Spirit, who is the divine

Minister to promote within us the love that we cannot generate by our own resolve or efforts. Insofar as the Christian is willing to judge sin in his or her life and walk by faith, God's Spirit will give that person the victory. He will truly take away wicked and selfish emotions and produce fruits pleasing to God.

F. Forgiveness with Kindness (4:32)

³²and be kind to one another, tenderhearted, forgiving one another, as God in Christ forgave you.

Possibly nothing is more responsible for disunity among God's people than an unwillingness to forgive. Even when people forgive a wrong, it is often parsimoniously. How often we hear Christian people exclaim, "I'll forgive, but I'll not forget!" Here God's Word is telling us to be forgiving, yes, and in doing so, to forget. This is what is meant by being kind and tenderhearted. Kindness and tenderheartedness cannot be disassociated from forgiveness. Indeed, the Greek tense means to *continue* to be kind. It means the *practice* of being kind one to another.

Why is it so difficult to forgive others for wrongs and slights? One of two reasons. It may well be that we have not become sufficiently aware of the enormity of our own sins. This is especially true if we think of sin as nothing more than a failure to obey the Ten Commandments or some set of social rules. Only when we become acutely aware that all self-centeredness, all self-glorying, all self-serving is wholly displeasing to God, do we begin to see ourselves for what we truly are. A second reason that forgiveness may be difficult is because we have yet to appreciate or we neglect to remind ourselves of the full and free forgiveness granted us through Christ Jesus. Paul uses two different words for forgiveness. In 1:7 he uses a word (*aphesis*) that has the meaning of sending something away. This conveys the fact that God has put our sins out of his sight. Here, however, he uses a verb (*charizomai*) that originally meant, "to be gracious to someone." It is the same word used in Jesus' story of the two debtors in Luke 7. One debtor owed fifty denarii, the other five hundred. Neither could pay, but we read in Luke 7:42 that the creditor *forgave* them both. The AV happily translated the word "frankly forgave" and the NKJV has "freely forgave." In Jesus' illustration of God's forgiveness, there is something especially elegant and charming. The human style is, "I'll forgive you, but I want you to know it is hard for me." In contrast, God's forgiveness has no reservations, no implication of grudging the act. The sinner, laden with guilt, is welcomed to God's forgiveness. Should it not be so with our forgiveness of one another?

III. Forewarnings for the New Life (5:1-21)

In these 21 verses the apostle moves from specific Christian behaviors to four contrasts between self-gratifying (fleshly) practices and doing what pleases God. The first verse is a brief preamble to all that follows. The contrasts that follow emphasize the proper path God wants each of us who has entered the new life in Christ to follow.

Some commentators see verse 1 as a conclusion to the preceding verse. Since God forgives, we should imitate His forgiveness. But the question is, What does "therefore" refer to? The English "therefore" can refer only to what precedes. But the Greek word translated "therefore" (*oun*) can introduce either a logical conclusion or the beginning of a new paragraph. Here it is much better to see the word as an introduction to new concepts. The preceding verses (4:25-32) include six injunctions, each with a reason. An entirely different construction is found in 5:1-21, obviously suggesting a different approach by the author.

A. Walking in Love versus Giving Way to Immorality (5:1-5)

¹Therefore be imitators of God, as beloved children. ²And walk in love, as Christ loved us and gave himself up for us, a fragrant offering and sacrifice to God

³But sexual immorality and all impurity or covetousness must not even be named among you, as is proper among saints. ⁴Let there be no filthiness nor foolish talk nor crude joking, which are out of place, but instead let there be thanksgiving. ⁵For you may be sure of this, that everyone who is sexually immoral or impure, or one who is covetous (that is, an idolater), has no inheritance in the kingdom of Christ and God.

A baffling question is Why did Paul think any mere human can hope to be an imitator of God, the God who is bathed in pure light, ineffable in His majesty and infinitude. Yet Paul leaves no doubt but that God can be followed in the Christian's daily life.

Everything Christ did in His earthly ministry was done in love. Paul used a delightful expression, "a fragrant offering and sacrifice to God" (or more literally, "an offering and sacrifice to God for a fragrance of sweet smell" to explain what Christ did in His love. Leviticus 1-6 describes five sacrificial offerings for the nation of Israel. The first three were "fragrant offering" sacrifices, not sacrifices for sin but voluntary sacrifices of worship. The last two were sacrifices for sin. The sin offerings picture most graphically what was accomplished by the death of Christ when His death became our death. His death was a final sacrifice which only He, as the sinless Son of God, could ever offer. On the other hand, His life and His willing submission to the cross, pictured by the fragrant offering sacrifices, provided a different benefit. Everything in his life's work was a willing, sacrificial offering of obedience to the Father. The obedience of our Lord manifested itself in unceasing compassion. He practiced constant concern for children, for sinners, for leprous outcasts, for the poor, for the sick, for the blind and crippled, yes, and for those in the upper reaches of society, such as Nicodemus and the centurion of Capurnaum, insofar as they were willing to receive him. That obedience led Him to endure suffering and hardship without complaint, since He knew that God had called Him to walk in such a path. That obedience, to which Paul referred by the Levitical fragrant offering sacrifices, provides an example for every believer, an example we are called to follow (1 Pet. 2:21).

Since believers are commanded to walk in love following Christ's example, it is definitely within each believer's ability. Someone may say, referring to another Christian, "I simply cannot be kind to that person." Or, "I can't help satisfying my natural desires in finding satisfaction outside my marriage." On the contrary, it unquestionably is within a Christian's power to act with regard for the best good of another, whatever the circumstances. After all, "In your struggle against sin you have not yet resisted to the point of shedding your blood" (Heb. 12:4).

Sexual immorality (Eph. 5:3) is a translation of the single Greek word *porneia*, the root of our word "pornography." In our English usage immorality can include such things as cheating and defamation of others, but this Greek word, more narrowly than our English word, stood for every kind of unlawful sexual intercourse, including prostitution, incest, adultery, and fornication. The world asks, "What's wrong with a sexual experience with someone to whom I am not married, so long as it is between consenting adults and one is careful not to acquire HIV or some other sexually transmitted disease?" For the Christian, the question remains, Can anyone engage another in a sexual practice outside the bounds of marriage without self-interest at stake and without considering the true needs of one's sexual partner? All such practices are without regard to the damage done to the conscience, the personality, and the future of the other person. Most of all, such practices fail to assume the responsibility for others that love demands. Hence they constitute moral perversion. The biblical standard of love demands fidelity in marriage and celibacy in singleness. For the Christian there are no other choices.

"Impurity" (*akatharsia*) is literally the word for refuse or dirt, but in a moral sense it is used for all sorts of impurity, certainly including vicious sexual sins. This would encompass such inhuman deeds as sexual abuse of children. Covetousness (*pleonexia*), which could be coveting someone's material possessions, is included here with sexual immorality, since a common root of sexual immorality is greedily seeking forbidden experiences. It underlines the selfish character of all sexual immorality.

What does Paul mean when he wrote that such things should "not even be named among" Christians, especially since he has just named them? He is using a common figure of speech to emphasize the depravity even of daydreams of such things. It is a rhetorical device exaggerating something to heighten the sense. A Christian who reads sexually suggestive materials, watches movies with titillating scenes of nudity and fornication, surfs the internet for sexually arousing pictures, participates in internet chat rooms with talk of sex, or participates with relish in discussing such things with others is paving the way for a practice of immorality.

The word "filthiness" (*aischrotēs*) could be translated "ugliness" or "obscenity." The words "Let there be" are not in the Greek. Verse 4 is not a new sentence, so "filthiness" continues Paul's injunction against sexual immorality, but here his injunction is against communicating *thoughts* of such evil. Most surely the apostle is not saying that the Christian is never to laugh or tell a good clean joke. What he has in mind is comedy that trades on sexual filth.

But why should he term a "covetous" person an "idolater"? A self-centered person lusting for what God has neither authorized nor provided is denying that God is caring and beneficent and hence is denying God Himself. This is the same species of denial practiced by those worshiping idols of wood, stone or metal.

Verse 5 states that no immoral, impure, or covetous person has any inheritance in Christ's coming kingdom. The statement appears to admit of no exceptions. Sadly, there are believers who at times most grievously fall into sexual or other sins. At first reading verse 5 seems to preclude forgiveness and places the eternal future of a sinning believer very much in doubt. Nevertheless sin does not disqualify a believer from having eternal life. Otherwise John could not have written as he did in John 10:28, "I give them eternal life, and they will never perish, and no one will snatch them out of my hand." He could not have written as he did in John 20:31, "but these are written so that you may believe that Jesus is the Christ, the Son of God, and that by believing you may have life in his name." Nor could Paul have written, adding no other conditions, "For by grace you have been saved through faith" (Eph. 2:8). The most faltering believer can be fully assured by these words and other passages of Scripture that affirm that salvation is by grace through faith alone.

Ephesians 5:3-5 conveys a stern message: any sexual immorality, even a suggestion of it, is utterly abhorrent to God. Nevertheless someone might wonder how verse 5 fits the context. The interpretation of verse 5 can go in one of two directions. Which is correct? As one possible interpretation, it could be describing immoral behavior of unbelievers, sins that deprive them of participating in Christ's coming kingdom of peace and rest. Instead of entering the kingdom, they will face the condemnation of God. This would connect verse 5 with verse 6, which tells of God's wrath coming on "the sons of disobedience." Verse 6 clearly refers to the fate of unbelievers. Another interpretation begins by connecting verse 5 with verses 3-4 and views the passage as a description of Christians who will enter but be deprived of an inheritance in the millennial kingdom. Both the HCSB and the NAB begin a new paragraph with verse 6, separating verse 5 from the fate befalling wicked unbelievers.

For the following three reasons, the authors accept the second interpretation as more in line with the context and Paul's insistence on salvation by grace.

First, according to 1 Corinthians 3:10-13, at the return of Christ a faithful and obedient Christian will receive rewards over and above God's free gift of salvation, rewards commensurate with his or her behavior as a Christian. First Corinthians 3:15 states that "if anyone's work is burned up," he will fail to receive rewards. This implies that some may genuinely trust in Christ for eternal salvation, yet as the "people of the flesh" (1 Cor. 3:1-4), they may be wholly devoid of faithful obedience. Does not this indicate that after our resurrection, some, though by grace received into glory, may miss all those rewards over and above salvation that God had planned for them? This brings up the question, Is it conceivable that any believer is ever completely lacking in good works? In Matthew 10:42 Jesus said that His follower who performs even the seemingly insignificant act of giving a cup of cold water to someone in need "will by no means lose his reward." Nevertheless a new believer, though delivered from the *necessity* of obeying the flesh, may nonetheless lack obedience to the commands of the Lord and continue to practice evils engaged in before conversion. Were this not so, there would be no need for the apostle's strict warning here and elsewhere.

Second, the word "inheritance" does not always refer to blessings given in salvation. In James 2:5 the description of those "rich in faith" refers to Christians who trust God in their daily lives.[86] These are they who become "heirs [inheri-

---

86 Zane C. Hodges, The Epistle of James, ed. Arthur L. Farstad and Robert N. Wilkin (Irving, TX: Grace Evangelical Society, 1994), 50-51.

tors] of the kingdom." Could not Paul have used the word in such a sense in Ephesians 5:5? It was part of language current in New Testament times, so it is at least possible.

Third, verses 5 and 6 seem to be disconnected. Verses 3-5 say, "Here are things you must beware of." The injunction in verse 6 has a different approach, saying, in effect, "These are the very kinds of evils that bring the anger of God upon unbelievers, so their sins should be absolutely loathed by you as well." In Ephesians 2:2 the expression "sons of disobedience" refers to unbelievers.

Surely every Christian needs to be fortified against the battering storms of temptation. Avoiding all obscene conversation and practices is possible through constant thanksgiving (v. 4). The one who continually acknowledges all the rich good that belongs to him or her in Christ and the truth of God's continuing loving supervision will find nothing but disgust with the practices of the flesh. Rather a thankful Christian will discover overwhelming satisfaction with all that is wholesome in contrast to behavior that stems from unwholesome fantasies and panders only to self.

Larkin points out that grammatically the last expression in verse 5 should read, "in the kingdom of Christ who is God."[87] There can be no doubt but that Ephesians teaches the deity of our Lord Jesus Christ.

B. Associating with the Wicked versus Discerning What Is Pleasing to the Lord (5:6-10)
⁶Let no one deceive you with empty words, for because of these things the wrath of God comes upon the sons of disobedience. ⁷Therefore do not associate with them; ⁸for at one

---

87   Larkin, *Ephesians: A Handbook on the Greek Text*, 111.

time you were darkness, but now you are light in the Lord. Walk as children of light ⁹(for the fruit of light is found in all that is good and right and true), ¹⁰and try to discern what is pleasing to the Lord.

The apostle continues the thought of God's unmitigated displeasure with sexual immorality, except that here his concern is the influence of those who in their unrepentant state have no expectation but that of fierce and final judgment.

Why did the apostle write this caution? Plainly enough, Christians need to understand first, how unrelenting is God's disapproval of such behavior. This does not mean that the believer who falls into immorality will lose his or her redemption, although a Christian whose life is consistently lived apart from the will of God can expect God's chastening in this life, the loss of rewards in the life to come, and even the loss of physical life in this world. Second, the Christian needs to understand the real danger of associating with those who engage in such frightful sins and to avoid social entanglements with any who would lead them into immorality.

In verse 7, "Therefore do not associate with them," Paul is doubtlessly thinking of those immoral people voicing the "empty words" (v. 6) and who by association are more or less identified with a local church or who, though not formally recognized as believers, want to consort with Christians. Then just as now, there are individuals who seek some personal gain from being with Christians and who put on a front to match. Paul is not thinking of non-Christian members of a community, people with whom one may need to associate in day-by-day activities to earn a living and to meet normal duties of citizenship, a matter he discussed in detail in 1 Corinthians 5:9-13. Paul is referring instead to unrepentant, wicked people with their friendly offers of social intimacy who are dangerously contagious. Certainly in our day the warning is every bit as applicable considering the libertinism popularized in our literature, on television, and in motion pictures, suggesting that everyone should be free to create a personal lifestyle, and that we should be accepting of those whose lifestyles may include immoral and sexually impure behavior.

Is verse 7 a command for the church to excommunicate such people? Not directly. The word which the ESV translates "associate" means to "cast ones lot with someone" or "share with someone." The HCSB translates, "do not partner with them," which better carries the sense of the word. The instruction here is not to a congregation for action it might take with respect to such people--although such action is not ruled out. Rather this is an admonition to individual Christians who might be caught up in the deceitful influence of immoral people. Believers are to watch out! They are to examine the deeds of others and stay free of their evil. This is not an order for Christians to become snoops, trying to ferret out the possible secret sins of others. Rather it is to observe what is plainly there to see.

Verse 8 is a cogent pictorial recapitulation of much that has gone before. "For at one time you were darkness" is not the same as saying that as unbelievers they were "*in* darkness." As non-Christians there was light around them, light provided by God. The difficulty was that their very being was darkness. Just as all of us, before faith in Christ came, the Ephesians had total inability to understand the nature of true goodness. "But now you are light in the Lord" means that knowing Christ in salvation, the Christian has moral insight that as an unregenerate person he or she did not know and could not experience. Having this light, it is more than reasonable that Christians should always live as those possessing such light. It is inconceivable that a Christian should want to live otherwise.

Beginning with the understanding that "light" refers to one who has received God's gift of salvation, the parenthetical statement in verse 9 amplifies this still further. The fruit produced by the light is "all that is good and right and true." Almost none are turned 180 degrees immediately upon receiving God's gift of salvation. As the Christian begins to live in the light, to one degree or another he or she will become a changed person. Furthermore a person does not become a Christian by being to some degree "good and right and true," but being a Christian can and should lead to these qualities.

As a Christian seeks to live a light-shining life, verse 10 says that he or she should try to learn "what is pleasing to the Lord." But has not Paul just told us what is pleasing to the Lord, namely, "all that is good and right and true"? What more is there to learn? Much more. Paul was quite aware of the many-faceted situations of life that seldom proclaim, "This is good, but that is bad." All of us live in a complex world where much comes in shades of gray, and right moral decisions require keen discernment. Only constant attention to the Word and seeking insight through earnest prayer and honest self-examination will grant the believer knowledge of what love truly amounts to in specific human situations.

C. Participating in Unfruitful Works versus Reproving Them (5:11-16)

[11]Take no part in the unfruitful works of darkness, but instead expose them. [12]For it is shameful even to speak of the things that they do in secret. [13]But when anything is exposed by the light, it becomes visible, for anything that becomes visible is light. [14]Therefore it says,
> *"Awake, O sleeper,*
> *and arise from the dead,*
> *and Christ will shine on you."*

[15]Look carefully then how you walk, not as unwise men but as wise, [16]making the best use of the time, because the days are evil.

Part of not becoming a sharer "in the unfruitful works of darkness" is to expose the wicked deeds of others by the light. How is the Christian to do this? Is it by a public proclamation of the sins of others? Some years back the late Dr. Carey Thomas explained how he built up the congregation in his large Pennsylvania Baptist church. He had a special technique for attracting droves to Sunday evening services, including members of the press. He considered his method biblical, based on this verse. He had somehow acquired informants who told him of graft, corruption, and lawbreaking in City Hall, on the police force, in businesses about town, and other places. He related how at every Sunday evening service he would recite some piece of this information to the audience and publicly rebuke the wrongdoers. This may be an effective way of getting the curious to come under the hearing of the gospel, but it is not what the apostle is directing Christians to do.

When Paul wrote that believers are to "expose" the "works of darkness," is this saying it is the believer's responsibility to expose the sins of the unsaved or expose the sins of backslidden Christians?

No doubt the apostle has in mind Christians dealing with Christians. This is in line with what is enjoined on Christians elsewhere in the epistles: believers are to correct or confront practices of sinning Christians (Gal. 6:1; James. 5:19-20). How is the correction to be carried out? We are not specifically told, although it certainly includes doing all that is "good and right and true." Such a life illuminates the flawed practices of believers who are living in the flesh. Further, exposure of sinning Christians through the example of godly men and women is often enjoined in the New Testament. Paul became an example to other Christians (1 Cor. 4:16-17; Phil. 3:17); Paul, Silvanus, and Timothy presented themselves as examples (2 Thess. 3:9); members of the Thessalonian church were examples to all the believers in Macedonia and Achaia (1 Thess. 1:7-8); elders are to be examples to the flock (1 Pet. 5:3). Are sterner measures called for? At times, most certainly. Preaching the Word of God itself brings rebuke, for this is one function of Scripture (2 Tim. 3:16). Timothy was ordered to rebuke those needing it, and this was in addition to preaching the Word (2 Tim. 4:2). He was to rebuke "before all" those who persisted in sin (1 Tim. 5:20). Paul called for the excommunication of wicked professing believers (1 Cor. 5:11). There definitely is a place for solemn, personal rebuke of sinning Christians, a responsibility mostly bypassed in modern churches.

At this point a caution is in order, although it is outside the immediate topic. If a personal or public rebuke is necessary, it should always be with genuine love and deep mourning, never with dominance or self-righteousness. There are mean-spirited pastors who have turned Christians away from the faith by publicly rebuking them for some sin without first having gone to them in private and having urged them in great sorrow and love to come to repentance. The excuse of these pastors may be, "I am striving for holiness in the church." That surely is a worthy goal, but holiness is meaningless without love. God is holy, but equally he is a God of love.

What is meant by the words in verse 13, "When anything is exposed by the light, it becomes visible?" This ought to be clear enough. Shameful things done in secret are no longer secret when exposed. The saints are light (v. 8), and are expected to walk as those who indeed are light. To the extent they do, their behavior brings conviction to believers who are living worldly lives. Without doubt, the Holy Spirit uses godly behavior to bring conviction to unbelievers as well. They see in faithful Christians an example of honesty and loving concern unknown in a world that lives only to gratify self interests.

"Therefore it says" in verse 14 introduces what may be part of an early Christian hymn. Who said it or who used the saying? There have been many guesses, but no one knows for sure. Paul's use of it, however, is significant.

"Sleeper" is not a euphemism for being dead. Nor are the words "arise from the dead" an invitation to come to spiritual light, that is, to find Christ. The context is about responsibility given to believers. To rise from sleep is most certainly a call to those fleshly Christians whose lives are almost indistinguishable from the unsaved of the world. The sleeper is one who at some time in the past received the light of salvation, but for some reason halted, being satisfied to be a carnal Christian experiencing no further enlightenment or spiritual growth. Some Christians look and act like those who truly are spiritually dead. The apostle calls Christians to rise up from a state of spiritual somnolence and enter the fruitful life that ought to be theirs. This appeal is no different from the lament Paul addressed to the Corinthians, "But I, brothers, could not address you as spiritual people, but as people of the flesh, as infants in Christ . . . Are you not of the flesh and behaving only in a human way?" (I Cor. 3:1-3). Until Christians genuinely commit their lives to the Lord, they will continue to be lacking in spiritual insight. They are not to be "as unwise but as wise" (Eph. 5:15). This verse continues to address the day-by-day spiritual practices of those who through faith are born again.

Verses 15-16 characterize how those living in the light are to carry out their responsibility. The ESV, however, along with most other English versions, follows a group of ancient Greek texts in which the word order makes "carefully" modify "look," as though a person is to carefully observe his or her conduct. Yet as Hoehner explains, other Greek texts have "walk" modified by "carefully."[88] Evidence shows that carefully more likely modifies "walk," not "look." So it should read, "Look then that you walk with care." Much more important is the admonition that each of us should walk with care than merely examining our walk.

This is the last of seven references to "walk" in the epistle, three of which are in Division C_1 and three in this division, its counterpart. Just as a driver needs to exercise great

---

88 Hoehner, *Ephesians: An Exegetical Commentary*, 691.

care on the highway, the Christian needs to exercise equal care in steering through human relationships. A driver talking on a cell phone, nursing a cup of coffee, or checking a global positioning satellite for directions while racing along at 70 miles per hour is inviting disaster. So the Christian by thoughtless or careless words can deeply wound another Christian. A dead fly in a bottle of fine perfume can turn it putrid (Eccles. 10:1), and likewise a foolish, seemingly trivial act can destroy the witness of a life that is otherwise marked by godly probity.

How can Christian people be taught to practice cautious living, learning to have a critical concern for the way their actions and speech impinge on the sensitivities of others? Most certainly it requires constant attention to the Word (2 Tim. 3:16). It also demands the mutual application of spiritual gifts (Eph. 4:11-16), something all too seldom experienced under the "efficient" organizational structure of many of our contemporary evangelical churches.

What exactly is meant by "making the best use of the time"? Exegetes have debated the question at length, but to the ordinary reader of the ESV, (and the NIV, NRSV, and RSV) there seems to be no issue. The problem is, the Greek reads, "redeeming the time," as the words are translated in the AV, NKJV, and a few others. The verb for "redeem" is *exagorazō*, which ordinarily means (in the middle voice) "to buy or purchase something." Some expositors try to make something theologically important out of the words. Nevertheless BAGD gives the meaning simply as "take advantage of any opportunity that comes your way."[89] For the Christian, those in Paul's day and much more so for us, opportunities

---

89   BAGD, 343.

for witness and service may be severely limited by the time we have left, for the number of our days or the Lord's coming may be nearer than we expect.

D. Debauchery versus Filling by the Spirit.

[17]Therefore do not be foolish, but understand what the will of the Lord is. [18]And do not get drunk with wine, for that is debauchery, but be filled with the Spirit, [19]addressing one another in psalms and hymns and spiritual songs, singing and making melody to the Lord with all your heart, [20] giving thanks always and for everything to God the Father in the name of our Lord Jesus Christ, [21]submitting to one another out of reverence for Christ.

The New Testament frequently refers to God's will. What is His will? How can it be known? Unquestionably the foregoing verses clearly express the basic foundation of the will of God. It is living in the light. It consists of a thoughtful and selfless love for others. The prudent believer will want to know and experience the will of God in every detail; the foolish and careless will pass it by.

Yet what is the answer for those of us who know what God's will is in principle, and who desperately desire to rise from among the dead and walk in it but simply lack the power to do so? Has not the apostle already told us in 3:16-19? If we missed it there, here it is in all its marvelous strength. Instead of seeking a fleshly resolution---getting drunk—believers are to experience God's ever-satisfying and glorious provision, the power of the Holy Spirit.

Verse 18 is not a prohibition against all use of alcoholic beverages. In many circumstances love for others may definitely exclude their use, but that is not the apostle's point here. What he is telling us is that *artificial means* for inducing release from tension, fears, boredom, weariness, and dissatisfaction are entirely opposed to God's will. What major problems confront believers? Temptation to sexual immorality, temptation to associate with those who practice immorality, temptation to engage in the unfruitful works of darkness. True wisdom seeks God's genuine remedy for the problems of life. Alcoholism was a major problem in Paul's day, and obviously it is today. In addition to alcohol we can include the numerous psychological releasers in widespread use in recent decades including various drugs, television and motion picture entertainment, gambling casinos, internet chat rooms, and others. Any device or medium to which one becomes habituated as an escape from reality is debauchery. Intoxication is a prominent example of an inappropriate escape.

"Debauchery" is a strong word. The NIV waters down its force by translating "which leads to debauchery." The Greek literally reads, "in which is debauchery," not that *leads* to debauchery. In the eyes of the world an occasional experience of getting high on booze is not debauchery ("Doesn't everyone do it?"). The world sees a homeless drunk as a debauched individual, but not the ordinary citizen who uses alcohol for release of tensions and is capable of handling his or her job and functioning tolerably well in society. But God sees it differently. For the believer, any effort to substitute an external release for the internal victory available through the Holy Spirit is debauchery.

"Be filled with the Spirit" is a misleading translation. A better reading is, "Be filled by means of the Spirit," for Paul is not writing about the Spirit being that with which one is filled but the action of the Spirit in producing a filling.[90] But then the question arises, With what is the Christian expected to be filled? Here we need to remember how the apostle used the word "filling" in his great central prayer. At 3:19 he prayed that Christians might be "filled with all the fullness of God." What does it mean in 3:19 to be filled with the "fullness of God?" Going back to 3:17, we find the explanation. It is to have Christ dwelling in the believer's heart with the consequence that the believer becomes rooted and grounded in love. According to verse 3:16, this is done through the work of the Holy Spirit. In exactly the same way in 5:18 it is the work of the Holy Spirit to fill the believer *with Christ*, to create a life in which Christ "dwells" in the believer's heart to produce true Christlikeness.

Chafer correctly observed that the Spirit's regenerating, indwelling, sealing, and baptizing ministries are granted each believer at the moment of eternal salvation.[91] Unlike these four ministries of the Spirit, "be filled by" the Spirit, because it is expressed by a present imperative verb, indicates that the filling is not an automatic bestowment at the time of salvation.[92] Rather, it is God's appeal for every believer to enter into filling continually--moment by moment.

What we have is God's saving work for the believer *in the present*. Paul wrote in I Timothy 4:16, "Keep a close watch on yourself and on the teaching. Persist in this, for

---

90 Wallace, *Greek Grammar Beyond the Basics*, 375, points out that there are no other instances where en plus the dative case after pleroō indicates content.

91 Lewis Sperry Chafer, *Systematic Theology* (Dallas: Dallas Theological Seminary, 1948), 6:174.

92 Hoehner, *Ephesians: An Exegetical Commentary*, 705.

by so doing you will save both yourself and your hearers." Amazing! Was Timothy's salvation insecure and dependent on his keeping a close watch on himself? Not at all! He had been justified for all time and given an indissoluble guarantee of his resurrection. We might term this "justification salvation." Yet just as the rest of us, he needed God's power for daily, salvation from the presence of sin and for the power to love others. This is what can be termed "sanctification salvation." Sanctification salvation is ours through being filled by the Spirit. (A third category may well be termed "glorification salvation.")

Is one filled by the Holy Spirit through the *practice* of voicing and singing the praises of God and giving thanks? (Eph. 5:19-20). Not at all! The usual sense of filling is that someone or something is responsible for the filling. So in Exodus 35:35 we read of Bezalel and Oholiab that "the LORD . . . has filled them with skill to do every sort of work done by an engraver." This is the natural sense here. It is the Spirit who produces spontaneous voicing and singing the praises of God. It is not the practice of voicing and singing the praises of God that leads to filling by the Spirit. To the extent that the Christian becomes filled by the Holy Spirit, he or she will be impelled to voice heartfelt worship in psalms, hymns, and spiritual songs.

This understanding should make a profound difference in the corporate worship of Christians. Worship services typically are planned with liturgies or readings, praise choruses and hymns, soft or lively background music as the circumstances seem to require, and careful, often emotional exhortations, all with a view to promoting worship. But this is backward. These things do not engender authentic worship. On the contrary, the person who is filled by the Spirit voices his or her worship independently of any external accoutrements. When Christian people fully understand their position in Christ and walk by faith, the Holy Spirit produces worship that springs from within. Such worship may well take advantage of a planned service of worship, but it is not human arrangements that produce true worship. Songs, prayers, preaching, and whatever else takes place in a worship service are of value only as they lead the believer to inner judgment of sin and greater faith. These are the conditions that truly allow the Spirit to produce a filling.

One need not try to make a precise distinction between psalms, hymns, and spiritual songs, for a clear distinction is not made in Scripture. We only note that they are praises for all that God is and does, and that they include (or ought to include) a teaching ministry (Col. 3:16).

Is the apostle thinking of corporate worship, or is he thinking of individual expressions of worship? Some degree of corporate worship is indicated here, for it is "addressing one another." Corporate worship is essential, for in 4:7-16 Paul wrote plainly of the necessity of corporate worship. Spiritual growth, he taught, involves both public ministry of individuals with speaking gifts and the ministry of every believer exercised toward other believers. Neither of these is possible in isolation. Yet the admonition is not limited to corporate worship, for the apostle writes, "always and for everything giving thanks."

The filling of the Holy Spirit is a process. As the Christian discovers through meditation on the Word where he or she has failed and genuinely repents of sin, and as one learns by experience to walk by faith, the Spirit is able progressively to fill the life with all the Father desires. Should any of us travel in a remote, hot desert, we need to carry a canteen full of water. If we begin with a canteen filled with debris, it needs cleaning out so the canteen has room for life-saving water. Similarly at conversion our lives were clogged by sin and fettered by mistrust, things that block the Spirit's power. Sometimes a large measure of sin and mistrust remain. Each of us needs to recognize our need and clear our hearts so that Christ might find full access.

Four results stem from being filled by the Spirit. These are expressed by a series of participles each dependent on the main verb, "be filled." These are "addressing one another," "singing and making melody," "giving thanks," and "submitting." The NAB, NIV, NRSV, and RSV make verse 21 a new sentence. Grammatically this is an error, but yet it catches the apostle's thought, for it is a *transition* clause. It is a vital part of the sentence beginning with verse 18, yet it is foundational for the verses that follow. Because "submitting" is so critical to the next division, it will be explained in detail below in connection with that division.

From verse 21 we move almost seamlessly into the next division with verse 22 dependent on the thought of verse 21.

DIVISION B₂ BE SUBORDINATE TO ONE ANOTHER IN AWE OF CHRIST
(5:22-6:9)

The correspondence between Sections B_1 (1:15-23) and B_2 (4:17 - 5:21) is fairly obvious. First, in B_1 Christ takes precedence over everything and everyone else. In view of being united to Him the believer is to stand in awe. In B_2 Christ's supremacy is the measure of every Christian relationship. Whatever conduct is advocated, it is in view of this relationship. Second, in B_1 Christ is the head of the life of the Church, and in B_2 He is the head of the ongoing life of the Church. In a parallel, the husband is the head of the ongoing life of his wife. Third, in B_1 Paul assures believers that they have been granted immeasurably great power. B_2 does not explicitly mention power given Christians, yet by asking them to do what is humanly impossible, God is obviously implying that this power is available to them.

It might be objected that verse 22 should not start a new division in the epistle, since it is closely tied with the thought of verse 21. Verse 21, as indicated in the discussion above, belongs grammatically to its three preceding verses. Furthermore, verse 22 does not even have a verb of its own. "Be subject" is the implied verb taken from verse 21. In most versions "be subject" is simply added to verse 22 by the editors.[93] Yet, as will be shown, "being subject" is the theme of

---

93 In many ancient manuscripts some form of the verb "to submit" is supplied, but most textual critics believe that the better reading is to omit it. See a detailed discussion in Hoehner, *Ephesians: An Exegetical Commentary*, 730, n.2.

5:22 through 6:9.

Most evangelical pastors, no doubt motivated by marital troubles they repeatedly hear when counseling their parishioners, feel duty bound to preach fairly regularly on the marriage relationship. Because of this, probably no passage of Ephesians provides texts for more sermons than verses 22-33. Many of those who address the marriage relationship from these verses interpret them to mean that the wife has a spiritual obligation to be fully submissive to her husband's wishes in view of his unquestioned superiority. Hodge took this position, justifying it with the following observation: "The ground of the obligation, therefore, as it exists in nature, is the eminency of the husband; his superiority in those attributes which enable and entitle him to command. He is larger, stronger, bolder; has more of those mental and moral qualities which are required in a leader."[94]

A diametrical approach that eases the feelings of moderns is to take Paul's instructions as applicable to the culture of his day but certainly not to ours. It is alleged that the command for the wife to be submissive was required by circumstances in Paul's day, but culture has changed. The thought that the husband should be the master and his wife less than equal, as if she were an inferior deserving of no more voice than a hired servant or a slave, is wholly inappropriate for the twenty-first century Christian. Insisting on the wife's submission, these interpreters point out, demeans her by failing to consider the knowledge and insight she has in her own right and hence is a direct violation of Paul's command for husbands to love their wives as themselves. The wife has the same freedom as her husband to direct and gov-

---

94 Hodge, *Ephesians*, 312.

ern the affairs of the family. The value of Paul's instructions resides in recognizing that his cultural approach provides a historical background that helps us understand his doctrine of Christ's relationship to the Church.

Proponents of the first view counter that here we are not dealing with mere sociological issues that belong to ages long since past. Application to the present day is indicated, they contend, by the direct comparison of the husband's authority with the headship of Christ over the Church. Consequently the husband has a solemn obligation to be the lord of his wife. He may consult his wife on decisions to be made, but ultimate choices and directions must always be his. The wife in turn is to acknowledge him as her master and acquiesce to his wishes.

Yet a careful observation of the first-century meaning of the words and a study of the content of the passage show *both* approaches fundamentally wrong! The second approach errs in supposing the instructions deal with no more than the culture of Paul's day. The apostle employed an intentional similitude between an ideal marriage and Christ's relationship to the Church, and this cannot be waived. It is as much a part of biblical teaching as any other doctrine of the epistle. On the other hand, the passage most definitely does *not* teach the lordship of the husband over the wife. To see what it does teach, we first must think carefully about the overriding principle found in verse 21.

I. The Overriding Principle (5:21)
[21] submitting to one another out of reverence for Christ.

As indicated above, this clause belongs to the preceding section, but it is discussed in detail here because of its importance for the interpretation of the husband-wife relationship. The short statement of verse 21 is a radical concept, but is the essential key to the following passage.

The connection of verse 21 with the preceding verses indicates its spiritual significance. Verse 18 has the command (as it should read), "be getting filled by means of the Spirit." Following this command are five verb forms known as participles, all part of the same sentence in the original. They are not independent verbs, but are controlled by the main verb "be getting filled." The person who is filled by the Spirit most surely (a) will be addressing others with psalms and hymns, (b) will be singing, (c) will be making melody, (e) will be giving thanks, and (f) will be "submitting." Whatever "submit" means, it is something promoted by the Spirit of God Himself. The implication is obvious. Someone not being submissive is not filled, that is, is not empowered by the Holy Spirit to live a life pleasing to the Father.

First, with respect to relationships between believers, one who is "submitting" is fulfilling the principle of love. This seems clear enough from the whole thrust of Paul's teaching about love, but the connection is plainly given in 1 Corinthians 16:13-14. Paul exhorts the Corinthian believers, "Let all that you do be done in love." This broad stroke covers the Christian's total behavior. Paul follows this with a specific instruction, namely, that members of the congregation are to "be subject" to the household of Stephanus and as well "to every fellow worker and laborer." Being "subject" by no means covers every obligation of love, but it is a significant part of an attitude that respects and recognizes the worth of others.

Second, in this particular place *subordinate* (as in the NAB) is a more precise English word for the original Greek word than the translation "submit" in the ESV.[95] Subordinate has a different connotation than either "subject" or "submit." Our English verb *be subject* has the meaning of bringing someone under the control or dominion of someone else. It carries the implication of surrender after opposing or resisting. *Submit* has the thought of yielding ones person to the power of another. Neither of these meanings quite fits the Greek word in the verb form that Paul used. Subordination is Paul's thought. Paul did not mean subjugation, for he certainly did not teach that one believer is to be brought under the dominating control of another believer. Furthermore it is a complete distortion to understand the word as "subservient," a common popular notion among Christians.

Third, being *subordinate* is an attitude expected of *all* Spirit-empowered believers. Those commentators are in error who consider that being subordinate does not mean mutual submission of each believer to the other but means one-directional submission to the spiritual authorities. It should be obvious that because of its grammatical connection with the command to every believer to "be getting filled," each

---

[95] The verb is *hypotasso*, which is used thirty-eight times in the New Testament with 23 of those occurrences in the Pauline Epistles. M. Barth's significant analysis, *Ephesians: Introduction, Translation, and Commentary of Chapters 4-6* :710, shows that when the verb is used in the active voice it carries the thought of subjection. In the active form of the verb, "the power to subject is attributed to God alone whether a person is subjected to God or another person, of whether a thing is subjected to a thing." But when Paul uses the middle or passive indicatives, participles, or imperatives of the verb, as in this passage, it has the sense of "subordinate."

of the five consequences of that filling *is necessarily for every believer*. There is no question but that it means mutual subordination. Men as well as women can be expected to meet its conditions, as can leaders of the local church. In whatever respect a wife is to be subordinate to her husband, God expects a pastor to be subordinate to the people he or she serves, the deacons and other leaders to be subordinate to the people and the pastor, the people to be subordinate to the leaders. Within the Christian assembly there are to be no exceptions.

This is precisely Paul's meaning. Each believer is to subordinate his or her interests and ambitions for the interest of Christ and his body. The word describes a voluntary attitude of giving in, cooperating, assuming responsibility, and carrying a burden.

Fourth, subordination must be carried out in fear of Christ. The word "reverence" in the ESV is the Greek word *phobos*. This is a word used to construct many English words: such as claustrophobia (fear of being in a shut-up space) and acrophobia (fear of heights). Does the word really mean *fear* of Christ? Yes. This is the proper translation of the word, a translation adopted by the HCSB, NASB, and the NKJV. Does it then follow that the Christian is to act in a certain way out of fear of what Christ might do to one? Not at all. Paul's instructions are not legalistic commands with a penalty for noncompliance. Rather this is the fear of *profound awe*, the astounding, overwhelming wonder that comes with a realization of the majestic glory of Christ revealed in 1:20-23. It is wonder made intensely personal when combined with the consciousness that one is unconditionally united to this Lord of all glory. It is a fear that combines astonishment with a sense of unbelievably great honor. That it is not a groveling,

slavish fear should be clear from Romans 8:15, "For you did not receive the spirit of slavery to fall back into fear, but you have received the spirit of adoption as sons."
. This species of fear is to be ours, since it is directed to the Lord of glory. Since it is, whatever position we are assigned in life becomes of no moment. We have no personal stake in our position or status except as we can use it to please the Lord. Are we called for the time being as a husband, a wife, a slave, a powerful industrialist, a worker on an assembly line, a medical professional, a youth in school, a field worker in a truck farm, or anything else? The worldly satisfaction or lack thereof amounts to nothing. The achievements and glories of this world are trivial, because we have seen and have become partakers of the astonishing glory of the Lord himself.

Fifth, what follows are all instances of what it is to be subordinate one to another. They are not separate instructions divorced from verse 21 but are examples that help illuminate what it means to be subordinate in real-life situations. Paul might have selected many other examples, but guided by the Spirit of God he chose three of pressing and recurring importance.[96] Most commentators consider the instructions "household rules" copied after the different household rules proposed by profane authors of the first century but think that Paul intended his to be superior.[97] Ernest Best imagines the

---

96 Wallace, *Greek Grammar Beyond the Basics*, 659, considers that making submission directly applicable to both halves of the three groups, husbands and wives, children and parents, masters and slaves, is an example of "exegetical gymnastics." But not, we believe, when they are seen as examples of an overriding principle applicable to all believers.
97 Hoehner, *Ephesians: An Exegetical Commentary*, 720-29, has an extensive discussion of the rules and scholarly speculations about them.

author of Ephesians to have been listing household rules, but to have been so out of touch with the life of believers that the author thought all Christians live in households which are entirely Christian.[98] Best and others totally miss the point. Paul is not listing rules. He is describing what it means for Christians to defer to each other out of fear of Christ, something that is fully attainable to believers through a common faith in Christ and the empowering of the Spirit.

"Defer" does well as a synonym of "subordinate." "Defer" means "yielding as through respect or reverence." Readers may have watched on television a committee hearing in the U.S. Senate in which each senator was given a stated amount of time to ask questions of the witnesses. The members of the committee were obviously in two camps, one Republican, the other Democrat. Each faction had its recognized spokesman. One senator's turn would come and he would say, "I defer to the Honorable Senator from North Dakota" (or some other state). That senator would then take an extra turn to press the issue at hand. Yet the senator who deferred was in no sense inferior to the one to whom he deferred. Similarly Paul is not saying that in any respect a wife is inferior

---

98 Best, *A Critical and Exegetical Commentary on Ephesians* Observation VI, 519-527. Wallace, *Greek Grammar Beyond the Basics*, 651, n. 94, thinks that 5:22-6:9 does not advance the argument of the book but is in fact a parenthesis to it. On the contrary, although it is definitely distinct from what precedes, it is not a parenthetical thought but advances the concept of the love each believer is expected to have toward others in the body. Furthermore, it is a nice reflection of the doctrines of Division B_1 (1:15-23).

II. Instance One: Wives and husbands (5:22-32)

A. Wives (5:22-24)

²²Wives, submit to your own husbands, as to the Lord. ²³For the husband is the head of the wife even as Christ is the head of the church, his body, and is himself its Savior. ²⁴Now as the church submits to Christ, so also wives should submit in everything to their husbands.

When Paul tells wives to be subordinate to their husbands, he is telling them that the husband's desires should take precedence over their own, just as the desires of the Lord. must always take precedence over one's own.

The words of verse 23, "for the husband is the head of the wife" has troubled many believers, especially women whose husbands have been brutal and inhumane. What do the words mean? Are they instructions that must be followed under any circumstance? What really are the metaphorical meanings for the Greek word "head." It is a word which had several metaphorical uses, over which Biblical scholars have recently been at odds with each other. Added to the confusion is the long tradition of the husband as the ruler of the family, a tradition easily enough understood since the husband was often outside the home as the breadwinner while the wife stayed home and tended to the raising of the children. Things have changed, of course, with the recent invention of effective contraceptives, formal education for American females through college, and opportunities for gainful employment of women outside the home. Nevertheless, the Christian should want to obey the Word of God.

"Authority over" is a common metaphorical meaning for "head" and seems to be the meaning here.[99] Christian men must be careful, however, not to read "rulership" into the word. God has decreed that the man should have a leadership position to establish order in the family and to avoid destructive Satanic influences.

"Now as the church submits to Christ." The church is responsible to obey the Lord. The wife has a corresponding responsibility to her husband, and this cannot be evaded. The last clause of verse 24 says the wife should be subordinate to her husband "in everything," indicating the extent the apostle had in mind. Any exception to Paul's instructions is not given here, for that would be outside his purpose of showing the principles expected to guide Spirit-led believers. Interestingly, the wife is to subordinate herself, not because her husband so demands, but of her own accord in obedience to the Lord. (verse22).

One problem comes in the words of verse 22, where Paul teaches that the wife is to defer to her husband "as to the Lord." We can well imagine a wife muttering, "But my husband is an airhead; he most certainly is not like the Lord." This is entirely possible. No wife has a perfect husband. Some husbands are insecure and incapable of making decisions. Others are impulsive and act without thinking. Some are possessed by wanderlust and move the family to a new

---

[99] Wayne Grudem, "Does Κεφάλη ("Head") Mean "Source" Or "Authority Over" in Greek Literature? A Survey of 2,336 Examples. *Trinity Journal* ns 6.1 (Spring, 1985):38-59. This is especially understandable in first century Greek culture where the husband was usually educated and the wife often illiterate. The wife needed recourse to her husband for information for which he was the authority, hence giving him "authority over" her in this respect. In view of verse 25, it cannot mean "bossy dominance."

town every year. Some are mother's boys who have never cut the apron strings. Some are indifferent, some inconsiderate. Others are good but not overly bright. The list goes on. Nevertheless the command is, as Weymouth's translation puts it, "as if to the Lord." It becomes a trivial matter for a wife to defer to her husband, even if he is wanting in a great many respects, when the wife realizes that her real status is her position as one fully united with Christ.

To a greater or lesser degree the wife's responsibility becomes murky when she is married to an abusive or a sinful and unrepentant husband. This is an issue that Paul deals with to some extent in 1 Corinthians 7. Here Paul is telling us the way a marriage ought to be and in the Lord can be. Nevertheless, it must be stated categorically, there is no reason for an individual or a Christian congregation to *accept as a believer* a husband who beats his wife or hurts her in other respects, even if he is a member of the church, even if he makes every outward show of piety, even if he is a deacon or a pastor. He may well be a born-again Christian, but if he is a wife-abuser, the church should not reckon him among the redeemed until he has genuinely and publicly repented. The same can certainly be said of a husband who is sexually or physically abusive to his children. First Corinthians 7:10-16 (see also Matt. 18:15-22) explains that a Christian wife is under no obligation to remain with an unbelieving husband. She might choose to remain in the hope of winning him to Christ, but certainly she ought to leave him if he is habitually abusive. Paul wrote, "For God has called us to peace" (1 Cor. 7:15). When there is no peace because a husband is cruel to his wife or children, whether physically or mentally, the wife can seek peace with the blessing of God.

The Christian wife's response to an unbelieving husband is the subject of 1 Peter 3:1-6. Peter's exhortation for a wife to defer to an unbelieving husband is her concern for his salvation, just as in 1 Corinthians 7:16.[100] Ephesians describes the peaceful conformity of each spouse to the other when each is walking in fellowship with the Lord.

B. Husbands (5:25-30)

25Husbands, love your wives, as Christ loved the church and gave himself up for her, 26that he might sanctify her, having cleansed her by the washing of water with the word, 27so that he might present the church to himself in splendor, without spot or wrinkle or any such thing, that she might be holy and without blemish. 28In the same way husbands should love their wives as their own bodies. He who loves his wife loves himself. 29For no one ever hated his own flesh, but nourishes and cherishes it, just as Christ does the church, 30because we are members of his body.[101]

One who understands the doctrine of Christian love must realize that here is a clear call for the husband to *subordinate himself* to his wife. Walter L. Liefeld wrote, "It is

---

100 See the discussion of I Peter 3:1-6 by Peter H. Davids, *The First Epistle of Peter* (Grand Rapids: Eerdmans, 1990), 114-23.
101 After verse 30 the AV and the NKJV insert after verse 30 the words, "of his flesh and of his bones." These words are properly omitted by all other modern versions, since they are lacking in the oldest manuscripts of the New Testament. See M. Barth, *Ephesians: Introduction, Translation, and Commentary on Chapters 4-6*, 637, n. 114, or any Greek commentary with a critical apparatus. By supposing these phrases are part of the original, many fanciful and unrealistic doctrines have come into being.

striking that there is no command here for the husband to rule his wife. His only instruction is to love and care for her."[102] A husband acting in Christian love will live and act not for the sake of gratifying his personal goals and ambitions but will seek the best good and interests of his wife. Surely this is asking the husband to defer every bit as much as Paul asks the wife to subordinate her interests to that of her husband.

A professing Christian college professor, an acquaintance or one of us, divorced his wife, leaving her heartsick and distraught. His explanation? "I just don't love her anymore." One who "loves" in the flesh can always expect to find his or her passions waxing or waning. The Christian, however, is capable of love that does not wane and that does not depend on the continuing physical attractiveness, amiability, and charm of a spouse. *Agapē* is not contingent on the appearance, character, or other qualifications of the one who is loved but on the power of the indwelling Holy Spirit. The command in verse 25 is a clear indication that love is something of which each believer is wholly capable. If it is lacking, it is because it is blocked by a heart that is resisting the Holy Spirit.

Husbands are to love their wives. The word love in verse 25 is a Greek present imperative. It carries the thought, "continue loving, without letup." This is the command, but how much? He is to love her to the extent of sacrificing his own life for her. He is to love his wife with total unselfishness. Verse 25 tells us that Christ *loved* the Church. The Church, made up of believers immersed by the Holy Spirit

---

102 Walter L. Liefeld, *Ephesians*, IVP New Testament Commentary Series (Downers Grove, IL: InterVarsity, 1997), 142.

into one body (I Cor. 12:13), was not in existence when Jesus died on the cross. Nevertheless He came into the world knowing in infinite detail all that the Church would be. His mind fully anticipated the total salvation of the Church and His death provided for it to the fullest extent. In these words, "gave himself up for her," we have a significant statement. It is a statement of the purpose and nature of Christ's death, which for the believer was both that of a substitute bearing the death penalty for sin and also of a powerful example.[103] On the cross Christ offered his life as a substitution for all (Matt. 20:28; 1 Tim. 2:6; 4:10; 2 Pet. 2:1; 1 John 2:21), even though the great mass of mankind rejects the provision. Also the Cross is exemplary for the Church (Heb. 12:2). In Ephesians 5:26-27 the apostle explains the consequence and purpose of Christ's sacrificial love for the Church. It set the Church apart for God, for this is the meaning of "sanctify." In this we have a statement of the high calling of the Church, a calling so easily prostituted by local congregations that become mere entertainment centers or social clubs.

How is the Church set apart? It is through having been cleansed by the death of Christ, which erased every trace of guilt for those who are a part of it. The statement of the Church's cleansing is followed by an illustrative figure, "by the washing of water." This is not a reference to baptism,

---

103   The preposition "for" is a translation of the Greek *hyper*. It can mean "on behalf of" or "in the place of." The meaning "in the place of" is not excluded here, for the substitutionary nature of Christ's death is expressly taught in Scripture (Matt. 20:28; II Cor. 5:21; I Pet. 2:24). Christ's death has this incalculable value for the Church, for no one enters the true Church apart from entering into the shelter of His death by faith. Yet in the death of Christ there is the additional power of His example of love (John 15:13).

for it is the entire Church, its members collectively, which is washed. It is a graphic expression emphasizing that the Church's sins (and they are many) have been washed away, that is, completely remitted.

What is meant by washing "with the word"? "Word" here is not a translation of the familiar *logos*, but the less common *rhēma*. Of the seven other times Paul used *rhēma*, all but once it referred to words that come from God or Christ. For example Romans 10:17 says, "So faith comes from hearing, and hearing through the word of Christ." It is reasonable to think that the apostle is using *rhēma* in the same way in Ephesians. Keeping this in mind, it is well to take the preposition "with" as signifying "in connection with." Hence "through the word" is saying that it is the proclamation of God's Word that brings the cleansing through which the Church is sanctified. Whoever comes into the Church, participating in its cleansing, comes through hearing and consciously believing the Word of truth! No one is born into the Church or comes into it by the actions of any other.

In demonstrative language verse 27 tells Christ's purpose in giving Himself up for the Church. It was "that he might present the church to himself in splendor, without spot or wrinkle or any such thing, that she might be holy and without blemish." What did the author intend to communicate by this description? Almost all commentators see the author using a figure of a bridegroom and a bride. Then the commentators debate how the figure corresponds to marriage practices in Paul's day. Did Paul think that Christ is now *betrothed* to the Church, the prospective bride making herself ready for the wedding at the day at His return? Or has the wedding already taken place with the Groom ministering to an often unfaithful wife, bringing her into submission as Hosea loved Gomer his wife and after her adultery finally bought her for fifteen shekels of silver and a homer and a half of barley? Or is it possible that Paul was thinking of the sequence of events in a Jewish wedding where the Church is thought of as being at some point in the lengthy celebration of the wedding? The words are taken to refer to a Jewish wedding ceremony where the best man presents the bride to the groom, but in this instance Christ is both the best man presenting the groom and He is the groom. This view of the Church as the bride of Christ has its origin in the Reformed (amillennial) interpretation of certain Old Testament passages, not in the writings of Paul. In fact Paul does not speak here or elsewhere of the Church as the bride of Christ or of Christ as the bridegroom. Second Corinthians 11:2 is not an exception, for in this passage Paul refers not to the Church, the body of Christ, but to the local assembly in Corinth that he himself had "betrothed" to Christ to present her as a pure virgin to her one husband. In Ephesians 5, instead of a betrothal or a wedding, Paul is making a simple comparison between Christ's consummate, ongoing love for the Church and the husband's responsibility to love his wife in the same spirit. In the same love that Christ has for the Church, the husband is continually to seek to further the best good, to promote, to adorn, and to beautify his wife.

Verse 28 does not mean that husbands should love their wives just as they love their own bodies, but they should love their wives as *being* their own bodies. We can hear the objections. "If I loved my wife as if I were she, I would never get to go hunting or fishing. You're making marriage a drag." Really? What did Christ say to Himself? "I'm going to skip the Cross, because there are a lot of interesting things I want to do. Peter and I have fished the Sea of Galilee, but I'd like to go up to Galatia and try some of the lake fishing there." No, the husband is to love his wife with no thought of himself or his interests. This does not mean that fishing is wrong. To someone stressed by the daily grind of the workplace it can be remarkably therapeutic. But if in any way it is undertaken at the expense of a wife, then the husband does not love as Christ loved the Church.

The final consequence of Christ's profound love for the Church is that she might be "holy and without blemish." These are the same words the apostle used in 1:4 of individual believers. Just as the individual has this perfect standing before God, even though his or her practices may be sadly inconsistent with such a standing, so the Church has and will continue to have a perfect standing, even though in its earthly manifestations it often seems to belie that standing. Christ purchased this perfect standing for believers individually. What is true of each believer is also true of all believers collectively, since believers are incorporated as the Church and made perfect through Christ's sacrifice of himself.

But how can every Christian husband fully love his wife, given the circumstances of some marriages? What if someone's wife is lazy, or a spendthrift, slovenly, frigid, garrulous, excessively fat, or a recluse? The interesting thing is that no human ever had as many blemishes as does the Church. It is made up of people who are frequently living in the flesh, people who are quarrelsome, people who are judgmental, people who pay little attention to the Lord. Yet Christ loved the Church, and continues to love it. That is astonishing. Here is instruction with powerful implications. Each man among us takes pretty good care of himself. God does not have to tell men to be good to themselves. That is stated in verse 29. *In the same way* men are to see that their wives have every opportunity to grow spiritually and emotionally. That includes giving her space, letting her do her own thing. It means helping her when she needs help. More than one Christian husband, whose wife works outside the home just as he does, will be asked by his wife to help with some domestic task or other and will respond, "No, that's your job." Not at all! A husband living in the will of God makes every effort to see that his wife's needs are met. Granted, a few wives will complain they have needs a husband is failing to meet when in reality their demands are selfish rather than expressions of true needs. A husbands response must always be through love fortified with genuine insight and understanding of the other person's inner thoughts and wishes. Yet love, when of God, never fails (1 Cor. 13:8).

C. Husbands and Wives (5:31-33)
31"Therefore a man shall leave his father and mother and hold fast to his wife, and the two shall become one flesh."
32This mystery is profound, and I am saying that it refers to Christ and the church. 33However, let each one of you love his wife as himself, and let the wife see that she respects her husband.

Here is the final key to a marriage relationship in the Lord. Again it is subordination of each to the other. It is possible, because *both are one*. To validate this point, Paul quotes Genesis 2:24. In quoting the verse, Paul does not mean that every part of the citation applies to Christ and the Church.[104] His purpose is served only by the clause, "the two shall become one," since his concern is the union between Christ and the Church.

Why did Paul not choose to cite Genesis 3:16, where God addressed Eve, "Yet your desire shall be for your husband, and he shall rule over you." This is as much a part of the Creation account as Genesis 2:24. If one passage vouchsafes the doctrine of a proper marriage relationship, it seems that so should the other. Since Genesis 3:16 asserts (or seems to assert) a dominance of the husband over his wife, should that not be the pattern for Christian marriages today? An answer is found in the following note on Genesis 3:16 in *Nelson's NKJV Study Bible*[105] "The word **desire** can also mean 'an attempt to usurp or control' as in 4:7. We can paraphrase the last two lines of this verse this way: 'You will now have a tendency to dominate your husband, and he will have a tendency to act as a tyrant over you.'" This understanding takes out of the picture the question of whether or not the verse represents a command to husbands. It is simply a statement of what marriage has so often become under the rule of sin. The passage does not define the marriage relationship for the Christian.

How is the unity of a Christian husband and wife

---

104 The verse is quoted from the Septuagint, an early Greek translation of the Old Testament. This is why it is not precisely like the text of Gen. 2:24 in our Bibles, even though the sense is the same. There are two insignificant differences between the text Paul used and current texts of the Septuagint, but Paul may have been using a text of the Septuagint unknown to us.

105 From Nelson's KJV Study Bible, copyright © 1997 by Thomas Nelson, Inc. Used by permission.

realized in practice? It is not unlike the mechanisms of communication that provide harmony within our physical bodies. The various parts of our body, organs as remote as the toes from the head, are in communication through the nervous and the endocrine systems. The master control for the nervous system is the brain. The master control for the endocrine system is the pituitary gland, which is located beneath the brain and is in communication with the brain. Through these controls, the body functions harmoniously. Correspondingly we need to communicate constantly with the source of our spiritual life, a subject addressed in 6:18. Also husband and wife need to be in communication with each other. Here is a sine qua non of marriage. Each partner should feel free to tell the other exactly how he or she feels. And the other should be able and happy to reflect those feelings with understanding and without censure. Openness is the avenue through which oneness and harmony can truly be experienced by the believer.

    In our physical bodies something at times will block an avenue of communication. Perhaps a nerve will be pinched followed by a painful neuropathy. Or an endocrine gland may be diseased and produce too great a quantity of a critical hormone or produce none at all. In an analogous way, some Christians are married to a mate who is spiritually handicapped. Apparently the situation is beyond remedy. John Wesley was the father of Methodism. He married Molly Vazielle, a wealthy widow. He agreed he would never draw on her fortune. It turned out she had an acid tongue, persisted in an unreasonably jealous disposition, and was given to temper tantrums. When she found he had employed in a different town a young female convert as a lieutenant, a woman who before her conversion had had three husbands without benefit of divorce, Molly suspected the worst and at every opportunity castigated him in public. They separated different times, and finally she left him for good. When she died a few years later, she left him only one thing: the wedding band.

Here is a call to walk by faith. A situation such as Wesley's would be intolerable if this life is all there is. But the Christian has the expectation of being with Christ in glory. Looking to that wondrous future the Christian can endure. The Christian can endure further out of a deep love for a disabled mate, a love abundantly provided by the Holy Spirit. Also, the Christian can endure by committing an intolerable situation to the Lord in earnest prayer, knowing that God will not fail and that He never gives His child a burden too great to carry.

Verse 32 begins, "This is a great mystery." The word "mystery" is used in the same sense it has in its other five occurrences in Ephesians. It is a secret previously unknown but now revealed. It is not the mystery of marriage but the mystery of the union of Christ and the Church. This is exactly the way Paul says he takes it. It is a "great" mystery because of its profundity. How could any human ever imagine something so great as the fact that the Church, which includes every believer, should be firmly and permanently united to Deity itself in the person of Christ? This same unity should and can obtain between a husband and wife, who in the eyes of God have become one. In spite of Paul's clear statement of what the mystery refers to, many have tried to derive from it a doctrine of the mystical nature of human marriage. The Latin Vulgate, translated by Jerome in the fourth century, rendered mystery by *sacramentum*. From this evolved the teaching of marriage as a sacrament, something that has no support in the original Scriptures.

Verse 33 begins with the word "however." The Greek word (*plēn*) can mean either "to sum up" or "in any case." It seems better to take it in the second sense. The word translated love is a strong imperative. "In any case, each one of you must continue loving his wife as himself."

In the preceding verses Paul did not seem to come down as hard on husbands as he did on wives. Coming to the end of his argument, Paul apparently considered men much more recalcitrant about showing love for their wives than wives about showing deference to their husbands. So now the apostle lets Christian husbands have no doubt about their obligation, however much he may previously have slighted the issue. The words "each one" state bluntly there are to be no exceptions. No Christian husband, whether by reason of his status in life or his professional or business obligations, can claim an exemption.

In turn Paul is now surprisingly soft toward the wives. The wife is to *respect* her husband. As pointed out in verse 21, we are to defer ourselves to one another in *fear* of Christ. That was the Greek word *phobos*, a noun. Here we have the verb *phobeō*, usually translated "to fear." The verb, however, is often correctly translated "reverence," or "respect," and in 5:33 "reverence" or "respect" is the preferred translation. The wife is to respect her husband, even if his human defects are painfully obvious. Why? Because he is one with the Lord Himself and he is one with his wife. If any readers are inclined to think that a wife should "fear" her husband because this is a possible translation of *phobeō*, fear then can have no meaning other than it has in 5:21. It is most certainly not slavish fear but the fear of profound awe that she is one with a husband who, as she herself, is one with the Lord of Glory.

II. Instance Two: Children and Parents (6:1-4)

¹Children, obey your parents in the Lord, for this is right. ²"Honor your father and your mother" (this is the first commandment with a promise), ⁴"that it may go well with you and that you may live long in the land." Fathers, do not provoke your children to anger, but bring them up in the discipline and instruction of the Lord.

In Greek literature of Paul's day, the word child (*teknon*) designated one who is a child in relation to a father and mother without reference to age. It was used for an unborn fetus all the way to an adult. In writing this command, Paul would not have had a small child in view, for quite likely he would have assumed that obedience would have been demanded of smaller children.[106] The "child" in view here is evidently one enjoying some degree of freedom in making his or her own decisions. It is one who has consciously confessed Christ in salvation and is fully capable of understanding the implications of Paul's message. The turbulent teen-age years were very likely on Paul's mind. As all parents come to realize, these are years when a developing

---

106 Lincoln, *Ephesians*, 398-402, has an interesting and extended survey of father/child relationships in the Greco-Roman world. The Romans granted the father absolute legal authority over his adult as well as his younger children, even to the point of allowing a father to decree a death sentence for either a young or adult child. The Greeks apparently considered the Romans extremists, but obedience of younger children to a father would have been demanded.

spirit of independence coupled with self-assertiveness often tend toward rebelliousness.

The word "obey" clearly carries the idea of deferring. The Greek lexicographers give the first meaning of obey (*hupakouō*) as "to follow instructions." In Colossiana 3:20 Paul asks that children obey their parents "in everything." In a number of New Testament passages the word is used for the total obedience a person is expected to render to God (Acts 6:7; Rom. 6:16-17; Heb. 5:9, 11:8). Does the word mean that a teen-ager or adult child is obligated to absolute obedience to his or her parents, or are there some exceptions?

The assumption in this section, as in the preceding instructions to a husband and wife, is that the parents are themselves willing followers of the Lord. If a Christian offspring has an unbelieving parent, and the parent asks the offspring to do something manifestly contrary to the will of God, that believer, even though living at home, if at all possible, should do what is right. A child working in a trade with a non-Christian parent may be asked to cheat a customer who comes to purchase an item. Or a college student who determines to leave his or her planned career to enter full-time Christian ministry may be forbidden to do so by an unbelieving parent. This puts a child in a terribly difficult position. We wish the apostle had elaborated further, but he did not. In Ephesians he is presenting principles for Christian action. The unholy demands of a godless parent bring an obedient child to prayer for an avenue of escape while maintaining love for the parent.

Four reasons are given for the deferment of children to a father. (a) They are "in the Lord." As believers they are united to Christ and hence united to believing parents. To fail to obey would be as unthinkable as for the muscles of an arm to refuse to consider a signal from the nerves that one's hand is resting on a hot stove. (b) "It is right." This recalls 5:3 where Paul spoke of conduct as "fitting among saints." In what sense is deferring to parents right? For one, it acknowledges in practice the doctrine that God Himself instituted the family with its structures. Above all, it is right in that hearkening to parents is the practice of love. (c) They have a commandment of God. (d) Although it is a subdivision of the third, the fourth adds the promise of a good life.

The apparent endorsement of the Ten Commandments as binding on Christians and this reference to the fifth commandment as specifically carrying a promise of an earthly reward convince some commentators that Paul was not the actual author of Ephesians. As we have observed, Paul could not have been more clear that the Law provides neither the ground of salvation nor a rule for the believer's daily living. On the other hand other scholars accept the Pauline authorship of Ephesians and use the passage to support the theological view that Paul taught that the moral law is indeed the rule by which Christians are to live.[107] Neither is correct. Paul is the author of Ephesians. And Paul did not teach that for the believer the law is the rule for the Christian's life. Why then did the apostle cite the fifth commandment to enforce the obedience of a child to parent? As Paul explained to the Christians in Rome, the Law is not foreign to righteousness:

Owe no one anything, except to love one another; for

---

[107] For example Thomas R. Schreiner, *Law and Its Fulfillment: A Pauline Theology of Law* (Grand Rapids: Baker, 1993).

he who loves his neighbor has fulfilled the law. The commandments, "You shall not commit adultery, You shall not kill, You shall not steal, You shall not covet," and any other commandment, are summed up in this sentence, "You shall love your neighbor as yourself." Love does no wrong to a neighbor; therefore love is the fulfilling of the law (Rom. 13:8-10). This does not say that obedience to the Law fulfills the obligation to love, but one who genuinely practices love fulfills the end, the purpose, for which the Law was given. Therefore it was quite appropriate for Paul to cite a command from the Law that, when kept, would constitute love for one's parents. Although the believer is not under the Law, the Law can be used to promote an understanding of God and his will for mankind. It can be studied with this end in mind (2 Tim. 3:16).

Commentators have worried about Paul's statement that the fifth commandment is the "first commandment with a promise," when the second commandment says that "the LORD your God" shows "steadfast love to thousands of those who love me and keep my commandments." At first glance this seems to be an earlier promise than the one that is part of the fifth. Yet the second commandment does not really include a promise. It is a statement of the character of Yahweh, a statement that applies equally to all the commandments. He is the one who judges iniquity but shows love to those who obey Him.

This promise of a long life associated with a loving regard for heeding our parents surely brings comfort to the believer. Yet the common experiences of life seems to say that this is not always so. Some who have little or no regard for parents live to ripe old ages and others who are genuinely solicitous of their parents' concerns happen to die young. Hendriksen's comment goes far toward resolving the apparent conflict between what the Scriptures promise and what we seem to experience.

> To be sure, obedience or disobedience to parents is not the only factor that determines a person's span of life, but it is an important factor. Disobedience to godly parents indicates an undisciplined life. It leads to vice and dissipation. This, in turn, *all other things being equal*, shortens life . . . In addition it should be borne in mind that though a disobedient child may live on and on and become a centenarian, as long as he continues in his wickedness *it will not be well with him*. He will have no peace![108]

But perhaps the principle point behind the promise is that obedience can be endured with joy when trusting in the Lord. This can be experienced by a believing teen-ager, even when parental orders seem unfair, suffocating strictness. There is a long life ahead.

Three verses are addressed to children but only one to fathers.[109] This seems disproportionate, since the burden for raising a good and obedient child falls more on the parent than on the child. Yet the ramifications of this single injunction are vast. At the outset it must be observed that parents are not excluded from the primary command to defer. In the parent-child relationship, this deferment takes the form of deep respect for the child or young person as someone made

---

108 Hendriksen, *Exposition of Ephesians*, 260 (italics his).
109 Occasionally the word "father" is used in the broader sense of parent. Did Paul use it here in that broader sense?

in the image of God and someone filled with rich potential for fruitful service. The respect requires discipline, for a child knowing no discipline grows up without a sense of responsibility and indeed without discernment of the rights of others. Children are not resentful of nor provoked by normal discipline. Rather, inside they genuinely welcome it, since it is evidence of their parents' genuine concern. Resentment comes when discipline is inconsistent: some minor infraction at one moment evoking a tolerant laugh but at the next a violent outburst often with severe punishment. A child is also provoked when discipline, even if consistent, is administered in a rage, is overly strict, or is physically abusive.

After a caution against harshness, Paul has a positive admonition to raise children in "the discipline and instruction of the Lord." The word "discipline" has the sense of "education" or "training." This education or training is to be that which looks to the Lord. This is not denigrating secular education but is emphasizing the need to teach our youth what is taught in God's Word. It necessarily includes manifesting the character of the Lord, for this also is educational. The genuineness of a professing Christian parent's faith is exhibited in his or her actions far more than in his or her words.

III. Instance Three: Slaves and Masters (6:5-9)

⁵Slaves, obey your earthly masters with fear and trembling, with a sincere heart, as you would Christ; ⁶not by the way of eye-service, as people pleasers, but as servants of Christ, doing the will of God from the heart, ⁷rendering service with a good will as to the Lord and not to men, ⁸knowing that whatever good anyone does, this he will receive back from the Lord, whether he is a slave or free. ⁹Masters, do the same to them, and stop your threatening, knowing that he who is both their Master and yours is in heaven, and that there is no partiality with him.

Christian slaves, servants, day laborers, bottom-rung employees, employees somewhere on a corporate ladder---surely all of these are encompassed in this address. These are to hearken with a full intention of doing what the boss requires. Subordination is again the key, but here there is a significant difference: *the subordination is to the Lord.* They are to consider themselves "servants of Christ." Christian slaves in Paul's day were not too likely to have Christian masters, nor today do many employees have the privilege of serving Christian employers. The Christian is never to be subordinate to an enemy of God. But being subordinate to Christ, the slave or the employee can render excellent service, since in reality the Christian is working for the greatest Master of all.

Unquestionably slaves and employees alike have often been exploited and humiliated by their masters or employers. Slaves have been cruelly tortured. One can expect nothing better from an unbeliever whose only interest is his or her personal gain. Even should a master be reasonably kind, the confinement of servitude is frustrating, particularly when the believer can envision much greater usefulness if granted liberty. What God is saying to the slave is simply this: "I am in control. The ultimate reward is in my hand. Look for my paycheck and meanwhile trust me, for I will not fail you", (Prov. 3:5-6).[110]

---

110 For an understanding of the Biblical doctrine of rewards see Bob Wilkin, *The Road to Rewards: Living Today in Light of Tomorrow* (Ir-

Will the reward be in this life or at the return of the Lord? The text does not say, except to indicate that it is future: "this he will receive back from the Lord." In this life there definitely are rewards of joy for the faithful believer. The Scriptures also tell of rewards over and above salvation that will be granted at "the Day" (1 Cor. 3:10-15). Possibly both are in the apostle's mind. Significantly, rewards are available to "slave and free," that is, without respect to one's worldly status.

Critics of our faith allege that Paul supported the institution of slavery. This is far from the truth and cannot be read from the text.[111] Paul took the social institutions of his day and showed how Christians should relate to them. The Church's task is not to reform the institutions of unbelieving society, but rather to bring individuals to a saving knowledge of Christ.

Given Paul's instructions here, critics also allege that it must have been wrong for slaves to flee slave owners in antebellum days and during the Civil War. No, the Christian should never choose to endure servitude for servitude's sake.

---

ving, TX: Grace Evangelical Society, 2003), and Paul N. Benware, *The Believer's Payday: Why Standing before Christ Should Be Our Greatest Moment* (Chattenooga: AMG Publication, 2002).

111 An excellent discussion of the issue of slavery in Paul's day is in Brian J. Dodd, *The Problem with Paul* (Downers Grove, IL: InterVarsity Press, 1996). Hoehner, *Ephesians: An Exegetical Commentary*, 800-804, has an interesting summary of the practice of slavery in Paul's day, which was quite unlike the antebellum practices in our American South. The terrors of American slavery are disturbingly described in the memories of Frederick Douglass, *My Bondage and My Freedom* with introduction and notes by Brent Hayes Edwards (New York: Barnes & Noble Classics, 2005).

A martyr complex does not honor the Lord; it only caters to the flesh. Paul told slaves, if they were slaves when they found Christ, "Never mind." But then he added, significantly, "But if you can gain your freedom, avail yourself of the opportunity" (1 Cor. 7:21).

Four verses addressed to slaves and only one to masters make it seem that Paul was supporting the rich and well-placed with a view to keeping slaves in their place. But this is a superficial comparison of numbers of verses instead of a comparison of the content of the words. There is no partiality with God, the apostle affirms, and in God's sight the master is equal with the slave. The greater number of verses addressed to slaves is in keeping with the temptation to despondency and sloth so likely to overtake one whose efforts all go to the enrichment of the powerful. The master faces a different temptation, that of disregarding the sacredness of the lives of those serving him. While it is appropriate that slaves be directed toward rewards that lie in the future, Christian masters must face their day-to-day responsibility toward those who labor for them.

Christian masters just as much as Christians at other societal levels are to be subordinate to other believers. Masters, however, have a greater responsibility when some of those they manage are not believers. Here they have a responsibility as well as an unparalleled opportunity to show the love of Christ and win to the Lord those who serve them. Above all, they do this by listening to their subordinates concerns and exercising the greatest degree of compassion toward them.

Paul does not condemn the status of one who happens to be a master. There is no spiritual profit in resigning a position of power to become impoverished or a slave. God has graciously allowed some to acquire wealth. He has allowed it so that they might unreservedly use their riches to deliver others from bondage, both materially and spiritually.

DIVISION A₂ . FIND STRENGTH IN CHRIST
(6:10-20)

Ephesians 4:25 - 6:9 with its long string of well-nigh impossible-to-reach God-given mandates can be altogether discouraging. God expects us to be Godlike. But who really can be Godlike? Continue to speak the truth, continue not to steal, continue to keep evil talk out of your mouths, continually refrain from grieving the Holy Spirit, be habitually kind to one another, continually walk in love, never ever even suggest sexually immoral actions, wives continue to defer to your husbands, husbands, continue to love your wives as your own bodies, to continue as a *habitual practice* doing the total will of God is what the Greek tenses say. Most of us can manage some of these things all the time. But can anyone continue in ALL these things? It seems impossible. It is difficult not to groan, "I quit!"

There are some Christian churches where people are constantly urged to resist sin by a mighty effort of willpower. These believers may struggle against some vexatious sinful practice, and for a time may even seem victorious, but their rate of recidivism is unacceptably high. If Ephesians ended with 6:9, it would be a dread-inspiring book. But then we come to 6:10 and the solution to the problem of "how to."

This division corresponds neatly to Division A₁ (1:3-14). The first division of the epistle describes things God has done once for all for every believer. The first division is a statement of God's commitment to every Christian. Division A₂ before us is a statement of how every Christian is indebted to be totally committed to God. This commitment is to be once for all in the same way that God, in total grace, has made his once-for-all commitment to us.

I. The Command (6:10-11)

¹⁰Finally, be strong in the Lord and in the strength of his might. ¹¹Put on the whole armor of God, that you may be able to stand against the schemes of the devil.

The words, "Be strong" can correctly be understood as "Be made strong." The process of getting strong is not self-powered. It is in "the strength of his might." There is supernatural power available to do what God wants the believer to do. The Christian meets the conditions; God supplies the power. This reinforces what the apostle prayed in 3:16, "that according to the riches of his glory he may grant you to be strengthened with power through his Spirit in your inner being." Lincoln nicely commented, "The decisive victory has already been won by God in Christ, and the task of believers is not to win but to stand."[112]

The new believer is spiritually reborn, but is a babe in Christ. Just as a new enlistee in the army must undergo basic training, for the new Christian a process of development must follow. This comes, according to 3:17, as Christ dwells in the believer's heart "by faith." Nevertheless, valid faith is not some amorphous thing; it needs direction. The Christian's armor provides that direction.

No one except a believer is expected to put on the whole armor of God. A person cannot participate in the armed forces of the United States without first enlisting. Similarly, for a person who is not spiritually born of God, an effort to put on the whole armor of God is an exercise in

---

112 Lincoln, *Ephesians*, 442.

futility. For them the armor is unavailable.

In contrast to the long string of verbs from 4:25 through 5:9, telling the Christian to continue doing certain things, we abruptly come to a different kind of verb. "Put on" is an aorist verb in the imperative mood. It is a strict command. Here is a sudden transition from the long string of commands to *persist* in doing certain things. The transition lets us know that we have come to a place where repetition is not expected. Consequently it has the force of *put on once and for all*, put on the armor of God with no thought of taking it off. This is a decision the Christian must make with the thought that putting it on is for good.

Here is the foundational condition for accessing God's power. Clearly there is a personal choice to be made. God's power is not gained through osmosis from regular church attendance. Religious exercises and ceremonies are no substitute. This is not a mere resolve to do better. To access God's power, every Christian is called to make a decision, and in making it, it is to be for life. Later one may fail to keep the decision. If so, it must be made again, and even again and again. Whenever it is made, in making it there are to be absolutely no reservations, no words in extra fine print that one hopes God will overlook. Furthermore the decision is to be made in faith, that is, without the supposition that failure inevitably will follow.

The decision is precisely the same decision that Romans 12:1 calls every Christian to make: "I appeal to you therefore, brothers, by the mercies of God, to present your bodies as a living sacrifice, holy and acceptable to God, which is your spiritual worship." This presenting of ourselves is not only what the Christian does to worship God, but it is crucial because of the nature of the enemy. Ephesians 6:12-18 tell us what is involved in such a total decision and why it is necessary.

II. The Battle Lines (6:12-13)

A. The enemy (6:12)
¹²For we do not wrestle against flesh and blood, but against the rulers, against the authorities, against the cosmic powers over this present darkness, against the spiritual forces of evil in the heavenly places.

Know your enemy! Many battles have been lost because an army lacked adequate information about an enemy's troop sizes and intentions. For Christians sound intelligence is even more critical. False intelligence leads to defeat.

The first item of intelligence for the Christian is that the real enemy is not human weakness, physical infirmities, lack of mental capacity, lack of funds, disagreeable personalities, unfair governmental regulations, repetitious and dull church services. Most of all, given modern psychological theories, the ultimate enemy is not our infant or childhood experiences, as damaging as these may have been. The real enemy is a host of evil spirit beings.

Satan is a reality. Paul regards him as a real person rather than a figure for self-deception or social influences, although self-deception and baneful social influences may certainly bear his signature. Satan is organized. The rulers, the authorities, the cosmic powers, the spiritual forces of evil are demons under Satan's control. False doctrines issue from Satan. Satanic control leads people to act in a multitude of evil ways. It may move governments and educational institutions to oppose Christian truth. People and governments are often the weapons, but the operators of the weapons, the ones against whom the Christian truly is at war, are spirit forces. *Hence our weapons must be spiritual weapons.*

The word "wrestle" points to hand-to-hand fighting. The hand-to-hand thought compels the reader to appreciate the severity of the conflict. The thought also brings to mind the danger of accepting everyday selfishness as inconsequential and tolerating sin as unsavory but unavoidable baggage. Sinful practices are not mere human infirmities. Back of them are the satanic rulers, authorities, cosmic powers, and spiritual forces of evil.

B. The armed soldier (6:13)
[13]Therefore, take up the whole armor of God, that you may be able to withstand in the evil day, and having done all, to stand firm.

"Take up" is a verb of command in the aorist tense. The implication is to take something at a point. Paul emphasizes the absolute necessity of a once-for-all decision in taking up the armor. If a Christian puts the armor on with no thought of laying it aside, however grim or confused the circumstances, he or she will be able to stand, will be victorious.

From the time in 202 B.C. that the Roman general Scipio Africanus decisively defeated Hannibal at the North African town of Zama, for more than five hundred years the Romans were the military masters of the Western world. Besides the skilled leadership of Scipio, a major factor in their success was the well-equipped and highly disciplined Roman legionary. Each Roman infantryman was trained for the most effective use of his equipment. The armor and the equipment could become burdensome. But when combat was impending, each was commanded to put on his armor. He wore it for his own good. It would have been unthinkable for any legionary to disregard an order. Paul frequently saw these legionaries, and no doubt he won many of them to Christ. Their armor and their military discipline made an impression that provided an apt illustration for Paul's readers.

"Withstand in the evil day." What day is this? Was Paul thinking exclusively about the great tribulation yet to come? It is difficult to believe he was, for in their day the Christians in Ephesus and elsewhere were facing imminent and real spiritual problems. The whole tenor of the epistle has to do with life in the here and now. It is any evil day. It is the day of spiritual testing, a day when testing may be painfully obvious or a day of subtle evil, but nonetheless a day of conflict.

"Withstand" is a rather bland translation for the verb Paul used (*anthistēmi*). "Stand your ground" (NIV) or "stand up to" better conveys the force.

"Having done all, to stand firm" is best understood as "having proven victorious over everything, to stand your ground."[113] "To stand" is a verb form (aorist infinitive) that has the sense of "to remain standing." The Roman soldier after an hour or two of violent combat would be utterly fatigued and possibly prostrate from exhaustion. Here the Spirit of God is reassuring the Christian that fatigue does

---

113 The verb is *katergazomai*. Hoehner, *Ephesians: An Exegetical Commentary*, 835-6, reasons that it means "all the necessary preparations having been made, stand."

not follow a continued effort to resist sin in God's strength, for the Christian can surely remain on his or her feet. Using the weapons God supplies, the Christian is invigorated, not weakened.

III. The Orders (Providing for the Combatants Every Need) (6:14-20)

A. Commitment to Truth: The Belt (6:14a)
¹⁴Stand therefore, having fastened on the belt of truth,

A total commitment to truth is a condition enabling the Christian to stand firm. For all believers there are times when failing to tell the truth or shading the truth saves from embarrassment. A temptation to disregard the truth for a self-centered reason is sadly common among us.

The legionary wore a leather apron that hung under the armor and protected the lowest part of the abdomen and the thighs. It is probably this of which Paul was thinking rather than a belt buckled on together with the sword or the officer's *cingulum*, a sash designating a high rank. What is critical, however, is not the imagery of what the soldier buckled on but the fact that the Christian is to buckle on *truth*.

Each of us who serves the God of truth must have a deep, continuing, personal commitment to truth (4:25). A life of faith in God is not really a life of faith unless it includes believing in the importance of truth, for our God is a God of truth. Seeking truth does not mean that we are to occupy ourselves with digging out the secret recesses of evil in the lives of others; that is God's business. Suspicion of others should never lurk in our heart. A love for truth allows us to be open to others and above board in our dealings with them. Truth means taking care not to deceive others, whether deliberately or by asserting as true things about which we lack information or which we know to be uncertain.

Does not "girded with truth" also mean that one is to be alert to the ever-present danger of self-deception? We act selfishly, then imagine some way to escape thinking of it as a sinful act. Once having made the rationalization, we come to believe its validity and feel free to indulge the selfish, untruthful practice again and again.

B. Commitment to Righteousness: The Breastplate (6:14b)
and having put on the breastplate of righteousness,

The metal breastplate together with the leather apron protected the entire front of the soldier's body. The figure of putting on the breastplate is a way of saying, "I'm committing myself to doing what is right. I may not know what is right in every circumstance of life, but when I put on the armor, I'm saying that doing what is right is my constant aim."

C. Commitment to the Gospel of Peace: Footwear (6:15)
¹⁵and as shoes for your feet, having put on the readiness given by the gospel of peace.

Paul did not specify what kind of footwear he had in mind, but likely he was thinking of the Roman *caligae*. These were leather half-boots tied to the ankles and shins with straps. The toes were free. The leather soles allowed for long marches, and, most importantly, were heavily studded to provide a strong foothold for throwing a spear or sword-fighting. If this is what Paul was thinking of, the word "readiness" might better be translated by the word "firmness," or "firm footing" (as in the NEB).[114] The noun "firm footing" (*etoimasia*) occurs only here in the New Testament. Some translations (NASB, NKJV) render it "preparation." Possibly these translations and the translation of the ESV miss the point of the *caligae*, which did not prepare or ready a soldier for battle, but made him able to stand his ground while engaged in battle. We might think of Psalm 121:3, "He will not let your foot be moved." The Christian is in a battle, but if he or she is fully informed of and committed to the peace God has provided, spiritual stability in the midst of the world's turmoil will certainly be promoted.

Is commitment to the gospel of peace a commitment to *proclaiming* the gospel with its message of peace to those who have not heard? Or is it a commitment to maintain peace among believers? It is a commitment to every facet of peace implied by the gospel of Christ. Peace must be maintained among Christians. With distressing frequency Christian people separate themselves from other believers over the most trivial issues. Quarrels and disputes break out, each one demonstrating that the disputants have yet to put on the whole armor of God. Even more distressing are those times when professed Christians are filled with public distaste for believers of other races, a species of "un-peace."

It seems strange, almost paradoxical, that in this passage combat should be linked to peace. The gospel of peace is the good news that peace from a justly outraged God belongs to the believer and will never be taken away. When this good news is fully accepted, the Christian can do battle against Satan without fear that condemnation is always

---

114 See interesting comments in M. Barth, *Ephesians: Introduction, Translation, and Commentary on Chapters 4-6*: 770 and 797-99.

threatening should he or she at some point fall into sin. The firm footing brings confidence that peace with God is offered to all and can be both lived and proclaimed fearlessly.

D. Commitment to Faith: The Shield (6:16)
[16] In all circumstances take up the shield of faith, with which you can extinguish all the flaming darts of the evil one,

A most effective offensive weapon was an arrow with some pitch-impregnated material at the head. The pitch was ignited and the arrow fired at advancing troops. Darts with pitch-tips were also used. The pitch would stick to the soldier's armament or clothing and burn with fury. A soldier suffering painful burns could hardly avoid flinging off his armor and running for the rear. In the first century two kinds of shields were available to the Roman soldier. One was a smaller round shield, the *aspis*, but if two missiles came simultaneously this would be of less value. The shield here is the *thyreos* (to the Romans a *scutum*) a large, door-shaped, rectangular shield 37 to 42 inches tall and 24 to 33 inches wide, made of wood, covered with leather, and with a handle in back. The NEB correctly interprets it as the "great shield." Before battle it was soaked in water so that it was immune to catching fire if struck by a flaming arrow or dart.

The ESV and the NAB read, "In all circumstances take up the shield of faith," the HCSB has "in every situation" and the NASB has "in addition to all," each carrying the same thought. Possibly an even better translation is "above all" found in the AV and NKJV. A daily walk of faith is foundational to a successful Christian life. The translation in the NIV, "In addition to all this," is grammatically possible but misses the whole thrust of Paul's teaching about faith in the Christian life. Faith is not merely an addition to other responsibilities. One cannot read the Epistles without realizing that a walk of faith is crucial to everything God wants in a Christian life. Other items in the armor augment, encourage, strengthen, and promote faith, but faith is necessary to all.

Evil influences, the flame-tipped darts and arrows of Satan, come from every direction and come constantly. Unless the believer is confident that God is in control, that God has his or her life in his hands, the Christian can easily succumb to the enemy. The Christian's resource is to commit to God's care every circumstance His wise providence brings or He allows. He knows long before any calamity arrives what one will be called to endure. He knows and uses it for the Christian's best good. Commitment to faith, taking up the shield of faith, is resting in His grace, confident that in the long run he or she will find God did not fail.

E. Commitment to Salvation: The Helmet of Salvation (6:17a)
17and take the helmet of salvation,

The Roman soldier had a bronze helmet lined with cloth or sponge for a cushioning effect. It could prevent his skull from being split with a swinging sword or fractured by the blow of a club. Without it, unconsciousness or death was almost a certainty. The helmet is a defensive part of the armament, but a most important part. How is it connected in Paul's mind with salvation?

Undoubtedly the apostle's thinking goes back to the corresponding section A_1 where His entire theme is the salvation granted the believer. Salvation with all of its blessings is a reality the believer simply must understand and keep in the forefront of his or her mind. It is an understanding of all that God in grace has done for the Christian. One of the enemy's most effective blows is false doctrine regarding salvation. Even if a Christian has the basics, ignorance of the full scope of salvation can leave him or her vulnerable. A believer can quickly give up when wallowing in doubt regarding his or her eternal security or constantly fearing that God is unwilling to forgive some dreadful sin. Protection from despair is achieved only by a sound understanding of God's promises.

F. Commitment to the Word of God: The Sword of the Spirit (6:17b)
and the sword of the Spirit, which is the word of God,

Two types of swords were in use, the large, broad sword (*rhomphaia*) and the short sword (*machaira*, the Roman *gladius*). For his illustration the apostle appropriately uses the short sword. Enemies of the Romans employed long swords, but because of their length they could not be wielded with the same dexterity and rapidity as the short sword. The Roman soldier could get in close and parry and thrust with great effectiveness. Probably the trained use of the short sword was more responsible for Roman success than any other item in his armament.

The believer's battle requires an effective sword. It is the Word of God that is effective in our battle, not human opinion, not dependence on church traditions, not modern psychology. Carrying our Bibles to church and occasionally reading them will not do. The believer needs to know the Bible, to study it, and to become a specialist in its truths.

We must go to God's Word for our teaching about God and His will, for reproof when we have gotten out of line, for correction when suffering from misunderstanding the will of God, and for training in living a righteous life. Furthermore each believer must learn to be "rightly handling the Word of truth" (2 Tim. 2:15), discriminating between directions addressed directly to us and directions that are commands not to us but to people of other times and circumstances. All the Bible is God's truth, and divine principles are unveiled in all of it, but confusion follows from a failure to recognize that prior to the Cross God was dealing with Israel by regulations of the Mosaic law, whereas for all believers He is now using love empowered by the Spirit.

It is not surprising that many Christians are dismally ignorant of the Scriptures when their pastors are more concerned with church organization, the conduct of the services, the finances of the church, denominational matters, political issues, and scores of other questions instead of becoming personal experts in the Word. Since commitment to the Word of God is indispensable for every believer, leaders in the Church should certainly lead in a continuing, intense study of the Scriptures, for only if they are committed deeply to the Bible will the values of the Bible and Bible study be communicated to others.

G. Commitment to Communication: Prayer at All Times (6:18-20)
[18]praying at all times in the Spirit, with all prayer and supplication. To that end keep alert with all perseverance, making supplication for all the saints, [19]and also for me, that words may be given me in opening my mouth boldly to proclaim

the mystery of the gospel, ²⁰for which I am an ambassador in chains, that I may declare it boldly, as I ought to speak.

Verse 18 seems to break with the thought of the Christian's warfare and move to a new subject, prayer. Yet with a little reflection, it becomes obvious that verses 18-20 do not constitute a new topic. Paul is still thinking of the believer's spiritual conflict. He does not make the analogy explicit, but the thought must have been in his mind that communication with headquarters is critical.

Some commentators have proposed that prayer is part of the Christian's armor. No, but it is associated with it. Verse 18 is not a new sentence in the Greek. It is connected with the main verb in verse 14. Verse 14, as we have seen, is a command that has the thought, "Stand with determination" or "Stand with finality." "Pray," in contrast, is a present participle that can be translated, "Be in the process of praying" or "keep on praying." Verse 18 can then be read in connection with the main command, "Stand . . . and as you do, keep on praying at all times."

In all organized combat, each soldier must be in communication with the officer leading and directing his unit, and that officer must be in communication with the officer over him. During actual combat a soldier is likely too busy to do more than attend to his immediate opponent. Nevertheless at every opportunity the soldier listens for commands and reports progress or lack of it. He can shout for help if he needs backup. He can signal the officer in immediate control if he has discovered a weakness in the enemy line. Warfare is never successful when it is each soldier for himself. For those who wrestle against the spiritual hosts of wickedness, it is essential that communication constantly take place between the Christian combatant and the Commander directing the forces against wickedness. In these three verses we have the soldier's instructional manual for communication. It includes four points for every Christian soldier and a fifth relating to the point man in the fray.

First is the when and where of prayer: "praying at *all* times in the Spirit." For many Christians prayer is for calamities, what may be called catastrophic praying. The Christian should be in constant communication, always aware of his or her own inadequacies and lack of knowledge and conscious of his or her total dependence on the goodness, omniscience, and power of God. Calamities seem most often to come upon us when we least expect them. The praying Christian is one whose faith prepares him or her with the confidence that God is in control whenever seeming misfortune overtakes.

What is meant by praying "in the Spirit"? This is not the human spirit, for it is prayer in a time of conflict when the believer is dependent on God. What then is it? Surrender of rational control? No, for the Christian is to "keep alert." This is the opposite of prayer consisting of a mindless, repetitively murmured phrase, even if it is repetition of the name of the Lord himself. Can it be prayer that observes a particular form pleasing to the Spirit? In many communions all public prayers are read from a text, or repeated by memory from a text. This is not necessarily wrong, and indeed, someone leading a congregation in prayer should not be praying randomly and disjointedly as thoughts pop into mind, for how can others meaningfully join in when the prayer is scarcely rational? Nevertheless 6:18-20 hardly sounds like a request for an ordered, preplanned liturgy. Here the apostle does not have in mind praying in a public service but the prayer of the individual. A Christian cannot be in a worship service at all times but is to be praying "at all times." "Praying in the Spirit" actually is equivalent to praying with the mind set on the things of the Spirit. Romans 8:5-7 says that to set the mind on the things of the Spirit is life and peace. This is an important key to effective praying. Paul's thought is, if the Christian sets his or her mind on self-gratifying goals, the Christian is hostile to God and certainly cannot expect a happy answer. Prayers are answered and bring peace to the soul when prayer is made according to the will of God, as John explained in 1 John 5:14.

Second is the variety of prayer: "With *all* prayer and supplication." What are some kinds of prayer? (a) Cries for help (Pss. 28:2; 31:9-10); (b) profession of faith (Mark 9:24); (c) plea for information, enlightenment (1 Kings 3:9; Ps. 119:169); (d) confession of sin (1 John 1:9; Dan. 9:15); (e) praise and adoration (Pss. 22:3-5; 145:1); (f) thanksgiving (Ps. 111:1; Phil. 4:6); (g) intercession (1 Tim. 2:2). Each of these categories may well be included in the prayers of God's people. "Supplication" refers to specific prayer requests. We can be specific; we need to be specific. A certain pastor regularly terminated his public prayers with this sentence, "And remember all those for whom we ought to pray but cannot call to mind." That shotgun approach took in a lot of territory and probably satisfied those in his congregation who felt left out. But if the Christian's heart is filled with love, it will not be quite so difficult to remember those for whom he or she should make supplication.

Third is the manner of prayer: "keep alert with all perseverance." "Keep alert" is literally "keeping awake." Of course we cannot be physically awake all the time. But we can pray "wakefully," not in rote phrases. Keeping alert means do not give up, do not get tired. Jesus said to His disciples in the garden, "Watch and pray" (Matt. 26:41). When praying in faith, it is easy to keep alert, and this includes bright curiosity to see how God is going to answer. It also includes an expectancy the answer will be forthcoming.

"Perseverance" can be a mark of faith, since it is waiting on God and trusting Him. Perseverance is not setting a specific time or following a rigidly prescribed program of prayer. Rather it is not giving up on prayer when an answer seems to be withheld. The Greek word translated "perseverance" means "to persist obstinately in".[115]

When is prayer a "vain repetition" (Matt. 6:7) and when is it "perseverance"? A vain repetition is a mindless recitation of some memorized phrases. Twice is too often for such supposed praying. In 2 Corinthians 12:8 Paul prayed three times that his thorn in the flesh would leave him. Does this suggest that three times is enough? No, because in Paul's case it was at the third earnest request he heard the divine answer: "My grace is sufficient for you, for my power is made perfect in weakness." It is time to stop making a specific request when an answer has been provided. Godly persistence in prayer means continuing until the answer is clear.

Fourth are some objects of prayer: "making supplication for all the saints." This includes believers of low station as well as high, one race as well as another, followers as well as leaders. This is surely a plea for interest in and concern for all those in the body of Christ. Obviously all of us know but the most minuscule proportion of all the saints. But we can pray for the ones we do know. Often the problem

---

115 Hoehner, *Ephesians: An Exegetical Commentary*, 858.

is we do not know the truly genuine needs of more than a tiny number of those we count as friends and acquaintances. This is a reason to become good listeners and to establish open communication with as many as possible. Then we can pray meaningfully for them. This means we need to try to put ourselves in the place of others and understand how they feel rather than projecting our feelings on them. To be truly empathetic, we ourselves need to be open to others so that communication can become a two-way street. People will be much more willing to share their prayer needs when we are frank about our own deepest concerns. This necessitates taking time to be with others in a manner that lets them know we care about them. Then we can begin to pray, if not for all, for at least a great many more.

One note of caution here. A certain pastor taught his congregation that they were not to pray for the unsaved. This verse was his justification. But Paul does not say pray *only* for the saints, but pray for all the saints. "All the saints" is appropriate to Paul's emphasis on the Church and a caution against excluding any saints from our prayers because of prejudice or personal distaste.

Fifth, we come to the special case of the point man, the Apostle Paul (Eph. 6:19-20). Paul asks for prayer for himself. It is instructive to note what he did *not* ask for. He did not ask for prayer that his chains might be loosened, that he might enjoy greater creature comforts, or that God might avenge him on his false accusers. Paul is confident that his imprisonment serves God's purposes (Phil. 1:12-14). His only fear was that he might not fully serve God in proclaiming the good news of Jesus Christ.

A point man for most of us is the pastor (elder) of

our church. Since he has been placed in a position of public prominence, surely he needs our prayers, and regularly so! If there were to be a human commanding general in the Church, and if somehow he could review the Christian troops in our community, how would he rate our prayer life? If he knew our hearts, would he be ashamed of our lack of preparedness and commitment to the conflict? Those aspiring to be faithful soldiers of the Lord can never afford to let praying slip by because we have too many other concerns occupying our minds--never!

CONCLUSION
(6:21-24)

After completing his letter the Apostle Paul concludes with a heart-warming note about his companion in the Lord's work, his beloved brother in the faith, Tychicus.

I. An Epistolary Matter (6:21-22)

²¹So that you also may know how I am and what I am doing, Tychicus the beloved brother and faithful minister in the Lord will tell you everything. ²²I have sent him to you for this very purpose, that you may know how we are, and that he may encourage your hearts.

More than one pastor would dearly love to have a Tychicus standing alongside him in the Lord's work. Tychicus was a companion of Paul who seemed always ready to serve. The first time he is mentioned in Scripture, he was one of the representatives of the Asian church who went with Trophimus from Greece to meet Paul at Troas (Acts 20:4). Tychicus and the rest of the party presumably went with Paul on his disastrous visit to Jerusalem. At least Trophimus was there (Acts 21:29), so we can suppose Tychicus also was there. After Paul was in Rome, Tychicus was available at Paul's bidding, for Paul planned to send either Artemas or him to Titus in Crete (Titus 3:12). Paul sent Tychicus to Ephesus from Rome, so it seems he must have been with the apostle during his final, difficult days in Rome (2 Tim. 4:12). Then he was the trusted bearer of the Colossian letter, undoubtedly of the letter to Philemon (Col. 4:7), and presumably of Ephesians.

What is significant is not only that Tychicus is an example of faithful service but that Paul referred to him with the utmost respect. He did not minimize Tychicus by terming him an "assistant minister," but rather he was the "faithful minister." He honored him before others, an example of Paul's injunction to all of us to "outdo one another in showing honor" (Rom. 12:10).

II. A Benediction (6:23-24)

²³Peace be to the brothers, and love with faith, from God the Father and the Lord Jesus Christ. ²⁴Grace be with all who love our Lord Jesus Christ with love incorruptible.

Paul concludes his letter with a benedictory prayer. In two respects the benediction is unusual among all of his concluding benedictions. First, it is a double benediction, the first part in verse 23, the second in verse 24. Second, it is not in the second person, "Peace to you," but in the third person, "Peace be to the brothers." Some commentators see the combination as evidence of an author other than Paul. But no; surely we can allow Paul this much freedom of expression. The combination is fully in accord with the more studied and formal nature of a letter written for circulation among a number of churches.

3 Three significant terms are on Paul's heart as he prays for the believers: peace, love, faith. Here he is not urging peace *with* God, for his audience is made up of those who have already found peace with God; they are brothers in the Lord. He wants them to have peace among each other. At the same time he wants them to have love for each other. Peace cannot come without love, and where Christians are

warring with each other love is manifestly missing. When love is present, peace will be there as well. The two words are intimates walking hand in hand. Why did the apostle add "with faith" instead of "and faith?" Doubtlessly because love presupposes a vital faith, just as does peace. What then is "from God the Father and the Lord Jesus Christ"? Is faith from God the Father? "With" before "faith" indicates that Paul was not thinking of faith as the gift of the Father. It is peace and love that come from God the Father. Faith is the necessary condition releasing God's freedom and power to produce peace and love.

The expression in verse 24, "all who love our Lord Jesus Christ with love incorruptible," is a way of referring to true believers. One who has recognized the depth of his or her own sinfulness and who has found forgiveness in the Lord Jesus Christ can scarcely avoid love for him. (at 1 Cor. 16:22 Paul says the same thing, only negatively.) The casual, cultural Christian who has the name but not the reality of faith certainly lacks love for him. Probably such a one is not among the ranks of true Christians at all. But for those who are unquestioned believers, the first word in Ephesians 6:24 is wonderfully true: there is grace, grace for every need, grace abundant.

The last word (*aphtharsia*) is translated "undying" in the RSV and others, but "incorruptible" in the ESV and others. Which is it? Grammatically it can be either. The word can refer to the Christians undying love for Christ, or it can refer to Christ, who Himself is immortal and incorruptible. Perhaps the choice is best left to the readers own convictions, although personally we think it is more likely the apostle assigned the word to the Lord. There have been believers, seemingly genuine, such as Demas, whose love was not undying and who gave up, having loved the world more. There were also the saints in Revelation 2:4, whose first love was in danger of being abandoned. May our own love increase day by day, for He has loved us and continues to love us incorruptibly and infinitely!

How finely Isaac Watts captured what we as believers so much need today:

> Am I a soldier of the cross,
>   A follow'r of the Lamb?
> And shall I fear to own his cause,
>   Or blush to speak His name?
>
> Must I be carried to the skies
>   On flowr'ry beds of ease,
> While others fought to win the prize,
>   And sailed thro' bloody seas?
>
> Are there no foes for me to face?
>   Must I not stem the flood?
> Is this vile world a friend to grace,
>   To help me on to God.
>
> Sure I must fight if I would reign;
>   Increase my courage, Lord,
> I'll bear the toil, endure the pain,
>   Supported by Thy word.

SPECIAL OBSERVATIONS

Observation I: Literary Structure in Ephesians

The type of literary structure exhibited in Ephesians has been described under different names: introverted correspondence, concentric inclusion, concentric structure, chiastic structure, complex inclusion, and palistrophe. The most commonly used term is chiastic structure or chiasmus. Our preference would be to use the term developed by E. W. Bullinger, "introverted correspondence," since it fits nicely with his classification of other types of corresponding structures found in biblical literature.[116] But because chiasmus is more familiar, that is the designation used here.

In a chiastic structure one subject is presented first. At another place, there is a corresponding subject. The corresponding subject is not a repetition of the first but to a significant degree is an amplification of or a contrast with the first. The first subject to be presented will have its corresponding member presented last. The second subject will have its corresponding member presented next to last. A chiasmus may consist of no more than two pairs of corresponding members. If it has three, the third subject has its corresponding member presented third from last. There may be three, four, five, or even more corresponding pairs. Often, as in our analysis of Ephesians, there is a central topic, which stands by itself. The central topic has special significance,

---

116 E. W. Bullinger, *Figures of Speech Used in the Bible: Explained and Illustrated* (London: Eyre & Spottiswoode, 1898) (also reprint, Grand Rapids: Baker Book House, 1968), 374-79.

for it is the key toward which everything else in the piece is directed.[117]

That such a structure should exist in Ephesians may be surprising to many English readers. Nevertheless ancient writers commonly strove for and appreciated carefully framed rhetorical styles. The styles of the Greeks and Romans differed from those favored by the ancient Hebrews. Was Paul trained in Greek and Latin rhetoric? That is debatable. He was well versed in the Old Testament, so it is reasonable to think that in a letter that was not an immediate response to a crisis and that called for carefully framed thoughts, he would naturally choose to use a formal Hebrew style. There seems little question but that Paul deliberately chose a characteristic chiastic pattern in writing Ephesians. The details go beyond what is exhibited here, since it extends to the use of key Greek words and phrases within the individual divisions.

Two recent scholars have developed detailed chiastic structures for Ephesians, P. S. Cameron in "The Structure of Ephesians."[118] and John Paul Heil in Ephesians: Empow-

---

117 For further illustrations of Paul's use of chiastic structures, see N. W. Lund, *Chiasmus in the New Testament: A Study in Formgeschichte* (Chapel Hill, NC: University of North Carolina Press, 1942); and Ian H. Thomson, *Chiasmus in the Pauline Letters*. For examples of Hebrew chiastic structures from Genesis, see Gordon J. Wenham, *Genesis 1-15* (Waco, TX, Word Books. 1987), particularly 22, 50-51, 99-100, 156-58; and Ian P. Fokkelman, *Narrative Art in Genesis*, 2nd ed. (Sheffield: JSOT Press, 1991).
118 P. S. Cameron, "The Structure of Ephesians," *Filologia Neotestamentaria* 3 (1990): 3-17.

erment to 'Walk in Love for the Unity of All in Christ."[119] The question is not whether there is a chiastic structure in Ephesians but whether the analyses of Cameron and Heil, both authors based primarily on repetition of words, or our analysis, based primarily on the sense of the divisions, represents what Paul had in mind. Both have an overall chiasmus (macro-chiasmus) within which are many subordinate chiasms (micro-chiastic units). In the macro units, both include unrealistic divisions. Heil, for example, considers 6:14-22 a basic macro unit, although separating 6:14-22 from the prior part of the Christian soldier's armor in 6:10-13 is unwarranted. Cameron unrealistically placed 3:14-4:6 in the same macro unit. Both ended a macro-chiastic unit at 5:20 when the sentence in the Greek does not end until 5:21. This is not the place for a detailed criticism, but possibly we have pointed out the kind of problems that in contrast make our analysis tenable.

Observation II: In Christ

Paul's use of the phrase "in Christ" is so frequent the reader should realize it has a special significance. We should think of it as a linguistic formula meaning "in unity with Christ." To list some examples, "in Christ," "in Christ Jesus," or "in Him" means our being the unending and total recipient of Christ's love (Rom. 8:38-39); being alive to Christ in the same sense that Christ is alive to God (Rom. 6:10-11); being the constant recipient of grace (1 Cor. 1:4-8); enjoying freedom (Gal. 2:4); having unity with all other believers (Gal. 3:28);

---

119 John Paul Heil, *Ephesians: Empowerment to Walk in Love for the Unity of All in Christ* .

having eternal life (Rom. 6:23); being uncondemned (Rom. 8:1); being delivered from the control of the flesh (Rom. 8:9); and being set apart for a holy purpose (1 Cor. 1:2). Additionally the expression is used with such verbs as "to speak," "to persuade," "to hearken," "to have confidence," and the like, with the sense that intimate union with Christ calls for a certain action. In many passages it is used almost as a synonym for "as a Christian" (e.g., 1 Cor. 7:39; Phil. 2:29; 1 Thess. 5:12; 1 Tim. 3:13). This usage does not contradict its significance as designating unity with Christ but is derived from it. Sometimes in Ephesians the expression is locative but serving as a sphere of reference (for example 1:20 and 3:11).. Other biblical authors often use the same "in him" phrase with a different sense. In Mark 6:3, for example, it has the obvious sense of "by him."

In 1892 Adolph Deissmann defended at length the formulaic meaning of "in Christ," seeing its meaning as "united with Christ."[120] He viewed Paul as a deep mystic in his use of the expression, although in doing so he somewhat etherealized Christ. Then in 1897 T. K. Abbott explained it as what the believer receives "By virtue of our union with Him, and as members of His body."[121] In 1906 B. F. Westcott described the expression as signifying "fellowship and vital union with Him, in whom the life of the Christian is ideally lived."[122] Recently F. F. Bruce defined it as "union with

---

120 Adolph Deismann, *Die neutestamentliche Formel, >in Christo Jesus,'* (Marburg: Friedrich, 1892).
121 T. K. Abbott. *A Critical and Exegetical Commentary on the Epistle to the Ephesians and to the Colossians* (Edinburgh: T & T Clark, 1897), 3.
122 B. F. Westcott, *St. Paul's Epistle to the Ephesians* (London: MacMillan, 1906), 186.

him."[123] Richard N. Longnecker defined Paul's use of the formula as "communion with Christ in the most intimate relationship imaginable."[124] It is interesting that in Philippians 2:1 the NIV translates the phrase by "united with Christ." This is exactly the meaning it should have. Yet in Ephesians 1:3 the NIV translates the identical phrase simply "in Christ." BAG terms it a "formula" for this "new life-principle: life in Christ."[125] The life-principle, as argued here, is that the believer is fully identified with Christ, that is, united with him in the eyes of the Father.

Some New Testament scholars are not agreed on Paul's meaning when he wrote "in Christ." Blass, Debrunner, and Funk comment, "The phrase . . . which is copiously appended by Paul to the most varied concepts, utterly defies definite interpretation."[126] Best claims that in Ephesians the meaning is instrumental (signifying "by means of Christ") in the following verses rather than locative ("placed within" or "united with" Christ): 1:3, 4, 6, 9, 10, 20; 2:6, 7; 3:11; 4:32.[127] He understands that Paul commonly used the expression to designate someone being placed within Christ, but along with a number of other authors he believes that in Ephesians the meaning must be determined from that epistle alone, since he supposes someone other than Paul was

---

123 F. F. Bruce, *Colossians, Philemon, and Ephesians* (Grand Rapids: Eerdmans, 1984), 254.
124 Richard N. Longnecker, *Galatians* (Dallas: Word Books, 1990), 154.
125 BAG, 259
126 *A Greek Grammar of the New Testament and Other Early Christian Literature*, trans. Robert W. Funk from 9th to 10th German ed. (Chicago: Univ. Chicago, 1961), 219 (4).
127 Best, *Ephesians*, 153-55.

the author. Nevertheless Larkin accepts the locative sense for each verse listed by Best as instrumental.[128] Muddiman claims that Ephesians is not consistent in the way "in Christ" is to be understood. Then he states, "occasionally the more profound (Pauline) sense of incorporation into Christ can hardly be denied."[129] He correctly understands how Paul used the term, but he thinks that much of Ephesians consists of additions made to Paul's original document by another hand.

In some places in the epistle it is not immediately obvious that "in Christ" has a locative sense. Ephesians 1:9-10 is an example. In verse 9, "in him" ("in Christ" in the ESV) can be understood of the intimate union of Christ and the Father. The meaning in verse 10 depends on what is meant by "all things" and what is indicated by "the fullness of time." If "all things" points to a unity of purpose (rather than a unity of all sentient beings, or all creation being swallowed up in God), then the locative sense is reasonable. The locative sense is also reasonable if "the fullness of time" points to the ultimate resolution of everything (1 Cor. 5:28) rather than the Incarnation. Possibly the best study of the expression, although one using the untranslated Greek text, is a study by J. O. F. Murray.[130] Any who are inclined to doubt the significance of the expression should study this work or the analyses by Larkin.[131].

---

128 Larkin, *Ephesians, A Handbook on the Greek Text*
129 Muddiman, *Epistle to the Ephesians*, 67.
130 J. O. F. Murray, *The Epistle to the Ephesians*, Cambridge Greek Testament for Schools and Colleges (Cambridge: University Press, 1933), lxii-lxxvi.
131 Larkin, *Ephesians: A Handbook on the Greek Text*.

Observation III. The Biblical Meaning of Love

Instead of one word for love, New Testament writers had available three primary words and used two of them. Then one of the primary words was formed into compound words. One is the verb *phileō* with its noun form *philos*. We recognize this word, since we often use it to make up English words, for example, philosophy, philanthropy, philharmonic. A second verb is *agapaō*. This does not appear to be used in the construction of any English word. Yet *agapē*, the noun form, has become fairly well-known through Christian literature. The third word was not used by writers of the New Testament, but it does occur in the Septuagint, the ancient Greek translation of the Old Testament. It is the verb *eraō* with its noun *eros*. We are familiar with it, since it is the origin of our English word "erotic." It is most regrettable that English has no real equivalents for these three words, because to translate each by the word love is to use the same word for diametrical concepts.

Possibly a feeling of strong passion is the only thing each word has in common. Whichever kind of "love" we might be experiencing, it may be accompanied by powerful and even uncontrollably intense emotions. The difference between the words does not lie in the fact that one has less and the other stronger feelings but rather in a much more fundamental character of the particular kind of love.

Eros speaks of a passion that covets or uses another person or other things for one's own gratification. Anders Nygren fitly termed it "acquisitive love."[132] It refers to the

---

[132] Anders Nygren, *Agape and Eros* (New York: Harper and Row, 1969).

kind of love that seeks only self-satisfaction, the will to possess, the will to experience self-gratification. Often it refers to purely sexual passion, but not necessarily. That the word is not used in the New Testament is not surprising, since by Paul's day it had become associated with some of the grossest kinds of immorality. Yet our English word "love," as it is so often used in novels and on the screen, portrays nothing more than the selfish passion of *eros*.

Although most Christians do not think critically about the meaning of love, they often are led to think about love in ways that do not seem at all like the lustful, bawdy practices of much of society. This is a very real and present danger for the Christian, who may not recognize *eros* for what it is. The Christian, "enlightened" by the investigations of modern psychology, may suppose that successful living hinges on self-esteem and self-interest. A pattern of self-esteem, for example, is alleged to provide an individual with a foundation for a compatible marriage relationship. So if someone possesses adequate self-esteem, an extramarital affair is presumed unnecessary for happiness. Supposedly it also provides a person with principles on which to adjust his or her personality to guarantee effective business and social relationships. Religious entrepreneurs have baptized the concept with biblical language and proclaim it from the pulpits as the key to a new understanding of Christian living. This is a deception. For all its proclaimed "heavenly" quality, it is nonetheless *eros*, because all that is self-centered, self-glorying, self-gratifying, belongs to *eros*.

In Paul's writing a term equivalent to *eros* is "the flesh." Used in an ethical sense, flesh is dominance or control of the soul by self-seeking, self-aggrandizing, and self-satisfying thoughts and practices.

Philos is totally unlike *eros*. Depending on the context it may mean "to kiss" or may carry the meaning "to be friendly." When the word is translated "love" in the New Testament, it represents feelings that appear in consequence of *a deep respect and whole-hearted appreciation of the worth of the person who is its object*, the kind of feelings that lead to a kiss of genuine friendship. It stands for an apprehension of the value of another person. It may even represent a passion that burns hot, yet not with self-interest but with esteem and adoration for the other person. When it is used for love within a conjugal relationship, it does not exclude sexual activity but sanctifies it with the devoted adoration that belongs to those who value each other.

It is helpful to note the occurrences in Scripture of *philos* (and its verbal form *phileō*). Negatively it is used of the self-adoring love indulged by the scribes and Pharisees, who "loved" to pray in public and "loved" the place of honor at feasts, the best seats in the synagogues, salutations in the marketplaces, and being called rabbi (Matt. 6:5; 23:6). This use does not change the meaning of the word. It is an example rather of what so many people highly prize, namely, themselves. It is an inwardly directed friendship, which our Lord rightly condemned. Contrariwise love with the right object is seen in God's love for Jesus: "For the Father loves the Son" (John 5:20). We who know God are expected to have this kind of love toward him (1 Cor. 16:22), which is nothing less than proper in view of His immeasurable excellence. This kind of love among believers is recognized as appropriate and normal (Titus 3:15) and is even commanded of one believer toward another believer (Heb. 13:1, where the

Special Observations

compound word *philadelphia* is used). Yet God is not said to have this kind of love for unregenerate men and women. How could He respect those who by deliberate sin have alienated themselves from Him? Nor is the Christian asked to have this kind of love for unbelievers.

Understanding *eros* and *philos* provides a necessary contrast for understanding *agapē*. This is love that is totally *other*-centered.

The essential difference between *philos* (verb: *phileō*) and *agapē* (verb: *agapaō*) is that while the first arises out of regard for the qualities of the person who is its object, the second arises from the innermost nature of the person who does the loving. *Philos* describes the passionate response of a soul stimulated by the excellent skills, the beautiful personality, or laudable character of another. *Agapē* is equally passionate loving that may have admiration and respect for the person who is loved, but requires neither, because it flows out of the heart of the lover. *Phileō* is to love someone for his or her virtue. *Agapaō* is virtue doing the loving. This is seen most vividly in 1 Timothy 1:5, where Paul wrote of "love that issues from a pure heart and a good conscience and sincere faith." The negative side is found in the example of Demas, who abandoned Paul, being "in love" with this present world (2 Tim. 4:10). His lack of a pure heart led him to a concern for what he could experience among the unredeemed.[133]

---

133 Many expositors consider that the *agapaō* word group refers to willed love more or less independent of emotion while the *phileō* word group refers to an emotional kind of love. This understanding of the two words seems to rest on the assumption that their meanings are defined by early Latin translations of the Greek words, the first with *diligo* and the

A person cannot make a decision to practice *agapē*. If one practices it, it is the result of a character that cannot help but practice it. If it is not part of his or her character, all the resolve in the world plus any number of rational or irrational arguments cannot lead to it. Nevertheless, it can become the character of the believer by the ministry of the Holy Spirit (Gal. 5:22; 1 Thess. 4:9). God tells us that we ought to love one another (1 John 3:16). If a Christian, lapsing into fleshly behavior, finds for some reason he has "fallen out of love" with his wife, he can will to love her, and by the power of the Holy Spirit can indeed do so.

Agapē is love that has the interests, welfare, rights, and good of the other person at heart without regard to one's own interests, welfare, rights, or good. *Agapaō* (to use the verb form) is to live for the sake of the other person instead of oneself. 1 Corinthians 13:4-7 is God's own definition of

---

second with *amo*. This interpretation was carefully developed by Archbishop Trench, *Synonyms of the New Testament* (London: Spottiswoode & Co.), 38-42. D. A. Carson in his book, *The Difficult Doctrine of the Love of God*, 25-30, takes issue with this point of view and concludes that the most appropriate translation for both is our English word love, for he supposes there is no real distinction between the two. He is right in denying that *agapĕ* cannot be reduced to unemotional "willed altruism." According to 1 Corinthians 13:3, believers may give their bodies to be burned or give all they have to feed the poor, clearly willed acts of self-denial, yet such might well be self-glorifying actions, totally without love. On the other hand Carson has not adequately demonstrated that there is not the meaningful distinction between *agapaō* and *phileō* summarized here. He only argues against *agapaē* being "willed love," in effect saying that since it is not, there is no difference between the two. In his otherwise valuable work, *Exegetical Fallacies*, 2d ed. (Grand Rapids: Baker, 1996), 51-53, he argues further that the semantic range of each word group is essentially synonymous, an issue with which we disagree. In any event it requires a larger study than is possible here.

agapē (required reading for every Christian!).

This does not mean *philos* cannot have many of these same qualities. Hebrews 13:1-6 tells us much the same about philadelphia (love + brother). One should have these feelings toward his or her brother and sister in Christ. A brother or sister in Christ ought to excite admiration, not for what that person is in the flesh but for what that one has become in the Lord.

What is so different and remarkable about *agapē* and in contrast to *philos* is that this love may be directed toward a human who does not deserve it, who has done nothing at all to merit it, someone for whom no excuse can be found. This is the significance and impact of Ephesians 1:5. God destined believers to be His sons by His own *agapē*. Paul emphasizes this throughout his letters. It never ceased to amaze Paul and should never cease being a source of wonder for us. God loves us. His love began ages before we ourselves came to be. For all the self-indulgent corruption of our souls, His love continues even until now, and will go on for all ages to come. His love stems from His very character, for "God is love."

Mankind is also expected to have *agapē* toward God (Luke 10:27). Most emphatically God deserves our best love. It is not as though someone can afford to be gracious toward Him as if He were undeserving of this kind of love. When the Scriptures speak of our *agapē* for God, the emphasis is on the selflessness with which we ought to give ourselves to him. This is the same selflessness with which he, prompted by no cause outside his own great infinite heart of love, gave Jesus for us. Therefore "We love because he first loved us" (I John 4:19).

Observation IV: The Church and Israel

Identification of the kingdom of God with the Church goes back to the fifth-century Saint Augustine. Following Augustine, the Reformers generally considered the Church the community of true believers, so this defined the kingdom. Most modern Reformed theologians give the kingdom a broader meaning than the Church alone, although the kingdom is considered to include the spiritual Church. Reformed theologian Louis Berkhof stated that the kingdom "represents the dominion of God in every sphere of human endeavor."[134] The kingdom is considered by Reformed theologians to be a present entity. It does not include a future, literal, earthly reign of Christ. It is the amillenial position.

In Ephesians 2:12 Paul seems to imply that the Church must be an extension of Israel. Gentiles suffer from being separated from the commonwealth of Israel. Reformed theologians reason that when Gentiles become believers and become one with believing Jews, the Church to which they now belong must therefore be the commonwealth of true Israel. The concept seems to receive additional support from Romans 11:24, where Paul writes of believing Gentiles being grafted into the "olive tree" from which unbelieving Jews have been severed. This reads as if the believing "church" of ancient Israel is the one into which believing Gentiles have been engrafted. Hence the New Testament Church is thought to be organically one with the "church" of ancient Israel. Yet interpreting both passages in this way suffers from a failure to recognize that although Gentile believers along with Jewish believers become heirs of the Abrahamic promises (Gal.

---

134 Berkhof, *Systematic Theology*, 570.

4:28), believers today are not under the covenant that God made with Israel through Moses.

Contrary to amillennial expositors, the Old Testament "church" did not have its beginning with Abraham (or with Adam, as some claim). There is no textual evidence for such a supposition. In the Septuagint, the word for church is *ekklēsia*. This is the common translation for the Hebrew word for congregation (*edah*). Israel is not termed a congregation until the Passover that marked the beginning of the Exodus (Exod. 12:3).

Following the Exodus God led the people by the Shekinah glory to the foot of Mount Sinai, and there he established His *direct, accessible rule* over the people. This rule over the congregation of Israel was a true theocracy (a God-ruled society) in which he, Yahweh, became the executive, the legislative, and the judicial head of the government (Exod. 25:8, 22; Num. 7:89; 23:21; Deut. 33:5; etc.).[135] This was the true kingdom of God, although in a preliminary, provisional form. As their Ruler He rewarded the people for obedience and chastened them for disobedience. His rule was manifested by miracles sustaining the people in their wanderings and giving them victory over their enemies. God established a system for His instructions to be communicated through the high priest. Within the tabernacle, the priest not only could hear the word of God but could also inquire of God to learn his will for the people.

---

135 In contemporary journalism, any society ruled by priests or imams is termed a theocracy. Such societies claim to be theocracies, for they claim that God is ruling through their priests or imams. The Scriptures do not claim rule by priests, only that the high priests of ancient Israel were able to communicate the directions of God the Theocrat.

The kingdom continued after the time of the judges, when God condescended to grant the people an earthly king. David was considered a "prince," that is to say, Yahweh continued to be the king, David and his successors being subordinate to him (1 Chron. 17:7). In times that followed, when the people and priests became corrupt, God communicated through prophets. Nevertheless the nation continued to be the kingdom of God (2 Chron. 13:5, 8; Isa. 43:15; 44:6; Ps. 68:24; etc.). In David's reign over the nation and that of his successors, the kingdom was expected to embrace God's spiritual as well as political expectations.

In no place was the kingdom ever defined as being other than what it was when established in the wilderness. Passages such as Psalm 80:1 are not exceptions. This Psalm addresses God, "You who are enthroned above the cherubim, shine forth, Before Ephraim and Benjamin and Manasseh!" There is no reason to consider the Psalmist as thinking other than of God's presence over the Ark of the Covenant.

The idolatry of the people finally reached a point beyond divine tolerance, so first the northern tribes and later Judah were taken into captivity. With the Babylonian captivity, the provisional kingdom came to an end (Ezek. 1:28; 10:1-22; 11:23; 14:3; 20:3, 31, Hos. 3:4). God's presence was no longer among the people in the holy of holies in the temple. After the return from captivity there was a nation but no theocracy. God was the Sovereign in heaven, but not an earthly king (Dan. 4:32, 35). As long as Yahweh was not ruling as their earthly king, neither were the people allowed to have a subordinate king in the line of David. Nevertheless the prophets foresaw a far more glorious kingdom in which the theocracy would be restored, only with far greater glory,

Special Observations

and Israel would be established in the land in peace (Jer. 30:3; 33:7-18; Mic. 4:7-8; Zeph. 3:14-20; Zech. 8:3-8, etc.). When Christ proclaimed that the kingdom was "at hand," the Jews naturally understood that the kingdom would be none other than what had been promised. Significantly Jesus never tried to correct their understanding. The conflict between Jesus and the Jews was not over the nature of the kingdom but about what was required for reception of the kingdom. The requirement was repentance and obedience to the law *from the heart*. Instead of willingly and gratefully accepting the conditions and trusting the power of God to enable them to meet the conditions, they rejected the offer and crucified the Son of David who made the offer. Consequently God turned to the Gentiles. Israel as a nation was set aside, but God has not forgotten and will not fail to fulfill the promises He made to Abraham and David (Ps. 89:3-4). [136]

From this, it should be clear that the kingdom is not at all equivalent to the Church. The kingdom was established initially for Israel and at Christ's advent was offered specifically to Israel. When, according to promise, the kingdom is established at the return of Christ, converted Israel will be awarded her place in the kingdom, for according to the obvious interpretation of Romans 11:15-17, 25-31, Israel as a nation still has a future. It will find salvation in Christ, and will inherit the Abrahamic and Davidic promises. Nowhere in the

---

[136] For a full exposition, see G. N. H. Peters, *The Theocratic Kingdom as Covenanted in the Old Testament, and Presented in the New Testament* (New York: Funk & Wagnalls, 1884). More recent studies of the kingdom are Alva J. McClain, *The Greatness of the Kingdom* (Grand Rapids: Zondervan, 1959), Stanley D. Toussaint, *Behold the King* (Portland, OR: Multnomah Press, 1980).

New Testament is the Church ever termed the kingdom.

The kingdom in the Epistles is in the future (Gal. 5:21; Eph. 5:5; 1 Thess. 2:12; 2 Tim. 4:1). Gentile believers in their resurrected state will reign with Christ in the kingdom (Rev. 5:9-10), for believers in their *standing* before God are translated into the kingdom (Col. 1:13). The Church is God's present work to make Christ known to the world and to bring believers into conformity with His will.

Two New Testament passages are frequently cited in support of the teaching that the Church is an aspect of a present kingdom of God. In John 3:3 Jesus says to inquiring Nicodemus, "Truly, truly, I say to you, unless one is born anew, he cannot see the kingdom of God." Supposedly this means that at spiritual rebirth one enters the kingdom of God. But read the passage from Nicodemus's perspective. From the Old Testament he knew only of the earthly kingdom expected by Israel. Jesus was not denying the validity of that expectation. He was simply saying, "If you have any hope of participating in that coming kingdom, you will need to be born again." No less is that the message for men and women today!

The apostle wrote in Romans 14:17, "For the kingdom of God is not a matter of eating and drinking but of righteousness and peace and joy in the Holy Spirit." This does not mean there is to be no earthly (millennial) kingdom. What Paul is saying is that when the kingdom is established, it will not be governed by the self-gratifying appetites of humankind. It will be a place of total "righteousness, peace, and joy." Since this is the believer's destiny, the believer should live today not for the sake of satisfying himself or herself with food and drink but should do what will promote righteousness, peace, and joy.

Special Observations

Observation V: The Church and The Law

In the discussion of Ephesians 2:14-18, several reasons are given for understanding the Christian not to be under the Law as a rule of life. Contrariwise, followers of both John Calvin and James Arminius are fairly unanimous in considering the moral laws of the Old Testament (primarily the Decalogue) to be the Christian's rule for daily living. Their reasons mainly go back to Jesus' use of the Law plus statements such as Matthew 5:17-20 and Luke 16:17, where Christ affirms the validity of the Law. Since there cannot be a conflict between Jesus and Paul, it must be that Paul had a different view of the Law than appears on the face of his epistles.

Why do these theologians give the statements of Jesus regarding observance of the Law precedence over what appears to be the obvious teaching of Paul? Because the Reformers, following Augustine, identified the Church with the kingdom Jesus proclaimed. If kingdom passages such as the Sermon on the Mount (Matt. 5-7) are instructions given by our Lord for the Church, then these words of Jesus define the use of the Law by the Church.

However, if one reads the Old Testament as it would have been read by Jews at the time of Jesus, a quite different picture emerges. The covenant God made with Abraham, Isaac, and Jacob took first place in Jewish thought. It promised to make of Abraham's posterity a great nation, to make Abraham the father of many nations, to give his posterity victory over their enemies, to bless Abraham personally and to make his name great, to give his posterity the entire land of Canaan and beyond, to make Abraham a blessing, and to be a God to Abraham. These promises, it must be noted, were (a) unconditional, (b) perpetual, and (c) without any indication of the time when they would be fulfilled.

When at the foot of Sinai God made Israel a kingdom over which He personally became the direct, accessible ruler (see Observation IV above), He gave the people the Law through Moses. In effect, the Law said that the *time* when the promises would be fulfilled was conditioned on the people's obedience to the Law. In other words the Abrahamic promises would be enjoyed when and to the extent the people met the conditions (Deut. 7:12-16; 19:8-9, etc.). If the people refused to obey, God would come down on them with terrifying judgments. Nevertheless even should the nation be scattered abroad by a judgment of God, the time will come when the promises will be remembered (Lev. 26:40-45; Isa. 65:8-10; Mic. 4:1-8, etc.).

As noted in Observation IV, the introductory form of the kingdom was removed at the time of the Babylonian Captivity, although a promise remained for the restoration of the kingdom. When Jesus came preaching the gospel of the kingdom, He proclaimed that the long-expected kingdom was now available to the people.

The Law, however, was still in effect. The kingdom with all its promised blessings could not be restored without the nation's obedience to the Law. Jesus, declaring the fact, upheld the Law in every detail (Matt. 5:17-20). The people, especially their religious leaders, were certain their manner of observing the Law was quite acceptable. Nevertheless Jesus showed, particularly in the Sermon on the Mount, what obedience to the Law truly entailed. The Law was to be obeyed not merely in externals but inwardly. For obedience to the Law, God's power was available to the people through the Messiah, if they genuinely wanted it. Had they received what was offered, they would see the kingdom in all its predicted glory.

The demands of the Law provide an explanation for John 6:15, where Jesus refused to allow the people to make him a king, a verse that amillennialists often cite as evidence that Jesus never intended to offer an earthly kingdom to Israel. Jesus perceived that the people "were about to come and take him by force to make him king," so he "withdrew again to the mountain by himself." Jesus came presenting the kingdom, but its reception did not depend on his assumption of kingship apart from their obedience.

Jesus' offer of the kingdom was a bona fide offer. There were no Old Testament prophetic elements that could not have been fulfilled within the lifetime of those then living. Unquestionably it would have been necessary for Jesus to have gone to the cross. The final winnowing of Israel (Daniel's seventieth week of tribulation) would necessarily have taken place. But the kingdom could have been realized within a few years.

The conditions Jesus presented were scorned. The leaders in their envy and hatred turned the people against Him, and He was crucified. His crucifixion, as explained in the exposition above, annulled the Law for those placing their trust in Him. It also brought frightful judgment on the nation with dispersal of the survivors throughout the Gentile nations. Because of their unbelief, God turned to the Gentiles to take out a people for His name, the Church of the Lord Jesus.

Meanwhile the kingdom is held in abeyance. When the Messiah returns and the remnant of the Jewish people "look . . . on him whom they have pierced," they will "mourn for him" (Zech, 12:10) and be restored apart from the Law, for He will have taken all their sins upon Himself (Zech. 13:1, Gal. 3:13). At that time Yahweh, Christ the Lord, will become "king over all the earth"(Zech. 14:9).

INDEX OF AUTHORS

The first number following the author's name is the page on which he is cited. The number in parentheses that in many instances follows the page number is the reference to the footnote when the citation is limited to the footnote.

Abbott, T. K., 271 (122)

Aristotle, 97

Arminius, Jacobus, 12

Athenasius, 15 (16)

Badger, Anthony B., 88 (41)

Barth, Marcus, iv. 13, 104 (51), 132 (62), 166 (76), 169 (77), 219 (95), 226 (101), 255 (114)

Barth, Karl, 15

Bell, Daniel H. Jr., 88 (40)

Benware, Paul N., 244 (110)

Berkhof, Louis, 282

Best, Ernest, ix, 70, 100, 222, 274

Blackman, Matthew L., 182 (84)

Bruce, F. F., viii, 139, 273

Bullinger, E. W., 270

Calvin, John, 11, 104

Cameron, P. S., 271

Carson, D. A., 279-80 (133)

Chafer, Lewis Sperry, 211

Davids, Peter, 226 (100)

Dawkins, Richard, 177 (81)

Deismann, Adolph, 273

Dodd, Brian J., 244 (111)

Dorsey, David, xiii, 122. 131

Douglas, Frederick, 244 (111)

Fokkelman, Ian P., 271 (117)

Gianoulis, George C., 17 (17)

Grudem, Wayne, 224 (99)

Harris III, W. Hall 155 (72)

Hays, J. Daniel, 105 (51)

Heil, John Paul, ix, 271

Hendriksen, William, viii, 121 (37), 154 (70), 241

Hodge, Charles, 121 (57), 199, 216

Hodges, Zane C., 199 (86)

Hoehner, Harold , iv, 22 (31), 119 (56), 132 (62), 136 (65), 179 (83), 207, 211 (92), 215 (93), 221 (97), 222 (99), 244 (151), 252 (113), 263 (115)

Larkin, William J., 2, 20 (19), 32 (23), 36 (26), 133 (66), 153 (69), 154 (70), 173, 200 275

Lewis, C. S., 84

Liefeld. Walter L., 226

Lincoln, Andrew T., 62, 73 (37), 112 (58), 121, 132 (62), 237 (106), 248

Index

Longnecker, Richard N., 274
Lopez, René A., 86 (38)
Lund, N. W., 271 (117)
McClain, Alva J., 285 (136)
Martin, Alfred, 88 (42)
Moo, Douglas J., 18 (17), 105, 180 (83)
Muddiman, John, 54 (29), 154 (71), 275
Murray, J. O. F., 275
Nygren, Anders, 276
O'Brien, Peter T., v, 132 (62), 135 (64), 148, 173
Olson, C. Gordon, 19 (18).
Peters, George N. H., 285 (136)
Pyne, Robert A, 182 (84)
Radmacher, Earl D., 62 (34), 113 (55), 122 (59), 172 (78)
Salmond, S. D. F., 26, 65
Schnackenburg, Rudolph, 189
Schreiner, Thomas R., 239 (107)
Snodgrass, Klyne, 13, 15, 41, 103 (48)
Strickland, Wayne G., 104-05 (51)
Taylor, Richard A. 154 (70)
Thomson, Ian H. 271 (117)
Toussaint, Stanley D., 285 (136)
Wallace, Daniel B., 86, 111 (54), 155 (72), 159 (74), 211 (90), 221 (96), 222 (98)

293

Wenham, Gordon J., 271 (117)
Westcott, B. F.., 273
Weymouth, Richard Francis, 35 (24)
Wilkin, Robert H., 243 (110)
Wilson, Edward O., 176

INDEX OF SUBJECTS

(The page number refers to a place in the text where the subject begins. The page number of a subject extending for more than two pages is followed by the symbol ff.)

Adoption	17
Agapē	279
Altruism	75
Am I a Soldier of the Cross?	269
Anger of the flesh	190
Anger, justifiable	184
Aorist tense (Greek)	xvii, xix
Apostle, meaning of	1, 157
Apostles and prophets	111
Armor of God, reason for	248
Armor to be put on once for all	249, 251
Association with unbelievers	202
Authorship of Ephesians	vii, ix
Baptism	149
Belief (See Faith).	
Blessings granted the believer	9 ff
Blood of Christ, significance of	25
Calling by God	55, 145

Character and purpose of the Epistle	ix
Chiastic structure, chiasmus	xxiii, 131, 270
Children and parents	237 ff
Christ the cornerstone	112
Christ, His indwelling	136
Christ's death, purpose and nature	228
Christ's love for the Church	231
Christ's purpose in filling the Church	61
Christ's purpose uniting Jews and Gentiles	99
Church the "bridegroom" of Christ	229
Church, the universal	x, 61, 66, 113, 142
Church, a new entity	119 ff
Church, one with believing Israel?	119
Church's cosmic witness	127
Circumcision	93
Circumstances of authorship	xii
Condemnation by God	77
Confidence of the Christian	98
Covenant of God with Israel	288
Credit before God	84
Cross a necessity to Christian message	98
Day of Redemption	139
Death	70

Index

Debauchery	210
Deity of Christ	200
Depravity of humans, universal	69
Dispensation	117, 146
Dominion of Christ	60
Election (Chosen by God)	11, 13
English text used	v
Enlightened by God	29
Evangelists	159
Faith	256
Faith defined	38, 88, 135, 256
Faith, presumed to be a gift	84 ff
Fear of Christ	220
Fellow citizens	110
Filling by the Spirit	210, 218
Flesh and eros general equivalents	278
Flesh explained	180
Flesh, its passions	75
Forgiveness with kindness	192
Fullness of Christ (of God)	138, 168
Gentile futility	176 ff
Gentiles despised by Jews	93
Gentiles, emptiness of their lives	95 ff, 285

Gifts, function of	169
Gifts, reciprocity of	170
God in control in battle against Satan	257
God, a self-determining being	33
God, His attributes	150
God's grace	23
God's power	33
God's product in salvation	89
God's purpose in making wisdom known	126
God's work	34
Good works prepared by God	90
Grace, definition	24, 83
Greek text followed	iv
Greek verb tenses	xvi
Grieving the Holy Spirit	188
Heavenly places	8, 82
Holy and blameless, meaning of	15
Honest work	186
Hope	55, n.30
Hostility of Jews toward Gentiles	101
Husband the head of his wife	223
In Christ," range of applications	272
In Christ"	6, 14
Inheritance	32

Index

Interpreting the Epistle	xi
Irresistible grace	81
Israel, her future	286
Jews despised by Gentiles	91
Kingdom of God in abeyance	290
Kingdom of God offered to Israel	289
Kingdom of God	282
Language of the Christian	188
Law and love	106
Law, its nullification	102
Law, Mosaic	288
Leadership, spiritual	165
Letter of Aristeas	101
Life in Christ	80, 193
Literary structure of the Epistle	xix, xxi, 273
Lordship of Christ	38
Love (agapē)	x, 136, 195. 227, 240
Love with faith	267
Malice	191
Marriage, Christian	217 ff
Masters	245
Mercy of God	79
Method of God in salvation	83

Ministry of leaders in the church	161 ff
Moral use of the law	103, n. 49
Mosaic law an obstacle to unification	100
Mystery, its significance	30, 119, 235
New self (the new man) put on	179
Nullification of the Law	102
Old self (the old man) crucified	182
Paul a prisoner	115 ff
Peace	148, 254, 267
Peace proclaimed by vicegerents of Christ	109
Peace through Christ	99
Philos, meaning of	278
Plan of God's grace	117, 124
Poor, the needs of	186
Power for the Christian	67
Prayer	259 ff
Prayer for leaders	264
Prayer for unsaved	264
Prayer, freedom of	110
Prayer, manner of	262
Prayer, objects of	263
Prayer, varieties of	262
Precedence of Christ	58
Predestination	19, 21, 34

Index

Present tense (Greek)	xvii
Principalities and powers	126
Product, divine	89
Prophets,	158
Purpose of the Epistle	ix
Recipients of the Epistle	xiv
Recipients of the Epistle	xiv
Reconciliation the key to unification	107
Peace resulting from unification	108
Redemption	25 ff
Reformed theology of the law	103, n. 49
Reproving wicked deeds	204
Responsibilities of the Christian	111
Responsibility of grace	126
Resurrection of Christ	57
Rewards for the believer	199
Righteousness, essential to Christian	254
Rulers and authorities	126, 250
Saints, identity	1, 3, 5, 110
Salvation, basic truth for the Christian	258
Salvation, meaning of	84
Satan, his purpose	127
Satan's control	250
Sealing of the Holy Spirit	35, 189

Sexual immorality	196 ff, 201
Sins	71 ff. 177, 180 ff
Slaves	242 ff
Sonship, placed as sons	17
Stewardship	117
Strength for the Christian	134
Subordination of married partners	219 ff, 232
Temple of God	113
Transgressions (See Sins)	
Trinitarian doctrine	149
Truth, essential to Christian armor	253
Truthfulness expected of believers	183
Unity among believers	167
Unity between Jews and Gentiles	99
Unity in practice	145
Unselfishness	146
Wesleyan view of election	13
Will of God for the Christian	209
Witness when confronted by difficulty	117
Word of God	258
Works, God's preparation of	80
Worship, corporate	218
Wrath of God	78

CPSIA information can be obtained at www.ICGtesting.com
Printed in the USA
BVOW010120310512

291113BV00004B/1/P